A Maske: THE EARLIER VERSIONS

JOHN MILTON

THE EARLIER VERSIONS

Edited by S. E. Sprott

UNIVERSITY OF TORONTO PRESS

Published by
University of Toronto Press
Toronto and Buffalo
Printed in Canada
ISBN 0-8020-5287-8
LC 72-97784

This book has been published
with the help of a grant from the
Humanities Research Council,
using funds provided by the Canada Council,
and of a grant from the
Publications Fund of
University of Toronto Press.

Contents

A Maske: THE EARLIER VERSIONS

Abbreviations and Acronyms

apostr. apostrophe

phaps perhaps

presum. presumably

emd emended

poss. possible, possibly

prob. probable, probably

Berg copy of *1637* in the Berg Collection, New York Public Library

Birch Thomas Birch 'An Historical and Critical Account of the Life and Writings of Mr. John Milton' *A Complete Collection of the Historical, Political, and Miscellaneous Works of John Milton* 2 vols. (London 1738) I vii–xiv.

BM British Museum

BMS A Maske, the Bridgewater Manuscript

Bright copy of *1637* (formerly Bright) in the New York Public Library

Cambridge copy of *1637* in Trinity College, Cambridge

Colman George Colman's revision of Dalton's version of the masque, in *Comus: A Masque. Altered from Milton ...* (London 1772).

Dalton John Dalton's adaptation for the stage, in *Comus, a Maske: (Now Adapted to the Stage) as Alter'd from Milton's Mask ...* (London 1738).

Dalton (1759) *Comus: A Masque. (Now Adapted to the Stage) as Alter'd from Milton's Masque ...* (London 1759).

Harvard copy of *1637* in Harvard University Library

Hunt. copy of *1637* in the Henry E. Huntington Library

JEGP *Journal of English and Germanic Philology*

JRUL *The Journal of the Rutgers University Library*

[MS^1] Hypothetical ms. of 'A maske' in Milton's hand and first state

[MS^2] later state of [MS^1] as revised by Lawes

[MS^3] final state of [MS^1] as revised by Milton

Newton Thomas Newton (ed.) *Paradise Regain'd ... To Which Is Added ... Poems upon Several Occasions* (London 1752).

PBSA *Papers of the Bibliographical Society of America*

Peck Francis Peck *New Memoirs of the Life and Poetical Works of Mr. John Milton* (London 1740).

Peck ms. a transcript *Comus* in Peck's hand, in BM Add. Ms. 28637, fols. 2^r–14^r, based on *1637* collated with TMS

Pforz. copy of *1637* in the Carl H. Pforzheimer Library

PM copy of *1637* in the Pierpont Morgan Library

PMLA *Publications of the Modern Language Association of America*

1637 first edition of *A Maske* (London 1637)

1645 'A Mask' in Milton's *Poems* (London 1645)

1673 'A Mask' in Milton's *Poems* (London 1673)

TMS 'A maske' in the Trinity College manuscript

TMS^1 first text of TMS, in Milton's hand

TMS^2, TMS^3 later states of TMS, after revision in Milton's hand

TMS^4 final state of TMS, after revision not in Milton's hand

Todd Henry J. Todd (ed.) *The Poetical Works of John Milton* 6 vols. (London 1801) V.

V&A Victoria and Albert Museum

Warton Thomas Warton (ed.) *Poems [of Milton] upon Several Occasions* (London 1785).

Wright William Aldis Wright (ed.) *Facsimile of the Manuscript of Milton's Minor Poems Preserved in the Library of Trinity College Cambridge* (Cambridge 1899).

Introduction

John Milton's *A Maske* has come down to us in five versions from his own lifetime and in later adaptations. The five versions are

TMS   'A maske', in the manuscript of Milton's minor poems in Trinity College, Cambridge

BMS   A Maske – the Bridgewater Manuscript

1637   *A Maske Presented at Ludlow Castle* ... , London, printed for Humphrey Robinson, 1637

1645   'A Mask', in *Poems of Mr. John Milton* ... , London, printed by Ruth Raworth for Humphrey Moseley, 1645

1673   'A Mask', in *Poems, &c. Upon Several Occasions. By Mr. John Milton* ... , London, printed for Thomas Dring, 1673

1645 and *1673*, which are much alike, have been reprinted, the former several times, and modern editions are properly based on them. Yet Milton in 1673 was not Milton in 1637, and *A Maske* in 1637 was not the same as 'A maske' in 1634. The present edition provides parallel transcripts of the three earliest and most dissimilar versions. In Appendix I are the words of songs of the masque, taken from manuscripts of Henry Lawes's musical settings. In Appendix II is the reconstructed text of a hypothetical manuscript of the masque that Milton probably wrote in 1634.

TMS –'A maske' in the Trinity College manuscript

'A maske' is preserved in the manuscript of Milton's minor poems and prose in the library of Trinity College, Cambridge. It probably formed part of a collection of books and manuscripts given to the library by Sir Henry Puckering in 1691, although a less likely origin has been proposed.[1] The leaves of the poet, mangled and scattered like the limbs of Osiris, were accidentally discovered by Charles Mason, a fellow of the College from 1725, in papers that he later said were Puckering's; they were gathered together by Mason and placed in a library volume of miscellaneous papers, from which they were removed in 1736 and bound to make a thin folio volume. This volume was not listed in the catalogue of manuscripts in 1697 because it did not then exist. A facsimile reproduction of the whole manuscript volume and a transcript by William Aldis Wright were published by Cambridge University Press in 1899; the Introduction records what is known of the history of the manuscript. Subsequent editors, including the present one, and many readers of Milton remain indebted to this notable publication. Slightly reduced, the Cambridge facsimile and Wright's transcript were republished by the University of Illinois Press at Urbana in 1943 in the first volume of *John Milton's Complete Poetical Works Reproduced in Photographic Facsimile*, edited by Harris Francis Fletcher. The present new transcript of 'A maske' is published by permission of the Master and Fellows of Trinity College.

---

1 M. Kelley 'Addendum: The Later Career of Daniel Skinner' *PMLA* LV (1940) 116-118.

The Manuscript

In the manuscript 'A maske' occupies seventeen pages, marked with odd numbers 13 to 29 possibly not in Milton's hand, plus two scraps. The leaves measure approximately seven and a half by twelve and a half inches. I do not know whether the first eight leaves make a quire, for the delicate condition of the manuscript forbids the necessary inspection; the seventeenth page holds the second epilogue, which (I shall argue on other grounds) was added to earlier material in 1637, and on the other side of the leaf is part of 'Lycidas', written in that year. Throughout the entire Trinity manuscript the order of the leaves, and so of the contents, and any conjectural dates of composition inferred from the order of the leaves, depend in part on Mason, who had found the limbs dispersed. The scraps are as follows. (1) On page ⟨18⟩ a marginal note (at lines 376-378 of the present edition) draws attention to a '[pa] per over [a] gainst'. A small scrap of paper measuring some three and a quarter inches by three quarters is stuck to page 19 on the inner margin near the foot of the leaf. From the letters written down it (456-470 margin) this paper is evidently the stub of a slip, the '[pa] per over [a] gainst', that contained an expanded passage (printed at *1637* 367-382) to replace the much revised earlier version 376-385 on page ⟨18⟩. The slip is not now with the manuscript, but it was seen in the eighteenth century by Newton, Warton, and Todd. Its text, reconstructed, is inserted in this edition at 386-402. (2) In the manuscript a part sheet some six and three quarter inches by four and a quarter is stuck to page ⟨22⟩ about two thirds down the leaf on a level with the marginal note 710, 739-740 on page 23 that reads in part 'that wch follows heere is in the pasted leafe'. The slanting upper and lower edges of the pasted leaf may intimate that it was cut from the middle of a leaf. In this edition its text is inserted at the point required (711-738). Both papers are discussed later in this Introduction on pp. 11, 9-11.

Except for a few words, 'A maske' is written throughout in Milton's hand, not elegantly but quite clearly, for the most part in moderately dense, slightly brownish ink. The pen did not maintain a constant state. In the song at the foot of page ⟨16⟩ it had become scratchy, but was remade or abandoned for a better at the top of the following page. At the end, over pages ⟨26⟩ to ⟨28⟩, it deteriorated into a sorry condition in which, after being dipped, it flooded and wrote thickly for a few letters, then suddenly dried and scratched a few thin strokes until dipped again. Normally, the writing is small though not cramped, and the closely spaced lines number about 65 to a page, although on pages ⟨26⟩ to ⟨28⟩ the writing is larger and looser, and the more widely spaced lines number as few as 55 to a page. The lines are not numbered, and there are no significant gaps in the text. There are, however, many emendations throughout. In this present edition an attempt is made to reproduce both original and emended readings (see p. 31).

Stages and Dates of Revisions in TMS

In the manuscript 'A maske' was left with readings that are ambiguous (e.g., 'm[i]ghty' 282, 'stoope' 1038), or were alternatives (e.g., 'ope's' 33, 'whome' 77, 'dusky' 122, 'thirst' 191, 'that syllable mens nams' 231, 'cell' 257, 'grow' 978, 'the end' 1039), or were unused in any other version (e.g., 'neerest & likliest' 109, 'goes out' 111, 'such tow' 316, 'Exeunt' 355, numerals under 'gladly banish' 454, 'moorie' 476, 'hallow farre off' 522, cancel lines through 'roaving robber' 526-527, 'his' 541, 'flighted' 595, 'w^ch' 678, 'heere sits' 844, 'distressed' 884, cancel lines through 901-904, 'at' 983). These inconclusive readings and the revisions made in the manuscript for other versions suggest that it was not long, if ever, intended as a fair copy but served Milton early and late as a working copy for private reference.

In this edition TMS refers to the manuscript without distinguishing any particular state of it. The revisions in it may be gathered into groups partly on paleographical grounds and partly as they were connected with the first writing in TMS, or with BMS, or with *1637*, or with later editions. This is basically a descriptive classification, though it will lead to conclusions. I adopt the symbol TMS[1] (probably from Miss Helen Darbishire, but not in her sense) to refer to the whole manuscript as it read after being revised during the first complete writing. Similarly, TMS[2], TMS[3], and TMS[4] are intended to refer to the whole manuscript after revisions were made at the respective stages, and by revisions for TMS[2] are meant the revisions that were made at that stage, though TMS[2] includes many of the revisions made for TMS[1].

TMS[1]

Developing a suggestion by Sir Herbert Grierson, John S. Diekhoff[2] argued that in much of TMS Milton was revising rough drafts. The regular writing and close, evenly spaced lines throughout most of the manuscript (e.g., 43-64, 603-630, etc.) also characterize known revisions such as the pasted leaf 711-738 and the second epilogue 1040–1089 and the last version of 'At a solemn Musick' that is elsewhere in the Trinity manuscript. The passage 8-22, more loosely written than its context and cancelled after it was completed, could thus have been a temporary departure from a paragraph, perhaps already in draft, on which Milton had embarked. Diekhoff also alleged other evidence. The cancelled word 'virgin' 111 might have been a verbal reminiscence of 'virgin' 169 from a passage already composed in draft though not yet transcribed. Sometimes Milton repeated a word and cancelled its *second* occurrence (301, 313, 524). None of these arguments seems to me very convincing. I should have thought that the last-mentioned practice pointed to Milton's writing out what he had composed in his head as much as to his revising a written version, or at least to the poet's composing while writing. More recently, in an important series of articles,[3] John T. Shawcross has argued that

TMS is mainly, if not entirely, a revised transcript of an earlier version of the masque which, if I understand him correctly, was presented at Ludlow, differed considerably from any version, including BMS, that we now have, and can be partly recovered from some of the original readings in TMS before Milton emended them. I do not agree with this hypothesis, for reasons that this Introduction will make clear. At the same time, there is nothing improbable in the suggestion that before or while writing TMS Milton drafted or worked out passages on sheets of paper that are now lost.

At the head of TMS[1], in Milton's hand, is the date 1634. This is naturally assumed to be the date of writing, as 1637 at the head of 'Lycidas' in the Trinity manuscript is the date at which that poem was composed. On the title page of BMS the masque is said to have been performed at Ludlow Castle on 29 September 1634, and this information is corroborated, presumably by Henry Lawes, on the title page of *1637*, where the date of performance is given as Michaelmas Night, 1634, though Lawes possibly gave 'October. 1634' as the date in his manuscript of the songs. TMS[1] was probably written earlier in that year. This widely accepted view is challenged by Shawcross, who sees TMS as a revised version written in 1637. Against his dating as it depends on handwriting I shall offer some considerations when dealing with TMS[3b] on p. 9. The date 1634 at the head of the manuscript is surely odd if Milton wrote it in 1637. It would mean that the version in TMS was substantially the version of 1634, or at least that Milton began with an intent of making it so; yet only seven lines after inscribing 1634 he started a passage of fifteen lines that had either not been in an earlier putative version of 1634 or that he now deleted from that version. More probably, he was writing in 1634, and TMS[1] is the earliest complete text of the work.

2 H.J.C. Grierson (ed.) *The Poems of John Milton* I (London 1925) xiv-xvi; J.S. Diekhoff 'The Text of *Comus*, 1634 to 1645' *PMLA* LII (1937) 705-727; 'The Punctuation of *Comus*' *PMLA* LI (1936) 757-768.

3 J.T. Shawcross 'Certain Relationships of the Manuscripts of *Comus*' *PBSA* LIV (1960) 38-56 293-294; 'Speculations on the Dating of the Trinity MS. of Milton's Poems' *Modern Language Notes* LXXV (1960) 11-17; 'Henry Lawes's Settings of Songs for Milton's "Comus"' *JRUL* XXVIII (1964) 22-28.

TMS^{1a}

From the beginning on page 13 Milton appears to have worked
fairly steadily ahead (despite troublesome passages at 8, 376, and
787) up to about line 885 at the foot of page 25 before the song to
Sabrina. The majority of emendations in this part of the manuscript,
and indeed throughout all of it, were contextual – that is, they were
made concurrently with the first writing of their context. Milton re-
formed letters as he wrote (he could hardly stop himself starting
'shepheard' with 'sph'), and he emended words, phrases, and lines
before leaving passages. Though often insignificant, these emendations are indicated in the text or notes of this edition; the reader may
assume that all emendations are contextual unless the contrary is spe-
cified in the notes by a reference to a category of non-concurrent revisions as distinguished in this Introduction. In doubtful cases, such
as 280-282, 677-678, 784-785, 801-805, I have been reluctant to
posit non-contextual revisions. Let us give the symbol TMS^{1a} to the
text in its first state as it was contextually emended up to 885.

TMS^{1b}

In the text up to 885 a number of emendations were made with
broader strokes of the pen or pens than were usual in the contexts
and with ink that sometimes appears less opaque, though it was probably the same. These are 'nam'd' 77, 'm[i]ghty' 282, 'some roaving
robber' 526-527 margin; probably 'the' 28, 'potent' 280; and possibly
'might[ie]' 82, 'hedge' 526, 'defence ... us' 530, 'iron' 534, and
'streame floud' 857. Just possibly 'fold' 541 and the emendations
in 'o̶r̶e̶r̶' 480 and in 860 also belong here. Some other instances of a
less dense line produced with the basic ink (e.g., 'unvanquish't' 489)
I take to have been contextual emendations for TMS^{1a}. On page 25
the pen was beginning to deteriorate. While it was thickening but not
yet scratching, Milton probably used it to review all he had written
from the start and to make the revisions listed above. Perhaps a
thicker but browner entry such as 'some roaving robber' 526 near

the foot of page ⟨20⟩ was blotted by him so that he might read on.
'S̶t̶r̶e̶a̶m̶e̶ floud' 857 could have been the first or the last of these revisions for TMS^{1b}. They are cited in footnotes in this edition.

TMS^{1c}

After reviewing to the foot of page 25, Milton probably recom-
menced to compose with the song to Sabrina at the top of page ⟨26⟩.
From here onwards the pen was more and more prone to flood and
thicken and now as well alternatively to dry and scratch. The text
from 886 to 1039, as it stood after being written and contextually
emended in this pen, may be referred to as TMS^{1c}. In this area I have
again assumed that emendations were contextual unless evidence or
argument to the contrary is unavoidable. TMS^{1c} was probably written
in 1634.

TMS^{1d}

When he had finished the epilogue at 1039, Milton apparently turned
back to the beginning yet once more and from there reviewed the
whole piece, emending from time to time in the flooding and scratching pen of TMS^{1c} of the final pages 27 and ⟨28⟩. At least, 'whome',
probably in this pen, is likely to have been written in 77 later than
the emendation 'nam'd' in the pen of TMS^{1b} on the same line, because Milton did not usually locate a first emendation far out in the
right margin nor usually insert a later emendation of another word to
the left of a first emendation (line 11 is a different case). The revisions
made in this review are 'shelter' 81, 'faire ... chast' 485, 'driving ...
guilt' 498; probably 'whome' 77, 'oft ... solitude' 412; and possibly
'ope's' 33, 'and give resounding grace' 269, 'for ... blind' 562, 'the'
and 'thaw ... spell' 880, 'in ... need' 884, 'Sabrina descends' 939, and
just possibly 'from' 64 and 'they all scatter' 171. The list does not
include 'cell' 257 and others made in an earlier scratchy pen of their
TMS^{1a} context on page ⟨16⟩, nor marginal emendations (e.g., 989 ff.,
1004 ff.) which could have been made contextually in the scratch

pen of pages 27 and ⟨28⟩. On these pages revisions for TMS^{1d} may, of course, look like contextual emendations in TMS^{1c}. With two exceptions the revisions listed above appeared (in some form) in BMS, including 'ope's', which in TMS is only an alternative to 'shews'. 'Whome' 77, another alternative reading in a scratch pen, was reproduced not in BMS but in *1637*. The emendation 'and give resounding grace' 269, written in rather larger letters and slightly darker ink than the context and in a scratching and flooding pen like that of 485 and 498, was printed in *1637* instead of 'And hould a Counterpointe' of BMS. The class and year of 'grace' are indeed uncertain. Nevertheless, although I cannot quite positively identify the pen, and of course Milton may have had a pen that scratched and flooded in 1637, I discern no clear instance of it in TMS^3 (but see below, p. 12). The asterisks with 'grace' are formed like those with 'floud' 857 for TMS^{1b}. 'Whome', 'grace', and the other emendations listed may be classed as revisions for TMS^{1d}. They are cited in footnotes in this edition. Some, if not all, would be dated 1637 by Shawcross because of Italian *e*'s that came from the pen of TMS^{1c}, though he does not refer to the pen as such; the fact that 77 and 269 were first used in *1637* might appear to support this date. However, as I pointed out on p. 4, other readings in the manuscript were left fallow, and I think these two lay in that condition from 1634. For the date of Italian *e*'s see below under TMS^{3b} on p. 9.

TMS^2

Some other revisions were made by Milton in a more cursive form of writing than characterizes the contexts in TMS^1 and with a different pen or pens. Since these emendations were incorporated in BMS, they must have been made before that was copied, but to distinguish them from those evolved in the first complete writing of the masque I class them as for TMS^2. All are cited in footnotes. On page 16 I shall argue that Milton probably wrote a fair copy [MS^1], from which BMS was

transcribed. Revisions for TMS^2 could have been made in connection with [MS^1], probably in 1634 soon after the revisions for TMS^{1a}.

TMS^{2a}

Some of the emendations in a more cursive form were made with a distinctly sharper and cleaner pen than that of TMS^1. They are 'flaunting' 587, 'restore ... back' 649, 'names' 669, 'and ... before us' 697, margin 896-901; and possibly 'the maine' 47, 'looks ... speaks' 270, 'and' 283, 'but' 693, and margin 834-835 with restoring underlines in margin 833-834. The marginal note 710, 739 probably belongs with these, for reasons explained below on p. 10. The five lines in margin 702-704 were possibly added with the same pen, ink, and rhythm of writing, for although the forms of the letters are not quite so large as in other entries in the class (e.g., 697), the diminution may have resulted from limits of space in the margin, as may a seeming trend to a softer pen. The lines could, however, have been written for TMS^{3b}, and in pen, ink, rhythms, and smaller forms they also resemble the pasted leaf (a) and the marginal note 740 below them for TMS^{3b}. However, since they appear in BMS, they may be taken to have been added in TMS for TMS^2; otherwise, they must have been written by Milton in [MS^1] and later transcribed as an insertion for TMS^{3b} – a possible sequence, but one that need not be assumed. Some other readings (such as numerals below 440) that I have taken for TMS^{1a} could have been made for TMS^{2a}.

TMS^{2b}

In a similar but perhaps more worn pen is the note in margin 379–382: '[in] ste[a]d of [ ] s do-wne [p]happs sōe [c]old banke is'. The pen and ink of this are not those of margin 376-378 for TMS^{3e}. The directive at margin 379-382 may have quoted from a version of the text 376-382 (or more) perhaps written for TMS^{2a} with the variant '[ ] s downe'; this variant was being cancelled by margin 379-382 in favour of the original reading of TMS^{1a} 379, 'phapps some cold banck[e] is'. The resulting emended and composite copy, though it presumably gave the version that appeared in BMS, could hardly have been [MS^1], into which Milton must have directly written the revision called for by margin 379-382; rather, the copy was probably a version on a loose sheet that was abandoned, and margin 379-382 cancelled, when [MS^1] was written from it, or still later for a longer version, the present vestigial '[pa]per over [a]gainst' for TMS^{3d} (see below, p. 11) and the revised copy for *1637*.

In the same pen and ink as margin 379-382 are perhaps the cancel lines through the passage 787-808 and just possibly some emendations that Milton made and cancelled when he was revising the passage; these are 'hence ... draft' 784-786 margin; 'm[ ] ie gua[r]d me' (margin), 'what grim aspects are these?', 'these ... monsters' (margin), 'wth ... disguises', 'bruage', 'whether deluded', 'hence wth ... kindnesse', and 'bru'd sorcerie' 801-805. The passage 787-808 provided material that was reworked into another that appeared in BMS but not in TMS^1, and reappeared enlarged in the pasted leaf TMS^{3b} 713-738 and in *1637*. The first revised passage would have been relevant in TMS^2 a few lines below the addition in the margin 702-704, which may have been made for TMS^{2a} before or independently of the longer addition, so that it did not need to be transcribed elsewhere with that. The addition may have been written for TMS^{2b} on a loose leaf (no longer extant) and copied into [MS^1], or it could have been written directly into [MS^1]. The pen and ink for TMS^{2b} could have been used for [MS^1].

Two lines 'by all the nymphs ... glance' inserted in the margin at 904-905 were presumably not for TMS^{2b} but for TMS^{1c}. Granted that the rhythm of the writing is slightly more fluent than in the TMS^{1c} context, that the pen looks a little softer than the scratchy one of TMS^{1c} and surely softer than that of TMS^{2a} margin 896-901, and that the ink, especially in 904, is perhaps slightly less dense than in the context. Yet we may assume that by this late stage in the writing of TMS^{1c} the pen had relented. Since the lines appear in BMS, though

with 'of ... daunce', they were probably in [MS^1], and read 'that ... dance' as in TMS. It would be more tedious to assume that they had been written with 'of ...' into [MS^1] and later inserted in TMS for TMS^3 with the revision 'that' for 'of' when copy was prepared for *1637*. Unused diagonal cancel lines through 901-904, probably for TMS^{1c}, show that the passage kept the poet in suspense earlier, and the writing in 'nymphs ...' need only reflect that.

The word 'Finis[.]' 1039, though not written with the same rhythm as those cited above for TMS^2, but blotted or showing a less dense ink possibly like that of cancel lines 787-808, was perhaps the final emendation Milton made for TMS^{2b} as he wrote 'Finis' at the end of [MS^1].

TMS^3

Emendations and additions that are distinguishable from TMS^1 and TMS^2 in pen, ink, and style of writing and whose readings were first reproduced in *1637* may normally be assumed to have been revisions made in 1637 when copy was being prepared for the first edition. All are cited in footnotes. They make up six sub-categories, some involving extended passages.

TMS^{3a}

The second epilogue 1040-1089, an expanded revision of the first 1004-1039, was written throughout in a lighter, rather greyer ink, in more even rhythm, and with more widely spaced lines than those of TMS^1. In *1637* this expanded version replaced the earlier ones of TMS^1 and BMS. 'That ... tree' and the cancel line at 1048 and the added line 'list ... true' 1062 in similar pen and style are probably in this ink, though they appear slightly darker. Six times the letter *e* was made in the Italian style ('happie' 1042, 'borne' 1048, 'scarfe' 1060, 'greene' (3rd) 1061, 'deepe' (3rd) 1065, 'Queene' (3rd) 1067) – of which more in connection with TMS^{3b}. The lines that cancelled the first epilogue and rubbed off on to page 29, and the emendation 'earths' and the numerals below 1029 in the first epilogue, are in the greyer ink. So too are 'unblemish't' 238, in a passage that appeared in public first in *1637*, and 'and' 424, in a passage thematically associated with the other two. Milton reconsidered the three passages (and possibly others) together. Perhaps the semicolon in 218 was inserted when the context was revised for TMS[3a].

TMS[3b]

The pasted leaf, whose physical appearance was described earlier on p. 4, contains a basic text 713-738 and an additional passage in the upper right margin 711-723. It will be convenient to refer to these two passages as pasted leaf (a) and (b) respectively. Pasted leaf (a) is written with a finer or cleaner pen and in a more cursive style than TMS[1], and in ink of a slightly paler hue than that of TMS[1] and slightly darker than that of the second epilogue TMS[3a], though the distinctions are fine. The ink of pasted leaf (b) is clearly different from that of (a); see below under TMS[3c] on p. 11. Pasted leaf (a) may be classified as a revision for TMS[3b] because its full text appeared first in *1637*.

The date 1637 is suggested by the handwriting. On eight occasions in (a) the letter *e* was made in Italian form ('baulme' 715, 'Thone' 716, 'borne' 717, 'some' 720, 'soone' 723, 'taste' 735, 'none' 735, 'appetite' (2nd) 737), rather than in the Greek ϵ that Milton normally used throughout TMS. There are also six Italian *e*'s in the second epilogue (TMS[3a]), and several in the draft of 'Lycidas' dated 1637 in the Trinity manuscript. Since the texts of the pasted leaf (a) and of the second epilogue appeared in *1637*, and 'Lycidas' was published in 1638, it is clear that Milton was using the Italian *e* before he went to Italy in April 1638; later he came to use it regularly. On this evidence, but without referring to pen and ink, Miss Darbishire[4] argued that he *began* to use it towards the end of 1637 while revising the masque and composing 'Lycidas', and dates around then have been assigned to his autograph marginalia with Italian *e* in copies of Aratus and Euripides. However, as H.F. Fletcher writes, 'the two forms [of the letter *e*] are treacherous bases on which to erect theories of chronological datings'.[5] Very occasionally Milton allowed the Italian *e*, including two bold instances in one line, in TMS[1] ('plum'es' 414, possibly 'providence' (1st) 354, 'Goddesse' (1st) 893, 'scene' (2nd) 980, 'towne' 980). On the basis of these last, together with Miss Darbishire's argument, Shawcross has maintained, indeed, that all or most of the masque was transcribed not earlier than 1637, including line 980, which I have classed as being in the flood pen of TMS[1c] for 1634. I do not think that these stray instances invalidate the probable argument for 1637 as the date of the clusters of Italian *e*'s in the pasted leaf, the second epilogue, and 'Lycidas' that are textually associated with that year. We need not, however, date TMS[1] so late. The clusters in additions to TMS should be distinguished from the strays in the body of the text. Since Greek ϵ remains preponderant even in the second epilogue, in 'Lycidas', and in the pasted leaf as a whole, including (b), Milton adopted the Italian form gradually. When he began to use it is not clear. Why should he not have slipped into one or two earlier instances in TMS[1] in 1634? The form was commonplace; other writers used it along with ϵ; he himself often wrote ϵ with an open upper loop, once ('change' 353) with an upper loop so large and open that the letter is virtually an Italian *e* with a hanging tail to

4 H. Darbishire 'The Chronology of Milton's Handwriting' *The Library* Fourth Series XIV (1933) 229-235; 'The Chronology of Milton's Handwriting' *Seventeenth-Century News* XI (Winter 1953) Supplement p. 11; *The Poetical Works of John Milton* II (Oxford 1955) 333 355-356.

5 Cf. H.F. Fletcher *The Intellectual Development of John Milton* II (Urbana 1961) 279-286; S.L. Sotheby, *Ramblings in the Elucidation of the Autograph of Milton* (London 1861) pp. 97-111, facing 124; M. Kelley and S.D. Atkins 'Milton's Annotations of Aratus' *PMLA* LXX (1955) 1090-1106; 'Milton's Annotations of Euripides' *JEGP* LX (1961) 680-687; 'Milton and the Harvard Pindar' *Studies in Bibliography* XVII (1964) [77]-82; Shawcross *PBSA* LIV (1960) 48-50.

convert it into ϵ; in TMS[1] he may just possibly have revised an Italian e to ϵ ('esteem'd' (1st) 557); under the influence of another common hand of his day he could produce a poor secretary e ('are' 704, possibly 'deceav'd' (1st) 246, 'when' 734) and a secretary c ('crownd' 956).

Spelling in the leaf does not decide its date but permits 1637. In four lines 730-733 in pasted leaf (a) that were absent from BMS but appeared in *1637*, 'againe' contrasts to 'agen' that Milton employed elsewhere in TMS[1], and *1637* sustains the contrast. This suggests 1637 for the leaf. In TMS[1] Milton spelled 'brud', 'balme', and 'balmy', but 'baulmie' in the second epilogue for TMS[3a]; in the pasted leaf we find 'brewd' and 'baulme'. *1637* keeps 'brewd', though it returns to 'balme' and 'balmie', probably by compositor's choice. BMS has 'balmie' to correspond with 'balmy' of the first epilogue in TMS[1] but reads 'brewd' and 'baulme' in the passage corresponding to the pasted leaf, along with 'Thone' corresponding to 'Thone' in the pasted leaf and in *1637* against 'Thôn' in TMS[1a] 790. If the pasted leaf is dated 1637 from its Italian e's but BMS is dated 1634 (see below, p. 17), Milton must have changed his spelling to 'baulme', 'brewd', and 'Thone' when writing a fair copy [MS[1]] in 1634. I admit that this is an uncomfortable hypothesis about a non-extant manuscript, and the common spellings lend some support to the view that BMS was written in 1637 after the pasted leaf (a); another factor, however, discommodes that view.

Attention must be paid to emendations in line 729 (see footnote to that line): 'Hence wth thy ~~hel brewd opiate foule brud~~ brewd enchauntments foule deceaver'. From these changes the pasted leaf (a) might be supposed to have been a first attempt to revise TMS[1] for TMS[2], for otherwise Milton was temporarily going back on himself. As Shawcross notes,[6] he appears to be working out the line on the pasted leaf. This consideration is the crux of a theory by Shawcross that BMS must have been transcribed after the pasted leaf (a) and, because of

6 *PBSA* LIV (1960) 50.

the Italian e's, in 1637, not 1634. Nevertheless, it is not certain that on this leaf Milton was working out the line for the first time. If the line had already existed elsewhere and in BMS as '[Hence wth thy brewd enchauntments foule deceaver]', Milton might quite naturally have reverted in the pasted leaf to 'hel bru'd' of TMS[1a] 784, then cancelled it, and eventually recovered '[brewd enchauntments]' from the prior version, just as elsewhere he frequently reverted to cancelled readings (e.g., 109, 199, 200, 281, 379, 475, 534, 587, 653, 833, 857, 998), or dropped one reading for another and later restored it (e.g., 1048; cf. 1014), and in *1637* he adopted readings that were common to *1637* and BMS but were not recorded in TMS (see later, p. 26). Possibly, then, 729 is a line reconsidered and reaffirmed from a version earlier than the leaf. Now notice is drawn to the leaf by the marginal note 710, 739-740: 'that w[ch] follows heere is in the pasted leafe begins ~~poore ladie~~ and first behold this &c.' Since the present pasted leaf begins not with 'poore ladie' but with 'and first behold', the note 710, 739 probably once alluded to an earlier pasted leaf that did begin with 'poore ladie', and 'poore ladie' in note 739 was probably cancelled and 'and first behold' 740 added to the note when the present pasted leaf was substituted for the earlier. The purpose in writing a second leaf was to revise the first, as by adding 730-733, which did not appear in BMS. If so, line 729 may have been worked out first on the earlier leaf. The note is written in a finer pen and more cursive style than for TMS[1a], akin throughout to those of the pasted leaf (a) but with letter forms a little larger and more flowing and less cramped than the leaf's, and by that much the more veering to those of TMS[2]. From hand, pen, and ink alone I should not certainly distinguish 710, 739 from the pasted leaf (a), nor 740 from 710, 739, but shades of difference support the hypothesis that best accounts for the emendation in 739-740, namely, that 710, 739 were written for the first leaf and TMS[2a] in 1634 and revised by the emendation and 740 for the present leaf and TMS[3b] in 1637. BMS was derived from the first leaf. The emendation in note 739 had nothing to do with the cancelling of the same words 'poore ladie' 720 in the leaf (a) for TMS^{3c}. I reject the unlikely speculation that the leaf (a) could have been begun with 'poore ladie' at 720 a third of the way down from the top edge and the lines 713-719 added above later. Although the lines above 720 are very slightly farther apart than those below, and the ink in some strokes is a little less dense and the rhythm of the writing a trifle freer, and the space between 'freindly' and 'or' in 719 may seem to have widened as if to accommodate the ascender of 'hast' below it in 720, yet Milton could have contracted his hand as it approached the foot of the leaf, and in any case the ascender of 'h' in 'hast' and what might be a comma before 'or' collided.

To sum up: the emending marginal note 739-740, together with the Italian *e*'s and the spelling, make it quite probable that the pasted leaf (a) 713-738 was written for TMS^{3b}. Its pen, ink, and cursive writing have close affinities with emendations for TMS^{2a}, and especially with margin 702-704, and the latter may possibly belong with TMS^{3b} if I have wrongly classed it with TMS^{2a}. Possibly 'at' 983 in a similar pen should be included here; it was used in no other version.

TMS^{3c}

The pasted leaf (b) or marginal additions 711-723 were written in a very slightly darker ink than that of (a), with a slightly rougher pen and in more angular forms. This passage was absent from BMS but appeared in *1637*. The emendations in 721 and 722 on the pasted leaf (a), and probably the line showing where the addition (b) fits, are in the darker ink. So, probably, is the line that cancels 'poore ladie ... refreshing' 720, a revision that in any case was made in association with the pasted leaf (b) and not with the revision of the marginal note 710, 739-740. The revisions 'foule brewd ... deceaver' 729 could be in this ink if they are not in that of pasted leaf (b). The same ink, or ink very like it, appears elsewhere, though with different pens. In the second epilogue the emendation 'Elysian' 1062 and a cancel line were added in this ink and with a sharp pen, thus show-

ing that TMS^{3a} was revised and that the pasted leaf (a) could have been written in 1637 and then revised by (b). Probably in the same pen, though just possibly in the foreign pen of TMS^4, are a circle round 'an' 775 and a large cross in the margin. Possibly in the same ink, but in a blunter, more scratching pen and in a different style of writing is the important marginal emendation 'benighted ... dungeon' 420-421, which was used in *1637* to replace the readings of TMS^1 and BMS. Obviously, Milton must have made these revisions after both those for TMS^{3a} and those for TMS^{3b}.

TMS^{3d}

The letters down the stub of the '[pa] per over [a] gainst' 456-470, and therefore the lost paper itself, were written by Milton with a pen which, although perhaps a trifle softer than that of TMS^1, I cannot identify in other entries. The ink was not that of the marginal note TMS^{3e} 376-378 directing to the paper. The cross at the beginning of 376 I take to be for TMS^{3d} and to be alluded to by the indecipherable mark 456 on the stub of the paper. I have reconstructed the '[pa] per over [a] gainst', inserted as TMS^{3d} 386-402, on the following principles. The letters down the stub 456-470, being initial letters of lines, show that the lines were those in *1637* 367-379, and the stub is extensive enough to have also contained the three remaining lines *1637* 380-382 in the passage. Hence the text of the page is that of *1637*, spelled and punctuated according to Milton's probable spelling and punctuation in 1637, and showing the emendations 'his' for 'the' 399 and 'such' for 'this' 402 reported by Newton, Warton, and Todd from observation of the page before it was removed, and retaining 'w^{ch}' 398 instead of 'For' that replaced it either for or in *1637*, since 'w^{ch}' is the word begun on the stub of the page at 469 and reported by Todd, though unrecorded by Newton and Warton, perhaps because they reported only cancelled readings.

Throughout TMS^1 and TMS^2 Milton often used asterisks to locate emendations. Neither those asterisks nor others listed below as for

TMS[3e] serve to date emendations; the crosses, however, belonged to 1637 or later. The view has been held[7] that Milton adopted crosses instead of asterisks from 1638 onwards, but the clear evidence of the cross with 'Elysian' 1062, a word introduced in the second epilogue for TMS[3c] and printed in *1637*, shows that he was using a cross by late 1637. None of the three clear crosses in TMS 122, 376, and 1061 is associated with material used earlier than 1637, and the mark at 678 may be not a cross but a cancelled tittle or accent. However, the mixed evidence cited under TMS[3e] and the asterisk at 238 for TMS[3a] suggest that in 1637 Milton was still using asterisks indiscriminately along with crosses.

TMS[3e]

Some emendations giving readings that were first adopted in *1637* appear in a lighter shade or shades of ink than that of TMS[1] and are also distinguishable by the pens and the rhythms of the writing. 'Lavish' 506 with '&' and an asterisk were made by a sharp clean pen; so was 'dusky' 122, which stands with crosses in TMS as an alternative reading, absent from BMS but adopted in *1637*. 'Close' 375 and 'Some say' 475 have tendencies to sharpness. Other emendations in less dense ink came from a broader pen than usual. The outstanding instance is 'majestie' 473 and the cancel line through 472 in ink that did not flow consistently. I do not think that this was the scratch pen that made 'and give resounding grace' 269, though if the latter was added for TMS[3] and not, as I prefer to take it, for TMS[1c], then 'majestie' is the only example of a thick pen in 1637 with which that of 269 could be compared. 'Majestie' may be dated 1637, I think, because it appears to have been added when the same word in TMS[1] had become smudged by the cancel line through 472, which was presumably drawn for TMS[3], since that line of verse was present in BMS but

7 M. Kelley and S.D. Atkins 'Milton's Annotations of Euripides' *JEGP* LX (1961) 684.

was dropped from *1637*. In a flattish though slightly less broad pen than that of 'majestie' and in ink of similar consistency is the marginal note '[r]ead the [pa]per over [a]gainst' 376-378. Since this is not in the pen and ink of the surviving letters down the stub of the paper TMS[3d] 456-470, it was probably written after the paper and when the paper was stuck to page 19. 'Majestie' just below the foot of the paper could have been written at about the same time. Possibly also in ink and blunter pen like those of margin 376-378 are 'soft' 597 and 'rich' etc. 598 (both with asterisks), *s* added in 'burnes' 153, cancel lines through 383-385, and presumably the lines in margin 384.

TMS[3f]

The following emendations are in ink that cannot be distinguished from that of the text of TMS[1], but since they were adopted first in *1637*, they may be taken as made for TMS[3] rather than as 'sleepers' awaked: *u* cancelled from 'glauncing' 99, 'prosperous' 295, *s* cancelled from 'begins' 501, *a* added in 'lêtherne' 668, *e* changed to *a* in 'currênt' 772, *e* and tittle added in 'mȳe' 811, *u* cancelled from 'boult' 813, and the second *e* cancelled from 'cheere' 977. The emendation '& be advis'd ... yet' 787 may be included here, although I cannot identify the slightly hard pen. The words were inserted at the end of a passage 769-787 that was absent from BMS but appeared in *1637* (see below, p. 22); presumably, they were written when the passage was revised for *1637* and at the same time as the change in 772. Since they are not in the ink with which other longer passages were reviewed for TMS[3a] or TMS[3b], their passage may have been revised separately from those. If the circle round 'an' in 775 was made for TMS[3c], the emendation of 787 and the review of 769-787 may have been earlier than it. Three other readings in the same passage are distinguishable by their being written at the ends of lines in a slightly more flowing rhythm than both their context in TMS[1a] and the insertion in 787. They are 'wth languish't head' 776, 'manship' in 'workmanship' 779, and 'complexions' 781. Since the ink is not appreciably different from that of TMS[1a], and in some other additions in the right margins in TMS[1] (e.g., 37, 690) Milton could write more loosely than in the text, these additions, if such they were, may be assumed to have been made contextually for TMS[1], though they do draw attention to themselves in a passage that Milton carefully reconsidered twice.

TMS[4]

At seven places in the manuscript words have been written with a fine pen, in small forms and a flowing style, and with seventeenth-century secretary *e*'s that indicate a hand not Milton's. Some are variants; some repeat the text, presumably to clarify readings. The related matter in the text is in no case cancelled but is usually underlined by the same fine pen. These readings, and the versions in which they first appeared outside TMS, are 'thirst' 191 (in no other version), 'when' 198 (in BMS), 'hov'ring' 237 (in *1645*), 'wild' 337 (in *1637*), 'pallat' 343 (first spelled thus in *1645*), 'perhaps some cold bank is' 379 above (in BMS), 'what if' 382 above (in *1637*). The last could perhaps have been written by Milton, whereas just possibly 'at' 983 (in no other version, though I think it was perhaps made for TMS[3b]) could have come from this fine pen, as could a small and fine caret in 224, and the circle round 'an' and the cross in the margin at 775 (though I have taken the last to be a revision for TMS[3c]).

Let us assume that all this work was of one date, that the intruder was a scribe, and the occasion some known version of the masque. Diekhoff thought that version the first edition, and Shawcross agrees.[8] The best argument for this view, I think, is that the additions above 379 and 382 would have been redundant after the '[pa]per over [a]gainst' had been written. Further, two of the certain readings (337, 382) were incorporated first in *1637*. Yet three (191, 237, 343) were omitted from *1637*. Possibly the latter were considered

8 *PMLA* LII (1937) 721; *PBSA* LIV (1960) 42 n. 7.

and rejected, for we have seen unused alternative readings in TMS[1]. As I shall argue, however, there is no need to postulate any scribe for *1637*. Alternatively, was a scribe revising copy for *1645*? The text of *1645* depends in part on *1637*, since both have common readings such as 'se'd' *1637* 200, '*Com.*' 260, 'quest'' 337, etc., but the text of *1637* was revised for *1645*, and TMS could have been reconsidered in that process. Two of the certain readings in TMS[4] (237, 343) were incorporated first in *1645*; 'thirst' could have been proposed but dropped and the others taken over from *1637*. Yet why should any scribe have been writing in Milton's private poetry book in 1645? Rather, the occasion most calling for an amanuensis was when copy was being prepared for *1673* and Milton, then blind, probably had his earliest version in TMS[1] read to him. This supposition most neatly accounts for the readings in TMS[4]. The text of *1673* was derived from that of *1645* with a few alterations sometimes making for the worse but occasionally restoring readings from TMS[1] such as 'you' TMS[1] 62, 'she' 485, and 'of' 522, just as TMS[4] confirmed readings of TMS[1] at 198 and 379. 'Thirst' was omitted, but so was its entire line; hence the alternative reading may have been proposed for *1673*, whereas there is no evidence that it was considered earlier. All the other certain readings for TMS[4] were used in *1673*, including the spelling 'pallat', which had first been employed in *1645*; all may have been adopted from *1645*. Possibly all, including 'thirst', originated with Milton, were considered for *1673*, and except for 'thirst' were confirmed.

BMS – A Maske – the Bridgewater Manuscript

Formerly at Bridgewater House in London, now at Mertoun in Roxburghshire, BMS is the property of the Duke of Sutherland, who has graciously given permission for this transcript to be made from it and published. Transcripts have previously been provided by H.J. Todd in

Comus ... (Canterbury 1798); by Lady Alix Egerton in *Milton's Co-mus⟨,⟩ Being the Bridgewater Manuscript with Notes and a Short Family Memoir* (London 1910); and by Harris Francis Fletcher in the first volume of *John Milton's Complete Poetical Works Reproduced in Photographic Facsimile* (Urbana 1943), which also supplies the only published facsimile. Though each of these transcripts and the wartime facsimile leaves something to be desired, all were and are of interest.

The Manuscript

The manuscript has been described by David Harrison Stevens in 'The Bridgewater Manuscript of *Comus*' in *Milton Papers* (Chicago 1927), pp. 14-20. It consists of twenty-four unnumbered folios, each measuring almost seven and a half inches by six. Originally, it had been stabbed and had tapes, but it has since been rebound in six gatherings with two additional folios of laid paper at front and back, without tapes, and in a skin cover, probably the original, ornamented in gold. 'Ashridge Library' is written in an unidentified hand on folio ⟨1ʳ⟩; the title in ornamental lettering occupies folio ⟨2ʳ⟩; the text runs from ⟨3ʳ⟩ to ⟨21ʳ⟩. A fine red line is ruled to form a margin down the left of each page; speech prefixes are also in red ink, now somewhat faded.

The Scribe

BMS is written throughout in a clear, regular, formal hand in two styles: secretary for most of the poetry, italic for speech prefixes, stage directions or parts of them, proper names, and an occasional word or phrase. Only one feature of this hand calls for comment. Of its three forms of small *s* two are the common long and short, but the third is taller than the short and is closely followed in most instances by a small half circle on its back and above the line, often looking like an accent over a following letter. It is merely calligraphic and may be found in other manuscripts such as those written by

Ralph Crane, a scribe of the King's Players, and in the manuscripts of the first book of *Paradise Lost* and of Lawes's songs. Since it appears within words (71, 111, 208), it evidently does not create a capital, though it possibly appears once with a capital *F* (18). Twice it appears in catchwords but not in the corresponding text-words (358, 880). It seems to be unrelated to pronunciation or prosody, and is not reproduced in this edition.

Todd[9] thought that BMS had perhaps been written by Henry Lawes, who said in the Dedicatory Epistle to *1637* that he had copied the work for its admirers. On the other side, Stevens, citing accepted specimens of Lawes's handwriting, was certain that the version as a whole was 'not the work of Lawes'. He did, however, find the hand of Lawes in the list of players on the title page and in stage directions at 177, 872-874, and 890 of the present edition, which looked to him like additions. Nevertheless, those at 177 and 872-874, together with the names on the title page, are written in the same italic style as that used throughout the manuscript, and on the title page the line 'The chiefe persons in the repʳsentacōn were', though less well written than most of the text, is in the same secretary style and hand, as is the stage direction at 890. Hence, one scribe wrote all the manuscript. The question is whether he was Lawes.

A quantity of material in Lawes's handwriting has survived, among it two brief letters in a somewhat illegible scrawl, presumably done at speed, and an autograph collection of songs[10] with hundreds of pages of music, each signed, and having the words of the songs written out in a regular, legible, flowing hand, which is, however, clearly that of the writer of the business letters. After inspecting these manu-

9 Henry J. Todd (ed.) *Poetical Works of John Milton* V (London 1801) 431-432.

10 BM Add. Ms. 36354 fol. 1; BM Add. Ms. 33965 fol. 58; BM Add. Ms. 53723; for facsimiles see *The Poems of Richard Lovelace* ed. C.H. Wilkinson (Oxford 1925) II; Willa M. Evans *Henry Lawes* ... (New York 1941).

scripts, I judge that BMS was not written by Lawes. Though some letters (capital *T*, for instance) were made with the same strokes and show about the same form, they are only what other writers of the time were producing. The musician could, one supposes, have embellished his calligraphy for a lord, but his workaday hand might be expected to betray itself in moments of inattention such as the scribe of BMS sometimes shows. In the accepted specimens his writing is characterized by large upward-curving tails to final secretary *e*'s (they wag their dogs), whereas in BMS, though tails to final *e*'s are indeed sometimes protracted and obscure punctuation, they come off the letters more horizontally than Lawes's and perhaps with the pen held at a different angle. Lawes habitually signed himself in italics, and his capital *H* in *Henry* was probably made with the same strokes as capital *H* in *Hemony* (635) and *Hellena* (678) in BMS, but his small italic *y* lacks the long tail running away to the left that characterizes small italic *y* in BMS. Gentlemen of the time (such as John Milton) affected italic signatures. However, on all this I stand open to correction.

The spelling confirms the view that Lawes did not transcribe BMS. In his versions of songs by Milton, Carew, and Lovelace in his music book, despite the various manuscripts from which these must have been derived, the spelling is basically consistent. Both Lawes and the scribe of BMS deployed the fulsome Elizabethan orthography that Milton sought to avoid, and in a number of its features they resemble one another, particularly in proliferated redundant medial and final *e*'s as in -*inge* (the scribe of BMS writes 'with vnwithdraweinge hand'). Yet the personal initiative encouraged by this fashion produced variants that allow the two writers to be distinguished. The most outstanding differences in habits and in a few words are set out in the following table, together with Milton's comparable usage in TMS[1].

It is unlikely that Lawes transcribed BMS. I do not know who did. Fletcher suggested that he was one of the elder Milton's professional scriveners, but he could have come from Lawes's circles.

Scribe of BMS	Lawes in songs	Milton in TMS[1]
-de (past participle) only once (30)	-de very frequent	-de absent
-esse frequent, -es sometimes	-es normal	-esse normal
-ie frequent, -ye(s) only 8 times	-ie rare, -ye very frequent	-ie twice as frequent as -y
v (medial consonant) normal	u (medial consonant) normal	v (medial consonant) normal
divine	deuine	divine
every (and everie, euerie)	eu'rye	every
spheare	sphære	spheare (and sphærie)
spiritt (and speritt)	spirritt	spirit
smale	small	small (and smal)

BMS *from* [MS[1]]

Along with its older spelling and some new unreliable punctuation, BMS introduces unique substantial variants from TMS[2] at 4, 7, 29, 57, 69, 71, 106, 158, 183, 191, 219, 224, 233, 240, 256, 276, 282, 300, 304, 317, 329, 365, 371, 393, 394, 396, 397, 439, 443, 457, 480, 482, 500, 575, 584, 613, 619, 629, 683, 699, 723, 742, 747, 753, 772, 775, 781, 831, 843, 846, 847, 848, 857, 861, 874, 891, 906, 945, stage directions and speech prefixes apart. Though a few of these readings may accurately reproduce others, whether errors or not, in the manuscript from which BMS was copied, most probably originated in slips in writing, involuntary revisions, misreadings, accidental omissions, and doubts on the part of the scribe of BMS. Few, if any, have authority for Milton's text; minor variants sometimes seriously conceal Milton's intended rhythms, for example at 34, 158, 168, 282, 541, 585, 713, etc. In some other cases, however, BMS varies from TMS^2 in readings that were later reproduced in *1637*; see 49, 85, 92, 113, 205, 291, 385, 434, 501, 523 (paragraph), 556, 750, 765, 771 (paragraph), 803, and possibly the speech prefixes in 201 and 493. These readings presumably derive from a source common to BMS and *1637*. Otherwise, apart from spelling and punctuation, and passages omitted or re-arranged, BMS reproduces the substantial text of TMS^2, and on some occasions it reproduces its very spelling, as in 'goverment' 48, 'dieties' 52, 'advent'rous' 102, 's'ed' 216, 'fardest' 225, 'rob'd' 261, 'loose' 288, 'noe salvage, feirce, bandite, or mountaneere' 426, 'vnblensh't' 431, 'sainctly' 454, 'of' 482, 'insteed' 532, 'ventrous' 612, 'letherne' 629, 'cease' 650, 'Couslips' 848, 'a shoare' 884, etc.

We may not, however, conclude that BMS was copied directly from TMS^2. I have pointed out on p. 4 that TMS^2 was left with ambiguous, alternative, and unused readings, and that it does not include some readings that appear in BMS and were adopted in later versions. We must therefore posit an intermediate manuscript, which was accurately enough copied from TMS^2 to have reproduced some at least of Milton's own spellings, and also included his afterthoughts. I suggest that this manuscript, which I call [MS^1], was written by Milton himself. A scribe could hardly have determined the ambiguous and supplied the revised readings from TMS^2 unless Milton had stood at his elbow; I detect nothing in the errors in BMS that points clearly to a third hand (unless there was a secretary hand, not Milton's, behind errors in 57, 183, 191, 317, 443, 747, 753); to suppose that Milton revised a scribe's copy is neither a neat nor a needed hypothesis.

[MS^1] was probably a fair copy written by Milton from TMS^2 (his 'foul papers') with variants now found in BMS and *1637* in common; revised by Lawes for [MS^2], it was probably used as the basis for the performance, perhaps for actors' parts and a prompt copy, if those were made, for copies transcribed by Lawes for his friends, and for

BMS; later (as I shall argue on p. 27) it was revised again by Milton for [MS^3] in connection with TMS^3 and used as copy for *1637*. The view that there was an intermediate manuscript was mooted by Lady Alix Egerton and by Diekhoff, but first seriously developed by Shawcross in an important article in 1960.[11] I think he is right, though I differ in details.

The stage directions in BMS are in the present tense rather than the past that was commonly used in published reports of performances of masques, but since they offer alternatives, copy for BMS was hardly prompt copy but an earlier version. The directions in BMS are more detailed and more polished in style than in TMS, but there is nothing in the additions that Milton himself could not have imagined and demanded. 'Appell glistringe' 120 could be his idea and diction. 'Looks in and speaks' TMS^{2a} 270 is more likely to have been added by him for TMS^{2a} and written into [MS^1] than borrowed by him from Lawes after [MS^2] had been returned. 'Spiritt' BMS 915 for 'Dæmon' recovers a term he had already used in TMS^1 3 and would adopt throughout *1637*. In short, the stage directions of BMS were probably a transcript of Milton's in [MS^1]. If Lawes wrote them, he was in a very undecided state of mind for the producer and leading actor of a show about to open. As Demon he did not know whether he would descend or enter (3) in Ludlow Castle Hall, and he needed to remind himself to come in with the brothers (760). As composer, he had not yet decided whether to set the epilogue or not (936), or whether to sing or not sing some octosyllabic verse (814); he spoke it, perhaps; at least, no setting by him is preserved, although, as Burney and others since have remarked, there must surely have been instrumental music that has been lost. At one time, indeed, Lawes may have been uncertain of the resources of the hall and the actors, but these directions all make sense if they are taken as alternatives offered to Lawes

---

11 Lady Alix Egerton *Milton's Comus* (London 1910) p. 31; Diekhoff *PMLA* LII (1937) 725; Shawcross *PBSA* LIV (1960) 46.

by Milton. In TMS[1] the speech for the Demon TMS 879-885 and directions 886-959 suggest that Milton intended that the Demon should invoke Sabrina in song, adjure her in verse, be sung to, and then bandy more verse between them, the last lines of the latter 944-959, or possibly all of them 924-959, to be sung or spoken as Lawes might choose. In BMS the alternatives 'The verse to singe or not' 814 after the song to Sabrina were extended to the first as well as the second passage of octosyllabic lines, and the end of the passage that might be sung continued to be marked, as in TMS[1], 'songe ends' 890. These directions are more likely to have been Milton's in [MS[1]] than Lawes's in [MS[2]]. This argument applies even if Milton was already writing for a wider public, as he was in *1637*. In the absence of extant music, we may assume that Lawes chose that all the verse here should be spoken, and Sabrina's song may have been spoken too, unless a setting of it has been lost.

The absence of capitals at the beginnings of lines in BMS may reflect Milton's usage. Perhaps paragraphs that are in BMS but not in TMS[2] were introduced by Milton in [MS[1]]; they were retained in *1637*. BMS shows a sprinkling of small slashes (/), probably not virgules, not in TMS or *1637*, but reproduced in this edition. In BMS they appear irregularly, often in conjunction with stage directions and with lyrics but also with the verse, always at ends of lines but not so as to indicate stanzas in song or pauses in speech or dramatic action, always except once with periods but not with every period even at the ends of lines, and not in association with any one person. The slash in the lady's speech at 223 may not suggest that the scribe found the end of a written line there in [MS[1]]. Slashes were used by other scribes, and they sometimes appear at the ends of stanzas or of songs in Lawes's manuscript transcriptions of the words of songs. Perhaps Lawes put some slashes in [MS[1]] as he went through it tentatively or copying, and they were transferred to BMS. Perhaps they are only leaning places of the BMS scribe.

Dates of BMS *and* [MS[1]]

BMS states that the masque was 'Represented' before the Earl and the Countess of Bridgewater on 29 September 1634. Presumably [MS[1]] was written shortly before that date. It is natural to suppose that BMS was inscribed as a presentation copy for the Earl or for Lord Brackley at about the same time or quite soon after. Shawcross must conclude that it was postponed until 1637 because he believes that TMS was not written until that year.[12] I have examined the evidence for this view on pp. 9-11 above. It seems to me unneeded and incommodious. It has Milton making at least three different new versions with fast, pernickety, and substantial revisions and reversals, late in 1637. Why was BMS prepared in that year? Was it because *1637*, despite its title page, was expected to differ from the version that had been played by Lord Brackley, to whom it was to be dedicated? If Shawcross is right, BMS did not preserve that version either. Was it because the poet wished to present a polished version? Then why not the *1637* text? From Lawes's point of view, if BMS was a presentation copy, it would seem redundant at any time after he decided to print a version and dedicate it to Lord Brackley, and if a copy of their masque was besought by the family at a time when the poet was believed to be about to change it, Lawes's public dedication of yet a second improved version to his Lordship was challenging. As I see the evidence, the title page of BMS was probably written after 29 September 1634, and BMS with or without the title page could have been written at any time between the completing of [MS[2]] by Lawes before the performance and the revising of it by Milton in 1637 for [MS[3]] as copy for the edition. I favour an earlier date as allowing the simpler transmission of the text. It might also have made BMS a pertinent memorial and even part of the celebration. Though the Countess is mentioned on the title page, her death on 11 March 1635 may not have set a terminal date for BMS (see below, p. 25).

12 *PBSA* LIV (1960) 50.

BMS *and Song Manuscripts*

Lawes's musical settings of passages corresponding to BMS 4-23, 229-242, 806-813, 916-923, 925-934, 937-948 are preserved in five songs with words in his hand in British Museum Additional Manuscript 53723 and in an unidentified hand in British Museum Additional Manuscript 11518. The music was edited from the former manuscript by Hubert J. Foss in *The Mask of Comus* ... (London 1937). No accurate transcript of the words in BM Add. Ms. 53723 has previously been published; the transcripts in Appendix I of this edition are published by permission of the Trustees of the British Museum.

In the headings of both manuscripts, October 1634 seems to be given as the date of performance, though BMS and *1637* give 29 September. It is unwise to assume a second performance. The punctuation of the headings may just possibly allow October to be taken as the month not of the performance but of some other event such as transcribing the music. Otherwise, Lawes may have used an Italian dating, or simply have erred in memory. The manuscripts themselves must have been later than [MS^1] or [MS^2]. Shawcross[13] has endeavoured to show that the music we have was revised from earlier settings that were possibly performed at Ludlow; I do not pronounce on this. He argues too that the revision was made in 1637 to accommodate the old settings to the new words provided by what I call TMS^1, and by using the songs, he attempts to go behind TMS^1 to recover some readings in what he thinks was the original masque in 1634. I do not think that his readings or interpretation of 'the basic Trinity MS transcription' can be sustained.

Aside from the interest of the music, the words in these manuscripts do supply some evidence relating to the copy used by the scribe for BMS. If we neglect Lawes's punctuation and spelling, BM Add. Ms. 53723 differs from BMS but repeats TMS^2 in the following substantial readings: 'feilds' ⟨1⟩,4 for 'field', 'Loue-lorne' ⟨2⟩,5 for 'love-torne', 'of y^e' ⟨2⟩,12 for 'to the'; it presumably derives from [MS^1] or [MS^2]. Yet in the prologue ⟨1⟩,1 Lawes's version agrees with BMS 4 in beginning 'from ye Heau'ns' against the beginning 'To the Ocean' of the epilogues in TMS^1 1005 and TMS^3 1041, and in the epilogue ⟨5⟩,9 Lawes's version agrees with BMS 945 in reading 'you' against 'yee' of TMS^1 1035 and TMS^3 1085. These readings were presumably either in Milton's hand in [MS^1] or in Lawes's as revisions for [MS^2]. It is difficult to see why Lawes should have changed 'yee' to 'you' in the thick of the second passage, especially since he wrote 'yee' at ⟨4⟩,10 with TMS 994, presumably from [MS^1]. It arouses suspicion to find these emendations in passages both derived from the first epilogue. Yet I do not think that Lawes had transcribed the epilogue from [MS^1] and substituted it in [MS^2], with revisions and in two parts, as new prologue and epilogue, because the spelling of the prologue and epilogue in BMS, where it deviates from TMS^2 towards Lawes's spelling, is probably only the spelling of the scribe of BMS, and in fact against Lawes BMS reproduces several spellings of TMS^2 ('odorous' BMS 17, 'chime' 946, dissyllabic 'Heven' 948), so that it was probably copied from [MS^1] in these readings. In sum, on textual grounds it remains an open question whether 'From the heavens' BMS 4 and 'you' BMS 945 were derived from Milton or Lawes. More of the prologue on p. 19.

The songs in the music manuscripts, whether derived from [MS^1] or [MS^2], also show variants that were probably in neither of these, since the readings deviate from TMS and BMS. Songs by other poets often show variant words when set by Lawes. In composing the music for *A Maske*, Lawes omitted passages corresponding to TMS 1015-1018 and 1023-1024 (Shawcross[14] thinks this 'perhaps ... the result of the use of early music but later words'), and his manuscript differs from TMS in the substantial readings 'garden' ⟨1⟩,6 for 'gar-

13 *JRUL* XXVIII (1964) 22-28.

14 *JRUL* XXVIII (1964) 25.

dens', 'Hyecinths' ⟨1⟩,13 for 'Hyacinth', 'thy' ⟨2⟩,4 for 'the', 'Transplanted' ⟨2⟩,13 for 'transported', 'ye next' ⟨4⟩,2 for 'next', 'Or'e' ⟨4⟩, 8 for 'on', and in repeating 'Sabrina' ⟨3⟩,1 and 'listne' ⟨3⟩,8. BM Add. Ms. 11518 agrees with BM Add. Ms. 53723 in these readings and in all other substantial readings except in having 'you' 4,10 for 'yee' and the unique 'Queen of Pity' 2,12 for 'Queen of parly', while 'Counterpoint' 2,14 has probably been emended from 'Counterpart' – readings that may have been attempts to render the songs suitable for chamber performances. Otherwise, this version of the words was probably copied from the other or from a source common to both and based on [MS^1] or [MS^2], perhaps a draft of the songs by Lawes. The songs could have been sung at Ludlow with the variant words in either of these song manuscripts, or with texts slightly nearer to Milton's, unless we take these versions to have been revisions made in October but represented as those of the masque at Ludlow, as the enlarged text of *1637* was ostensibly represented.

Major Variants in BMS

1

The prologue 4-23 was absent from TMS^1, or rather formed part of the original epilogue TMS^1 1005-1026 and of the revised epilogue in TMS^3a and *1637.* To serve in a prologue the opening phrase 'To the Ocean' of the epilogue had to be emended to 'From the heavens'. Since the latter is the reading in the manuscripts of the songs, the prologue was presumably sung at Ludlow, and here BMS does give the arrangement of the masque for the stage. Who made this arrangement looks to me uncertain. I argued earlier that on textual grounds the question remains open whether Lawes or Milton introduced 'From the heavens'. Since Milton preferred to have no prologue in versions before and after BMS, the presumption is that he did not put it in [MS^1]. This argument will lose a little of its thrust as we examine other passages in which he evidently revised his judgments. Besides,

we are not to imagine that the poet wrought one seamless robe that the composer tore and patched to play in. Lawes and Milton may have worked in close collusion to make a masque,[15] and as Diekhoff[16] said, the idea of mentioning the Hesperian gardens at the beginning had entered Milton's mind when he wrote TMS^1. However, the absence of an initial stage direction in BMS suggests that the prologue was dubbed in, the more so because in TMS^1 Milton thought that the epilogue might be spoken or sung, and he might have offered the same alternative for a prologue made of part of it. (Contrary arguments will occur to the reader.) On the whole, I suspect Lawes of the prologue, because his interest is proven by his having set it to music. If Milton wrote [MS^1] without a prologue, Lawes may have written a note at the beginning for [MS^2] to refer a reader to the epilogue and revised the epilogue accordingly, for if he had written out a prologue, the prologue in BMS would probably betray his spelling; he may also have set the prologue to music from [MS^1] and after he had revised for [MS^2], for if he had shortened it in the music first, he might perhaps have transcribed the shorter version as prologue. (I speculate.) See below, p. 30.

2

In the Sabrina passage 815-910, twenty lines assigned to the Demon in TMS and in *1637* are distributed between the two brothers, twelve being in the octosyllabic verse that Milton permitted Lawes to sing or not. Since Lawes presumably decided not, one tends to assume that he, and not Milton, redistributed the lines to occupy the other speaking actors, and the somewhat perplexing textual evidence admits of this interpretation.

The speech prefixes in the passage are punctuated differently from those elsewhere in BMS. In TMS prefixes at the beginnings of lines of

15 Cf. J.G. Demaray 'Milton's *Comus*: The Sequel to a Masque of Circe' *The Huntington Library Quarterly* XXIX (1966) 245-254.
16 *PMLA* LII (1937) 725.

verse are located in margins and normally all prefixes are followed by periods except for '1 Bro:' TMS^1 443, '2 Bro:' TMS^1 536, and 'La:' TMS^{3b} or TMS^2 702. In BMS initial prefixes, except for the first two (122, 175), are also located in margins (not as in this present edition), and initial and medial prefixes are normally followed by colons, except at 201, 332, 418, 487, 583, 654, where final punctuation is omitted, perhaps by the scribe, who in 418 has perhaps shifted a colon of [MS^1] from prefix to text (cf. 360, 583). Since Lawes would surely not have revised all or nearly all the prefixes throughout the work in so finicking a manner as to introduce final colons, these were possibly contributed to BMS by the scribe, or more probably were used normally by Milton in [MS^1] as he used them occasionally in TMS^1 and TMS^{3b}. (The periods in *1637, 1645,* and *1673* could be printers' and not reflections of Milton's.) Let us pass on to punctuation within prefixes. Throughout TMS^1 Milton wrote '1 bro' and '1 Bro' indifferently and probably '1 bro' in the '[pa] per over [a] gainst' for TMS^{3b} 396; presumably, then, he wrote '1 bro' and '1 Bro' for [MS^1]; for [MS^2] a numeral '1', especially in a margin, could conveniently have been emended to 'el', presumably by Lawes, to signify the elder brother. In BMS colons normally appear after 'el' but are omitted in two cases where the prefix appears in mid-line (360, 402) and in four cases in the margin (819, 823, 827, 909). These are four out of the five cases where the elder brother is assigned speeches given to the Demon in TMS^1, and all five cases, including 891, spell *'br'* instead of *'bro'* that is usual elsewhere except at 483 and 497, where the scribe has spelled *'b'*, perhaps to shorten the lines. Were there colons after 'el' in [MS^1] or [MS^2]? To proceed, I anticipate the conclusion of a later argument on p. 27 that the compositor of *A Maske* may have had medial colons in his copy and that that copy, as far as the colons were involved, was presumably [MS^1] or [MS^2]. If so, it seems that either Milton used a medial as well as a final colon in '1: Bro:' in [MS^1], though there is no instance of his using a medial colon in TMS, or more probably that

Lawes introduced the medial colon, willing to conform to Milton's final colon, when he emended '1' to 'el' or rather to 'el:' for [MS^2]. Now to return to the four cases in which medial colons are absent: if Milton wrote these as '1 Bro:' and Lawes emended '1' to 'el', why did Lawes not add a colon after 'el' as he perhaps did elsewhere? One answer is that Milton had not given the speeches to the brothers, but when Lawes did, he normally omitted medial colons in his original contribution, though he put them in when revising Milton's prefixes. Whence, then, the colon within the fifth reassigning prefix in 891? After this line was allocated to the elder brother, the address 'lady' became inappropriate and was emended to 'sister'; since 'lady' was written but deleted in BMS, the redistribution of parts had perhaps not been made in [MS^1], nor the emendation for [MS^2], though the latter is unlikely to have been overlooked by Lawes, or at least by Lord Brackley, in a performance. Since Lawes apparently did not set the passage, it was presumably spoken at Ludlow; if the *faux pas* stood uncorrected in [MS^2], perhaps he, and not the brothers, spoke the lines after all, and 'sister' 891 was contributed to BMS by the scribe, along with the colon in 'el:' in the same line.

Passages Missing from BMS

Fundamental differences arise between BMS and all other versions by reason of its omitting six passages that appeared in TMS:

1 TMS^1 218-250   the lady's soliloquy on chastity (not at BMS 223)
2 TMS^1 769-787   Comus to the lady against virginity (not at BMS 725)
3 TMS^3 730-733   the lady to Comus on 'baites' (not at BMS 690)
4 TMS^1 211-213   the lady's simile of a votarist (not at BMS 218)
5 TMS^1 674-678   the Demon on haemony (not at BMS 634)
6 TMS^1 873-874   the Demon on Sabrina and the cattle (not at BMS 793)

These have usually been taken as cuts, probably made by Lawes, to shorten the time of performance or lighten the young actress's role.

They could, however, have been made by Milton while he continued revising and composing, as other poets have done, to arrive at the form and meaning of his work. Textually, the question of whether Milton or Lawes made the cuts involves the question of whether the passages were omitted from [MS^1] by Milton or were included in [MS^1] by Milton but deleted by Lawes for [MS^2]. Where they appeared in TMS^1 and again in *1637*, there is a slight initial presumption that Milton wanted them and put them in but Lawes took them out. However, they are not necessarily all of a kind, and each must be examined on its own evidence. I argue that they were probably excluded by Milton.

1

In BMS 223 before the place of the lady's soliloquy on chastity TMS^1 218-250 a half-line is left hanging. Aesthetically, this may not look like Milton's work, even if elsewhere the writing in TMS sometimes faintly suggests that he may have left a half-line incomplete before returning to it (e.g., TMS^{3b} 729, TMS^1 776, 779, 781). The half-line in BMS is followed by a slash. As I intimated on p. 17, this slash does not show that the scribe found nothing more written on the line in [MS^1]. It could have fallen from him without aid or have been copied from one made for [MS^2] by Lawes, who slashed his song manuscript and could have slashed a passage out of [MS^1] if a passage had been there. When we return to TMS, we see that a semicolon in 218, at the point where BMS breaks off, is crowded and could have been inserted, possibly for TMS^{3a}, and that 'unspotted' 238 was emended to 'unblemish't' for TMS^{3a}, which shows that Milton resorted to TMS to prepare the passage for *1637*, though not that it was absent from [MS^1]. In TMS^1 231 the reading 'that lure night wanderers' was underlined, not cancelled, and accompanied by an alternative reading 'that syllable mens nams'. The alternative was, in fact, accepted in *1637*, but its pen and ink, and the rhythm of the writing in at least 'that' seem to me to be those of TMS^1; the loss

of a letter in 'nams' can be paralleled both in TMS^1 ('shaps' 230, 'wolvs' 576) and in TMS^3 ('lims' 712, 'flams' 714) and in 1637 in 'Lycidas' ('leavs', 'flams'). The alternative does not prove, any more than do the emendations for TMS^1 in the passage, that the lines were not in [MS^1], but it shows that Milton was in some unresolved doubt, probably in 1634. (He was still revising for *1645*, where 'hovering' was substituted for 'flittering', the alternative being entered for TMS^4, possibly as late as 1673.) However, in TMS we notice a small mark in the left margin in between 250 and 251, that is, just below the last line of the omitted passage. This mark is indecipherable to me but gives the appearance of having been made by carrying the tail of '&' (which ends below the line in Milton's handwriting) sharply back to the left and then upwards at a right angle. Normally, one might overlook this mark as insignificant, but the coincidence of its falling at the end of the passage omitted from BMS is striking, and it may have meant that the passage coming down to 250 was in some sense thought of as set off from what would follow (perhaps with a kind of anachronistic scholar's dipple). It has also the appearance of being written lightly in the same pen and ink as '&', that is, for TMS^1 in 1634. If so, we uncover another argument for thinking that the passage was omitted from [MS^1], namely, the very slim chance of Lawes's having independently cut a passage from [MS^1] that ended exactly where Milton had placed a mark in TMS^1. This mark does not prove that in TMS Milton was inserting a passage into a speech that he was transcribing, but only that the passage had his attention (perhaps he thought then of omitting it); otherwise, why the (possibly inserted) semicolon in 218 and the half-line in BMS 223? Apart from the semicolon, no earlier mark signifies a beginning of a passage to be cut (unless in a review the possibility was tried by a long dash after 235; ink from page 15 shows through below 'wth' 222). If the passage was omitted from [MS^1], it was added, not restored, to [MS^1] for [MS^3], presumably on a separate sheet, where it was copied out by Milton from TMS^1 with one revision for TMS^3.

2

The diatribe of Comus against virginity TMS^1 769-787 was also probably omitted by Milton from [MS^1]. In TMS^1 it is followed without break by the passage 787-808 that was cancelled and made use of in revisions in earlier parts of the scene that I take to have been made in 1634 since they are in BMS. Again it seems much more probable that TMS^1 769-787 was absent from [MS^1] than that Lawes independently cut from [MS^1] exactly the passage that in TMS ran on into other material cancelled by Milton. The whole of the scene between the lady and Comus gave Milton trouble from nearly the first line to nearly the last, and he is quite likely to have omitted the passage about beauty when he decided to shift the succeeding passage. No mark or reading in the passage in TMS^1 indicates that it was to be cancelled. The pen and ink of '& be advis'd ...' above 787 are probably not those of the context, but I cannot identify them (query TMS^{3f}); the emendation was made sometime after 787 was cancelled for TMS^2, and 'young' rather than 'yong' was more likely to have been written by Milton in 1637 than in 1634, though 'yong' reappears in *1637*. The suspiciously high number of emendations for TMS^3 in the passage suggests that it may have been worked over in 1637 to a greater extent than might have been needed if a copy had been present in [MS^1]. On p. 29 evidence will be drawn from the text of *1637* in favour of this conclusion.

3

The four lines of the lady's refusal of Comus's 'baites' TMS^{3b} 730-733 were not in TMS^1 or BMS but appear in the pasted leaf (a) and in *1637*. Their absence from BMS suggests that they were not in [MS^1], since any assumption that Lawes cut them for [MS^2] is pure conjecture. Furthermore, they appear in conjunction with other revisions. One is at a loss to account for Milton's needing to write the pasted leaf (a) unless he wished to make substantial alterations to the version of [MS^1] or [MS^2]. In fact, his hesitation about the place to

begin, about 729, and later about 720, for which he substituted pasted leaf (b), shows that the whole passage continued to trouble him, and it is, of course, part of that scene between the lady and Comus which, as I have observed, he quite thoroughly revised. In the upshot the only important difference between BMS and the leaf (a) was the four lines on 'baites'. Perhaps his adding these to the version in [MS^1] fulfilled his intention to revise, though it did not glut it, as leaf (b) shows. To suppose that the four lines had been in [MS^1] but were cut by Lawes for [MS^2], and that Milton wrote the pasted leaf (a) to restore them, though feasible, is not neat.

Once we have weakened the possibility that Lawes cut the longer passages above for dramatic purposes, we must ask why he should have tinkered with the following brief and scattered passages. We are entitled to suppose that any of them in which Lawes is not strongly implicated was omitted by the author from [MS^1]; their absence from BMS needs no other explanation, and if they were restored by Milton from [MS^2] for [MS^3], only one was unrevised in the process, though this argument is not conclusive.

4

The three lines of the lady's simile of the evening like a votarist TMS^1 211-213 give no textual indication of whether or not they were in [MS^1], but since they are separated from the longer cut passage 218-250 by only five lines, Milton possibly omitted them from [MS^1] along with that. Lawes might have cast them out as Popish, but so could have Milton; perhaps only Milton might have thought that they introduced an incongruous image.

5

The textual evidence is scarcely richer in the case of the Demon's six lines of verse about haemony TMS^1 674-678. The reading 'that' in *1637* 663 restores the original 'that' which had been emended to 'w^{ch}' in TMS[1] 678 but does not show whether the restoration was made in [MS[1]] or for [MS[3]]. Two of the lines in TMS[1] were added in the margin and themselves revised. This passage, then, gave Milton some second thoughts, and perhaps he was in enough doubt to have omitted it from [MS[1]]. If he put it in, Lawes could have dropped it because of its elliptical syntax, but why dispute this specimen (and perhaps the next) out of many others?

6

Two lines about Sabrina and the cattle TMS[1] 873-874 also troubled Milton if we judge from the fact that they were omitted from BMS and then only one was restored in *1637*. It is not clear that this one could have been more easily restored by Milton for [MS[3]] if both lay (under Lawes's condemnation) in [MS[2]] than if he had reconsidered both in TMS[1]. Demon Lawes could have balked the syntax in 873, but the nice clarification of the meaning and euphony of the passage could have been the author's in [MS[1]].

Authority of BMS and [MS[1]]

To conclude: although BMS is not 'the actual stage copy which was used in the original presentation', as has been alleged, it is of greater interest and authority than has usually been assumed, because it probably indicates the form and contents of Milton's first fair copy [MS[1]] of *A Maske* and suggests that the differences between that and TMS[1] and *1637* are due to Milton rather than to Lawes. In order to expose the consequence of this hypothesis to fuller scrutiny, I have reconstructed the text of [MS[1]] but put it in Appendix II as being wholly conjectural.

1637 — A Maske (London 1637)

Copies and Editions

Copies of the first edition of *A Maske Presented at Ludlow Castle ...* (London 1637) are now rare and expensive collectors' items, though more than a score have survived. I have collated the following: British Museum C.34.d.46, C.12.g.34, 161.d.72, Ashley 1166; Victoria and Albert Museum 6591.26.52.3, 6591.26.52.12; Bodleian Library Malone 302, Malone 195(3); Trinity College, Cambridge; Berg Collection, in the New York Public Library (formerly Huth-Clawson copy); New York Public Library (formerly Bright copy); Pierpont Morgan Library; Carl H. Pforzheimer Library; Harvard University Library, said to have come from the library of Lord Powis, the owner (in 1923) of Ludlow Castle; University of Illinois Library; Elizabethan Club at Yale University; Henry E. Huntington Library. I have examined all these at first hand except the two last, of which I have used films.[17] The volume has also been reprinted by the Elston Press at New Rochelle, New York, in 1902 (from the present Huntington copy); by Dodd, Mead, & Company at New York in 1903; and by the University of Illinois Press in 1943 in the first volume of *The Complete Poetical Works of John Milton in Photographic Facsimile*, where Harris Francis Fletcher has described the University of Illinois copy in detail.

The present edition is based on the copy in the Carl H. Pforzheimer Library in New York, with permission from the Carl and Lily Pforzheimer Foundation, Inc. on behalf of the Carl H. Pforzheimer Library. This copy was formerly in the Bridgewater Library, until it was purchased by the Henry E. Huntington Library in 1917, and passed in

---

17 I am grateful to Mr Carey S. Bliss, Curator of Rare Books at the Henry E. Huntington Library, for checking some readings in the library's copy, and to Dr John D. Ripley for similar services in England.

the following year to Herschel V. Baker, and in 1919 to Carl H. Pforzheimer. It has been rebound, possibly about the beginning of the nineteenth century, in a leather cover stamped on the front and back with the Bridgewater crest; extra end leaves were added, on the first of which is the bookplate of the Bridgewater Library. The original title page has the numeral ⌊6.⌋ written in ink in a three-sided box. This shows that the quarto was originally the sixth of a collection of works bound up in one cover, many volumes having come down from the Bridgewater Library with the contents numbered thus. On the title page of the Pforzheimer copy other cancelled and illegible manuscript entries could have been shelf marks or less probably dates or purchase prices.

The Pforzheimer copy could have been presented to the first Earl of Bridgewater, or to Lord Brackley, the elder brother in the performance, to whom *A Maske* was dedicated by Lawes, and who succeeded to the earldom in 1649. This pleasing speculation is tolerable in view of the copy's long association with the Bridgewater Library. On the other hand, it could have been acquired in some more pedestrian way and at a later date. The second Earl, indeed, inscribed 'Liber igne Author furca dignissimi' in a copy of Milton's *Pro populo Anglicano defensio*, but his outburst could not have been earlier than 1651, and in any case the library contained books of many shades of opinion.

The Pforzheimer copy contains ten emendations in pen and ink, recorded in this present edition in footnotes at 27, 56, 80, 144, 238, 437, 463, 494, 516, 815. The style of these is a script carefully made with serifs to imitate print; consequently, the hand is difficult to identify. It has been thought to be Milton's, and after inspecting the original, I see nothing to disprove this supposition. The word 'by' at 27, less carefully scripted than some other readings, could be in his writing hand; the emendation at 815, where 'contemptu[ous]' of *1645* is substituted for 'reproachful', would support Milton's claim if the copy could be shown to have been in the Bridgewater Library much before 1645. On the other hand, all the emendations could

have been made from *1645* except 516, and that invited itself. Hence the possibility that Milton did not insert them must be kept open, and would become a strong probability if their ink were proven to be identical with the not dissimilar ink of the library marks on the title page.

Printing

A Maske is a 4°: A^2 B-E^4 F^2, but B3 is missigned A3, and in Huntington B3^v is missigned A. Its contents are: $A1^r$: title page. $A1^v$: blank. $A2^{r-v}$: 'The Epistle Dedicatorie'. pp. 1-35: text. F2^v: blank. Catchwords are present throughout, though D3^v has '*Eld:*' for the textword '*Eld.*' and E3^v has '*Thick*' for the textword '*Thicke*'. Misprints and variants of spelling are distributed over the formes in such a way as to suggest that one compositor set the whole piece. Various states under press correction are in BM C.34.d.46, V&A 6591.26.52.12, Bright, PM, and Huntington.

The paper was of mixed stock, as Fletcher pointed out, somewhat poor in quality, and sometimes creased so badly as to flaw the impression, especially in BM 161.d.72. In the Pforzheimer copy there are perhaps four different watermarks, though the paper and inking are better than in several other copies. Inking was uneven in the edition and individual copies; in all copies examined some letters, and rather often punctuation marks such as commas and hyphens, partly or wholly failed to print. Type shook loose, notably in Malone 302.

The anonymous printer, says W.R. Parker,[18] was 'most probably' Augustine Mathewes, who used the border and ornamental capital *T* of the first page of *A Maske* in books printed by him between 1630 and 1633. Officially, a Star Chamber decree of 11 July 1637 gave rights to Mathewes's colleague Marmaduke Parsons, who also used the border and capital in books in 1638, but actually Mathewes continued to print, according to Parker, until 1653. In addition, as Parker

18 'Contributions toward a Milton Bibliography' *The Library* Fourth Series XVI (1936) 425-438.

points out, John Raworth, who received rights by the same Star Chamber decree, used the border and capital in the 1640s. Indeed, Fletcher states in his photographic edition that Raworth printed *A Maske*, for a small *k* with a low right-hand upper bar appears in *A Maske* and in Raworth's books. Raworth's *k* may be seen, for example, in Edward Boughen's *A Sermon Concerning Decencie* (1638); in W. Sclater's *Sermons Experimentall* (1638) it appears along with the border of *A Maske*, fol. A2ᵛ, which Raworth used elsewhere. Mathewes had also used this border and *k* – for instance, in L. Uthalmus's *Fascicvlvs* ... (1636) and (if he printed them) in [Peter Heylin's] *A Coale* (1637) and in Samuel Ward's *A Collection* ... (1636), which has an italic *e* in the preface like that in *A Maske*, fol. A2. Possibly Raworth acquired the *k* and one or both borders from Mathewes; owing to the changing relations between these business men in 1637 and 1638 I am unable to determine which printed Milton's work or precisely when.

The first edition of *A Maske*, anonymous but prefaced by a Dedicatory Epistle from Henry Lawes, was published at London by Humphrey Robinson with the date 1637 on the title page. It has been thought to have been in print as early as 1635 because in the Epistle Lawes has been taken to imply that the Countess of Bridgewater was still alive, whereas she died on 11 March 1635.[19] The inference, however, is unnecessary, and in *Ayres* (1653) Lawes wrote to the daughter in much the same way of her 'ever Honour'd Parents' although he knew by then that they were both 'deceased', the Earl of Bridgewater having died in 1649. As a preface to 'A Mask' in *1645* Milton inserted a letter dated 13 April 1638, in which Sir Henry Wotton refers to Milton's having sent him a copy of the work on 6 April, 'intimating ... (how modestly soever)' who was the author. Wotton continues:

> For the work it self, I had view'd som good while before, with singular delight, having receiv'd it from our common Friend Mr.

R. in the very close of the late *R*'s Poems, Printed at *Oxford*, wherunto it was added (as I now suppose) that the Accessory might help out the Principal, according to the Art of *Stationers*, and to leave the Reader *Con la bocca dolce*.

The *Poems* referred to were probably those of Thomas Randolph, which were published in quarto at Oxford with the date 1638 on the title page. A copy of *A Maske* was perhaps bound up with them by Wotton's friend, John Rouse, as Warton conjectured and most have agreed (though Robert Randolph and Humphrey Robinson have also been less plausibly proposed),[20] or by a stationer, as Wotton came to think. The copy in Trinity College, Cambridge, is now, and the Pforzheimer copy was formerly, bound with other works in accord with a common seventeenth-century practice. The collations of Milton's and Randolph's books do not suggest that they were ever continuous, though Randolph's *Poems* are followed by his plays *The Mvses Looking-Glasse* and *Amyntas* with an independent set of signatures,[21] so that Milton's anonymous *A Maske* with its own signatures need not have roused suspicion when following the others. It was not entered in the Stationers' Register, but no information about relations between the Oxford publisher Francis Bowman and the London publisher and possible printers of *A Maske* suggests that the volume was not published by Robinson in London as its title page purports, or that there was any other edition.[22] Though Wotton saw it with Randolph's *Poems* 'som good while before' 6 April 1638, how much

---

19 W.M. Evans *Lawes* p. 109.

20 *Notes and Queries* First Series VII (1853) 7 111-112 140; Logan P. Smith (ed.) *The Life and Letters of Sir Henry Wotton* II (Oxford 1907) 381 n. 5.

21 Though F. Madan (*The Early Oxford Press* Oxford 1895 p. 209) writes, 'The signatures run through the entire work'.

22 As on the basis of Wotton's letter there was thought to be by Thomas Birch (*A Complete Collection of ... Miscellaneous Works of John Milton* 2 vols. London 1738 I xiii) and Francis Peck (*New Memoirs ... of Mr. John Milton* London 1740 p. 212).

before is uncertain. It might not have been published until 1638[23] if the date 1637 on the title page referred to the legal year that ran to 24 March 1638. Wotton could have seen it late in 1637, as his ambiguous phrase certainly allows, but only if the date 1638 on Randolph's *Poems* was proleptic. Probably it was published late in 1637 and seen by Wotton in 1638.

1637 from [MS³]

To the compositor are due certain standardized features such as capitals to begin lines of verse and commas before conjunctions (though Milton sometimes used these in TMS), along with much of the punctuation, including gratuitous errors, though he probably preserved some of the punctuation of his copy text. He also contributed his own sometimes inconsistent spelling, which is midway in character between those of Milton and the scribe of BMS, but he frequently reproduced Milton's spelling in TMS, and in general 1637 is closer to Milton's intentions than is BMS. After corrections had been made in the printing house, a score of significant but mostly obvious printer's errors remained (27, 56, 80, 83, 104, 144, 238, 313, 437, 446, 463, 494, 603, 765, 788, 804, 874, 916, 1017, 1048).

In 1637 the passages that had been shifted or suppressed for BMS have been restored. The material of the prologue of BMS has been returned to the epilogue, the speeches that had been distributed among the brothers are given back to the Spirit, and the cut passages have reappeared; the whole text has undergone light revision, a few lines have been omitted, and new passages have been interpolated. Obviously, the compositor could not have worked from BMS, even if such a presentation manuscript had been made available to a printer, but has set type from a copy text that was a revision of TMS. This may be seen in detail if the identical substantial readings of TMS² and

23 Cf. Shawcross *PBSA* LIV (1960) 53; but see W.L. Edgerton 'The Calendar Year in Sixteenth-Century Printing' *JEGP* LIX (1960) 439-449.

1637 are compared against readings in the lines in BMS that I cited on p. 15 as unique substantial variants of BMS from TMS²; in these cases 1637 has restored correct readings that had been corrupted in BMS, and readings common to TMS² and 1637 probably indicate readings of the copy text for 1637. How closely 1637 and therefore its copy text were sometimes derived from TMS² may be judged from the faithfulness with which 1637 reproduces spellings used by Milton in TMS² in cases such as 'ope's' 21, 'blu-hair'd' 36, 'buisnesse' 183, 'se'd' 200 for 'sed', 'venter' 243, 'yong' 515, '*Chimera's*' (apostrophe) 540, 'greisly' 626, 'sease' 679, etc.

The copy text for 1637 clearly depended on [MS¹] because 1637 agrees with BMS against TMS¹ in significant readings at 33, 69, 76, 97, 189, 307, 408, 422, 453, 521, 576, 841, 856, 895; among minor features, it agrees in paragraphing at 53, 252, 543, 862; in spelling 'spets' 145, 'se'd' 200, 'th'event' 430, 'oth'' 466, 'o' 530 and 585, 'ceas't' 574, 'said' 890, 'a shoare' 974; and in punctuation at 43, 410, 429, 469, 490, 521, etc. In these readings, especially those of them that were sustained in 1645, concurring 1637 and BMS probably indicate true readings of [MS¹] that had been introduced by Milton in 1634 as revisions from TMS not marked in TMS. Again, the stage directions in 1637 have been adapted from those in [MS¹], partly to accord with formulas common in plays printed to be read, and notably to remove permissiveness.

Revisions for [MS²] are also involved in 1637. To close speech prefixes, 1637 used periods, though [MS¹] may have had colons, but within speech prefixes 1637 used colons in '*el(d):*' in nine cases (376, 500, 503, 509, 517, 532, 535, 607, 682 (catchword)) and periods in only five (348, 426, 438, 640, 683). Since colons appear in '*el(d):*' in corresponding passages in 1637 500 ff. and in BMS 481 ff., they are likely to have been in the corresponding passages in a common source, and if there, possibly in some other places in that source. What should that common source have been but [MS¹] or, as I argued earlier, Lawes's revisions for [MS²]? The final periods in prefixes in 1637 and the five medial periods in *'el(d).'* were probably introduced by the compositor; the printer John Raworth used periods with speech prefixes in Thomas Heywood's *The Rape of Lvcrece* (1638) (as had Edmond Allde in printing the first edition in 1608) and in Philip Massinger's *The Dvke of Millaine* (1638) (as had Bernard Alsop in the first edition of 1623), but the compositor of *A Maske* possibly had colons in his copy text, because he set the catchword *'Eld:'* but the textword *'Eld.'* at 682-683.

Equally clearly the copy text for *1637* went beyond [MS^2]. In *'And give resounding grace'* 259, and in 'Whom' 65, *1637* resumed unused readings of TMS^{1d}. Further, in the following readings and passages it depended on TMS^3: 'duskie' 112, 'burnes' 143, 'un-blemish't' 230, 'prosperous' 286, 'close' 366, 367-382, 'Benighted ... dungeon' 401-402, 'and' 406, one line omitted after 449, 'Some say' 452, 'Begin' 480, 'and lavish' 485, 'soft' 578, 'rich' 579, 'leather'n' 652, 705-739, 'currant' 774, 'a' (possibly) 777, 'mine' 792, 'chere' 997, 1026-1073, 'The End' 1077.

The simplest way to explain these facts is to suppose that Milton revised [MS^2] for [MS^3] to provide copy text for *1637*.[24] No evidence in the latter or elsewhere requires us to posit a copy's having been made from [MS^2], much less a copy by a scribe. When variants were introduced into BMS by its scribe, the true readings remained in [MS^2] and did not need to be corrected by Milton for *1637*, and copy for the new readings and passages in *1637* could have been written by him for [MS^3] in margins of [MS^2] and on additional sheets, especially if, as earlier arguments suggest, [MS^2] was in fact relatively un-cluttered by deletions and emendations by Lawes. As Milton revised for [MS^3], he referred back to TMS^2, adopted some of its readings, and intermittently revised it for TMS^3, though not so as to make TMS^3 a complete copy for or of the version in [MS^3]. [MS^3] thus consisted of [MS^1] in Milton's hand, lightly revised for [MS^2] by

24 Cf. Shawcross *PBSA* LIV (1960) 48.

Lawes in 1634, and revised again by Milton in 1637 by his emending, deleting, restoring, or adding readings and lines, sometimes in accord with TMS^1, TMS^2, or TMS^3 and sometimes not, and by his inserting new material not in BMS or TMS. [MS^3] was probably written before his letter to Diodati on fame [? 23 November].

New Readings in 1637

Readings in *1637* but not in TMS or BMS, if not obvious misprints and particularly if reproduced in *1645*, probably derive from [MS^3], where they were revisions or additions by Milton, though one or two (e.g., 337, 516) might have been compositor's contributions in *1637* that were later accepted or unnoticed by Milton for *1645*. The sub-stantial readings in this class are 'yee' 50, 'hath' 136, 'mine' 185, 'the' 216, 'off' 244, 'them' 310, 'wild' 328, 'further' 337, 'For' 378, 'wild' 421, 'controversie' 428, 'Yet' 429, 'brother' omitted 434, 'there' 448, 'But' 485, 'off' 501, 'father' 516, 'Swaine' 520, 'did' 586, 'That' 663, 'Ile' 683, 'forgerie' 732, 'and' 771, 780, 'showne' 779, 'sampler, and' 785, 'which' 859, 'there' 993. Two of these (421, 663) revert to deleted readings in TMS^1. Similarly, stage directions in or omitted from the following lines in *1637* have probably been re-vised or deleted by Milton for [MS^3] from those in [MS^2]: 99, 100, 161, 259-260, 512, 685-690, 848-851, 905-906, 929, 979-980, 1000-1004, 1013-1014, 1025. In stage directions and speech prefixes throughout *1637* the Demon of earlier versions is referred to as Spirit, a change which probably reflects Milton's revisions for [MS^3]. In the scene with Sabrina the octosyllabic verse 906-928, 980-999 is given to the Spirit, not the brothers, and the lady is not addressed as sister; these features reflect rather [MS^1]. Paragraphs at 25, 1062, 1068 may have come from [MS^3]. So may some punctuation. To judge from Milton's habits in TMS and from the variants between that and BMS and *1637*, the poet's punctuation in [MS^1], especially at the ends of lines, was probably light. In *1637* numerous periods and commas, especially at the ends of lines, probably came from the printer, but most of the semicolons, except for two probable print-er's errors (83, 916), had in all likelihood been added by Milton in [MS^3] for *1637*, and were retained in *1645*. Question marks in 502 and 535 may have come from [MS^3], though the one in 469 possibly remained from [MS^1]. Wrong apostrophes in 'quest'' 337 and 'direct'' 841 possibly derive from some peculiarity of [MS^3]. In *1637* dashes appear after 227, 346, and 847. Since they were not in BMS, they were possibly not in [MS^2], and since the first, which is long, corre-sponds to another, also long, in (presumably) TMS^1 235 in a passage that was first used in *1637* and retained with a dash in *1645* and *1673*, it may have been added by Milton for [MS^3]. So, then, may the others, and in the passage ending with the dash at 346 Milton re-vised 'wide' and 'furder' for [MS^3], and after the dash at 847 he re-vised the stage direction. The fact that each of these last two dashes has an incorrect apostrophe in its neighbourhood is perhaps fortui-tous. Not so the long dash after the motto on the title page of *1637*.

Passages in 1637 but not in BMS

Passages in *1637* but not in BMS must have been derived from [MS^3], whether from insertions in [MS^2] for [MS^3] with or without benefit of TMS^3, or from restorations for [MS^3] of passages originally in [MS^1] but cancelled for [MS^2]. In type the former might be expected to reflect Milton's spelling in 1637, but the relatively few differences between that and his spelling in 1634 are only occasionally eminent in *1637*, as perhaps in the passage corresponding to the pasted leaf, and may have been obscured by the compositor of *1637*, as 'eternall' of the second epilogue in TMS^{3a} 1053 became 'æternall'. Typographi-cal peculiarities of these passages in *1637* do not distinguish them from the remainder of the work in print, as might have been the case if they depended on Milton's hand but the rest on a scribe's, or vice versa. The following are the passages, with some comment on their origins and transmission.

Passages Common to *1637* and
TMS^1
but Omitted from BMS

1

1637 203-205 – the lady on evening as a votarist. Nothing in *1637* shows whether this derives from [MS^1] restored for [MS^3] or, as I think more likely, from an insertion for [MS^3]. If the passage was added with the one on chastity that follows, both might have been written out on a separate sheet with the intervening lines 206-209, but the text of *1637* does not indicate this. In the intervening passage 'far' 208 is a unique spelling in *1637*, and it is not Milton's spelling; 'farre', which is his spelling, also appears in *1637* 1053 in the epilogue derived from TMS^3 and [MS^3], while 'stolne' at *1637* 210 repeats TMS^1 and BMS; yet we need not impute 208 to a scribe.

2

1637 210-240 – the lady on chastity. The text of *1637* has been set from copy that was an accurate version of TMS^1 ('ayrie' 223, 'Shoars' 224, dash after 227, 'beleeve' 231), incorporated the revi-sion 'unblemish't' 230 made for TMS^{3a}, and improved on TMS^1 both by adding 'the' 216 where TMS^1 had omitted it (the caret there I have taken as possibly for TMS^4) and by spelling 't'whom' 232 (cf. *1645*) for 'to' whome' of TMS^1. These facts do not in themselves show whether copy for *1637* derived from [MS^1] restored and revised for [MS^3] or from new copy inserted for [MS^3]; on p. 21 I argued from a marginal mark in TMS^1 that Milton had perhaps omitted the passage from [MS^1].

3

1637 658-663 – the Spirit on haemony. Whether this passage was in [MS^1] or not is an open question, though I have argued on p. 23

that it was probably not. *1637* departs from its usual spelling in 'dayly' 661 and 'swayne' 660, both of which could have come from Milton ('soyle' is inconclusive), and 'That' 663 has reverted to the original reading of TMS¹ before it was emended in TMS¹ to 'wᶜʰ'. Here again *1637* could have been set from [MS¹] restored for [MS³] or from a passage newly inserted for [MS³] – probably from the latter.

4

1637 767-768 – two lines on the forehead of the deep, telescoped in BMS, but restored here to read as in TMS¹ and presumably as in [MS¹].

5

1637 771-789 – Comus against virginity. On the basis of its location in TMS¹ I argued on p. 22 that the passage corresponding to this was probably omitted by Milton from [MS¹] and inserted by him for [MS³] in association with an unusually high concentration of revisions for TMS³. This conclusion is supported by the fact that the text of the passage in *1637* has no fewer than seven readings which, since they are not marked for TMS³ but were sustained in *1645*, were probably written by Milton for [MS³]; they are 'and' 771 (a reversion to the original cancelled reading of TMS¹), 'a' 777, 'showne' 779, 'and' 780, 'sampler, and' 785, 'another' 788.

6

1637 885 – the Spirit on Sabrina and the heards. One line is printed of two that are in TMS¹ but not in BMS; whether it was restored or inserted for [MS³] is an open question.

Passages Common to *1637* and TMS³ but Omitted from BMS

1

1637 374-382 – the brothers on the uncertain fate of the lady. These lines were in the '[pa] per over [a] gainst', whose stub is in TMS³ 456-470 and whose reconstructed contents are inserted in this edition at 386-402. The passage was set for *1637* from lines inserted for [MS³], based on the '[pa] per over [a] gainst' and including the emendations in it, and involving the cancelling in TMS of three lines on Persephone for TMS³ 383-385.

2

1637 712-720 – Comus on nature's gifts. These lines come from the pasted leaf (b) TMS³ 711-723, with two others emended as a consequence in pasted leaf (a) at TMS³ 721-722, while one was cancelled in (a) at 720 and omitted from *1637*. The passage must have been inserted for [MS³], and the original lines in [MS²] must have been emended, or cancelled and transcribed as part of the insertion.

3

1637 731-734 – the lady on baits. These lines are in the pasted leaf (a), which I have argued was written for TMS³ᵇ; if so, the lines were probably not in [MS¹] but were inserted for [MS³]. The spelling 'againe' 733 in *1637* differs from 'agen' elsewhere in *1637* and in this respect corresponds with 'againe' in the pasted leaf (a) 732 in contrast to 'agen' elsewhere in TMS¹, suggesting that copy for the baits passage in *1637* was [MS³], written in Milton's 1637 spelling. The reading 'forgerie' at *1637* 732 differs from 'forgeries' in the pasted leaf (a) 731, but may have come from [MS³] and was sustained by *1645*.

4

1637 813-840 – the lady's peroration on the doctrine of virginity. No earlier version of this passage is forthcoming. If a version was written for TMS³ and inserted in the Trinity manuscript, it had disappeared by the eighteenth century, or is not mentioned by Birch, Peck, Newton, Warton, or Todd. Spellings that do not appear elsewhere in the text in *1637* are 'deere' 824, 'beene' 825, 'nerves' 831, 'o're' 837. 'Deere' is not Miltonic but Lawesian, and 'beene' also appears in Lawes's Dedicatory Epistle 28. Yet since the compositor produced unique spelling variants elsewhere (e.g., 'Dark' 142, 'Deep' 767, 'streight' 845), and 'o're' is possibly a variant of Milton's (TMS 480), we need not assume anything other than that *1637* was set from copy that Milton wrote and inserted for [MS³].

5

1637 1034-1037, 1046-1047, 1049-1061 – additions in the second epilogue. These lines are all contained in TMS³ᵃ and must have been added to [MS²] for [MS³], but whether a newly transcribed version of the whole epilogue 1026-1073 was substituted for the old is uncertain. If the first part of the original epilogue of TMS¹ had been written at the start of [MS¹] to make a prologue, Milton might have found it convenient to write out a new copy of all the revised epilogue for [MS³], in which case we might hope to find that *1637* reflects features of the second epilogue in TMS³ in lines that are common to the first. If [MS¹] had kept the original epilogue entire and at the end, Milton might merely have written out the revised and new parts to be inserted into the old for [MS³], in which case we might hope to find fossils of the old version of TMS¹ in *1637*. In many cases the spelling of the epilogues in TMS¹ and TMS³ is the same, or differences have been concealed by the compositor's habitual spelling in *1637*. However, in the epilogue in TMS¹ Milton had spelled 'æternall' 1015 (cf. 638) and 'sphærie' 1036, whereas in the revised epilogue for TMS³ he used 'eternall' 1053, 1073 and 'sphearie' 1086; *1637* also has 'æternall' 1038, 1058 and 'Sphærie' 1071, though outside of the epilogue it reads 'eternall' 619 for Milton's 'æternall' of TMS¹; perhaps, then, the compositor set the first 'æternall' 1038 of the epilogue from [MS¹] (which we may assume to have followed TMS¹) and kept the same spelling for the second 'æternall' 1058, though he would have found 'eternall' there in [MS³] if that followed TMS³. (Throughout the work he wavered between *æ* and *e* ('Præsident', 'Presidents', 'præsent', 'presence'), though Milton in TMS¹ normally used *æ*.) This suggests that Milton did not rewrite the whole epilogue for [MS³], and possibly, therefore, that in [MS¹] the epilogue had been entire, as I speculated on p. 19. The paragraphs in *1637* at 1062 and 1068 were perhaps derived from [MS³] but would not have required the final passage in [MS¹] to have been rewritten. The punctuation after 1029 and 1033, though possibly from TMS³, more probably came from [MS¹], since BMS also punctuates the lines; the comma in 1026 could have been added for [MS³]. Perhaps then the wrong parenthesis after 1048 resulted from overcomplicated insertions for [MS³].

Omissions from 1637

There are a few other omissions from *1637* besides the lines that were cancelled in the course of the revisions listed above.

1

1637 after 428 – five lines of the elder brother's yearning for a ruffian to kill, not cancelled for TMS³ but presumably struck out of [MS²] for [MS³].

2

1637 after 449 – one line about yawning dens, cancelled for TMS³ and presumably struck out of [MS²] for [MS³].

3

1637 99, 158, 161, after 259, 906, 979 – stage directions not cancelled for TMS[3] but presumably struck out of [MS[2]] for [MS[3]].

Authority of 1637

It has been alleged that *1637* was not authorized by Milton. If the above conclusions are essentially sound, then though he did not acknowledge his authorship at the time, and apparently did not correct the edition while it was being printed, yet he had prepared the copy text, and indeed probably wrote it.

This Edition

In the present edition new transcripts of the three earliest versions of 'A maske' are printed in parallel columns, that of TMS on even-numbered pages, those of BMS and *1637* in the first and second columns respectively of odd-numbered pages. Gaps in the texts resulting from this procedure are not in the originals.

TMS

This edition, based on a first-hand inspection of the manuscript under daylight, electric light, and ultra-violet light, aims to reproduce the text of TMS as accurately as modern type will allow without preserving calligraphic variants in the original such as long and short *s*. Many nuances of handwriting are smoothed away in type. For example, in Milton's hand a majuscule may be larger in size than a minuscule but perhaps not obviously different in form, and letters such as *C, L,* and *Y* may sometimes be taken as capitals or not. Milton's inconsistency in this is a feature of his writing and his spelling whose subtlety cannot be reproduced in print. I have not standardized the original spelling and punctuation and not consciously corrected; where I thought that an interesting consequence might follow

my exercise of judgment, there is a footnote. Milton did not distinguish capital *I* from capital *J*, and these have both been printed here as *I* in the fashion of the printer of *1637*, whereas Wright distinguished them. In Milton's handwriting the syllables of words, especially prefixes, are sometimes detached, and words may be unevenly spaced. I have regularized spacing, except in a few possibly significant cases (e.g., see notes to 218, 509, 637, 639). Asterisks are generally given their own spaces in addition to spaces between letters that they filled up when inserted in the manuscript; apostrophes are generally printed before final *n* and before *d* and *t* in past participles, whether Milton wrote them before or above the letters. His slanting margins, sometimes redressed by himself, are straightened here. Students of handwriting, spelling, and prosody will, of course, return to the autograph (with some help, I trust, from this edition).

Emendations and insertions in the manuscript are reproduced. Usually Milton deleted an unwanted word or line of verse by drawing a horizontal pen line or lines through it, sometimes almost or wholly obliterating it; all such cancellations have been normalized as single horizontal lines scored through type, leaving all decipherable readings legible. Occasionally Milton cancelled a passage by diagonal lines; these have been reproduced to show the limits of the lines and thus of the passages to be cancelled, but the spacing of the type does not allow the courses of the original lines to be exactly followed. Sometimes Milton revised a letter or word by reshaping it or writing what he wanted through it; in this edition the final version of such an emendation is printed *in situ* and the original in a footnote. Usually Milton cancelled what he did not want and inserted the revised reading between lines of verse or in a margin, sometimes with a caret, asterisk, cross, or linking line to indicate its place in the text; such insertions and symbols are reproduced as nearly as possible in the locations they occupy in relation to original readings in the manuscript. To insert one or two lines of verse, Milton normally used the broad and irregular right margin, and there also he inserted three passages of several lines each; all these are printed where he wrote them. Two passages on scraps of paper have been inserted where they belong in the verse; the conjectural text of the '[pa] per over [a] gainst' is at 386-402, and the text of the pasted leaf is at 711-738 (see above, pp. 11, 9). Conjectural readings by the present editor are in square brackets [], interpolations in pointed ⟨⟩, the symbols themselves and the spaces they make not being Milton's.

In the manuscript the lines are not numbered; here they are numbered down the right-hand edges of left-hand pages. The numeration is applied to all *basic lines of writing* on each page of the manuscript, excluding foliation but *including stage directions*. Emendations and additions, even of whole lines of verse, when written between basic lines of writing or in margins, are not counted as extra lines except where they establish additional lines on a page at a place where basic lines are absent. TMS is a document whose contents make their own dimensions, which are different from what may be called the prosodic dimensions of the poetry. The resulting numeration differs from the numbering by lines of verse that is common and useful in other editions. To facilitate reference, the standard numbering of *lines of verse* in *1645* is printed in **bold-face** type down the left-hand edges of even-numbered pages.

In the Trinity manuscript the rectos of the leaves occupied by 'A maske' carry odd numbers from 13 to 29 in their upper right-hand corners. Whether or not this numeration is Milton's, to indicate pagination of the original it is reproduced in **bold-face** type (and even numbers are inserted) to the right of opening lines of the original pages. The pagination of the present edition does not correspond to that of the original.

BMS

The present edition provides a type transcript of the final version of the manuscript, neglecting variant forms of the handwriting. For small *s* see above, p. 14. Majuscule *L* is sometimes difficult to distinguish from the minuscule; the letter is printed as a capital if the perpendicular is tall and the spur to the left is marked as a distinct loop (828, 837) and arbitrarily in all speech prefixes '*La*' ('*Ladie*'), where in the original it is often ambiguous. Since the hand is not the author's, occasional obvious re-formations of letters have not been recorded. Roman type represents the secretary style, italic the italic. Spacing between words is regularized, but run-together words are printed as such.

Cancelled material is cancelled as in the original but so as to remain legible. Where emendations were written through first versions, the revised versions are printed in the text, the first in footnotes. Conjectural readings by the present editor are in square brackets [ ], interpolations in pointed ⟨ ⟩.

Speech prefixes are regularly printed to the right of the margin, irrespective of their locations in the original, where all except those at 122 and 175 are in the margins; otherwise, lines are indented and divided as in the manuscript.

In the manuscript the lines are not numbered; in this edition the numbers down the *right side* of the columns of BMS indicate the *numbers of lines of writing* in the manuscript, *including stage directions* but excluding title page and catchwords. In the original no unusual spaces were left between lines; in this edition the lines of verse in BMS are spaced so as to lie level with the corresponding lines in TMS. The relation of a line in BMS to the standard modern line number may be found by referring to the numbers of *lines of verse* in *1645* printed in **bold** down the *left* of TMS on the facing pages.

Folio numbers, absent from the manuscript, are supplied here in pointed brackets ⟨ ⟩ to the right of the first lines of its pages. Catchwords, present in the manuscript except after 100 and 227, are printed here on the right margins of columns immediately below the lines they follow.

1637

In the present edition the text of *1637*, based on the Pforzheimer copy (see above, p. 23), is printed in the right-hand columns of odd-numbered pages. Peculiarities of seventeenth-century type are not preserved. Where type failed to print in the Pforzheimer copy, the present transcript has been corrected from other copies that have been cited in the notes. Mere typographical variants (such as worn type) in the Pforzheimer copy have not been recorded, but other significant variants are reported in notes. (Fletcher's edition provides a description of the University of Illinois copy.)

Spelling, punctuation, italics, lineation, and indentation of *1637* are preserved, but italic punctuation is regularized. Spacing between words is also regularized; at 641, 697, and 701 run-together words are noted.

In the original the lines are not numbered; in the present edition the numbering down the *right* of the columns records *lines of print* in *1637*, exclusive of title page, epistle, page numbers, and catchwords, but *including stage directions*. The standard modern line number may be found from the numbers of *lines of verse* in *1645* that are printed in **bold** down the left of the transcript of TMS on the facing pages. The text in *1637* in the original was printed without unusual gaps between lines; in this parallel-text edition the lines are set level with corresponding lines in TMS, and the resulting blank spaces in the column are not in *1637*.

Page numbers, printed in *1637* in parentheses at the centres of the tops of pages, are set here in parentheses after the first lines of original pages. Catchwords are printed here on the right margins of columns, immediately below the lines they follow.[25]

S.E. SPROTT
June 1966

---

25 Some of the expenses of preparing the typescript for this edition have been defrayed from research funds of Dalhousie University.

Postscript

This edition depends on my examination of the manuscript of 'A maske' in Trinity College, Cambridge, in the autumn of 1965, and the Introduction, transcripts, notes, and appendices were all completed by mid-1966. A long delay in publication affords an opportunity to take note of editions that have appeared since that date. In December 1969 the manuscript underwent restoration, and in 1970 it was photographed; a facsimile of the whole Trinity College manuscript, along with Wright's transcript, was then published by the Scolar Press at Menston, Yorkshire, in 1970, and again in 1972, when some emendations were added to the transcript. The Scolar Press has conferred a boon on students of Milton, but an unwary reader may be advised that the new gammatype facsimile, though superbly clear, is not subtle, and obscures some variations in inks and in penstrokes that were apparent in the manuscript, which remains the highest authority. Removal of mending paper from the leaves has permitted a few letters of writing and some marks to appear in the Scolar facsimile (at TMS 259, 392 margin, 406, 945 of this present edition). These were hidden in 1965 and are not included in the present transcript. On the other hand, the Scolar facsimile does not show some letters that were visible in the manuscript in 1965 (TMS 21, 131, 260-261, 420, 678, 702, 746, 758). Otherwise, the new facsimile does not reveal any substantial material not recorded in this present edition. I have not seen the manuscript since the summer of 1968, and my transcript should be regarded as a report on 'A maske' as it was read shortly before the manuscript was restored. In 1968 another edition of the Bridgewater Manuscript was published by the Press of Case Western Reserve University at Cleveland, Ohio, in John S. Diekhoff's *A Maske at Ludlow*. Diekhoff's transcript corrects some of the errors of its predecessors. In the present volume no notice outside of this Postscript is taken of the three recent editions. (S.E.S. November 1972)

Symbols

italics as in original

ASTERISK * as in original (in TMS with some emendations)

CROSS x as in original (in TMS[3] with some emendations)

CARET ^ as in original

SLASH / as in original

PARENTHESES ( ) as in original

BRACKETS [ ] added to contain editor's conjectures

POINTED BRACKETS 〈 〉 added to contain editor's interpolations

UNDERLINING as in original (in TMS to restore cancelled readings)

~~THROUGH-LINING~~ through readings cancelled in original
   by one or more horizontal lines or heavy scoring

DIAGONAL LINES THROUGH TEXT as in original to cancel passages

FREE LINES as in original (usually to locate insertions)

LINE NUMBERS: roman, to right of text
   in TMS nos. of lines of writing (see p. 32)
   in BMS nos. of lines of writing (see p. 32)
   in *1637* nos. of lines of print (see p. 33)
   in Appendix I nos. of lines of writing
   in Appendix II nos. of lines of print in this edition

LINE NUMBERS: bold, to left of text
   in TMS nos. of lines of verse in *1645*
   in Appendix II nos. of lines of verse in *1645*

NUMERALS IN TEXT as in original (in TMS 25, 27, 351, etc.,
   to revise order of lines or words)

m̄ n̄ ꝑ as in original

Texts

TMS – 'A maske' in the Trinity College manuscript
BMS – A Maske – the Bridgewater Manuscript
1637 – A Maske (London 1637)

A Maske ⟨2ʳ⟩

Represented before the right

hoᵇˡᵉ. the Earle of Bridgewater

Lord president of Wales and the

right hoᵇˡᵉ. the Conntesse of 5

Bridgewater./

At Ludlow Castle the

29ᵗʰ of September 1634

The chiefe persons in the repʳsentacoñ were./

The Lord Brackley 10

The Lady Alice ⎫
⎬ *Egerton./*
Mʳ Thomas ⎭

Author Jo: Milton.

A MASKE

PRESENTED

At Ludlow Castle,

1634:

On Michaelmasse night, before the

RIGHT HONORABLE,

IOHN *Earle of Bridgewater, Vicount* BRACKLY,

Lord Præsident of WALES, And one of

His MAIESTIES most honorable

Privie Counsell.

Eheu quid volui misero mihi! floribus austrum

Perditus ⸻

LONDON,

Printed for HVMPHREY ROBINSON,

at the signe of the *Three Pidgeons* in

Pauls Church-yard. 1637.

---

6 *Slashes here & elsewhere are in the original.*
11 *Lady*] *L poss. minuscule.*

TO THE RIGHT   *A2*^{⟨r⟩}

HONORABLE,

IOHN *Lord Vicount* BRACLY,

Son and heire apparent to the Earle

                           of Bridgewater, &c.   5

My Lord,

His Poem, which receiv'd its

first occasion of birth from your

selfe, and others of your noble

familie, and much honour from   10

your own Person in the performance, now

returns againe to make a finall dedication

of it selfe to you. Although not openly

acknowledg'd by the Author, yet it is a

legitimate off-spring, so lovely, and so   15

much desired, that the often copying of

it hath tir'd my pen to give my severall

                                                   friends

4 Earle] Earle. *Hunt.*

friends satisfaction, and brought me to a   ⟨A2ᵛ⟩

necessitie of producing it to the publick

view; and now to offer it up in all rightfull   20

devotion to those faire hopes, and rare

Endowments of your much-promising

Youth, which give a full assurance, to all

that know you, of a future excellence.

Live sweet Lord to be the houour of your   25

Name, and receive this as your owne,

from the hands of him, who hath by many

favours beene long oblig'd to your most

honour'd Parents, and as in this repræ-

sentation your attendant Thyrsis, *so now*   30

in all reall expression

Your faithfull, and most

humble Servant,

H. LAVVES.

18 *Running title to fol. A2ᵛ is* The Epistle Dedicatorie.

A maske   1634.   **13**

the first scene discovers a wild wood   2

A Guardian spirit, or Dæmon

⟨With **BMS 4-23** cf. **TMS 1005-1026**⟩

1-885 *basic text TMS[1a]; exceptions noted.*
2 *poss. inserted, but presum. TMS[1a]; wood] prob. no period.*
3 Guardian] u *emd from* a.

<table>
<tr><td>A Maske./   ⟨3^r⟩</td><td>A MASKE   (1)</td></tr>
</table>

A Maske.╱   ⟨3ʳ⟩

A MASKE   (1)

PERFORMED BEFORE

the Præsident of WALES

at *Ludlow*, 1634.

The first sceane discovers a wild wood, then a guardian spiritt

or demon descendes or enters. ╱

The first Scene discovers a wild   5

wood.

The attendant Spirit descends or enters.

From the heavens nowe I flye

and those happy Clymes that lye   5

Where daye never shutts his eye

up in the broad field of the skye. ╱

There I suck the liquid ayre

all amidst the gardens fayre

of Hesperus and his daughters three   10

that singe about the goulden tree. ╱

there eternall summer dwells

and west wyndes with muskye winge

3 *period poss. comma.*

1   Before the starrie threshold of Ioves court

                   my mansion is, where those imortall shapes   5

                   of bright aereall spirits live insphear'd

4   in regions mild of calme & serene aire ~~where the banks~~

7-22 *emendations & cancel lines TMS[1a].*
7 aire] *period poss.*

about the Cederne allyes flinge

Nard and Casias balmie smells   15

Iris there with humid bowe

waters the odorous bankes that blowe

Flowers of more mingled hew

then her purfld scarfe can shew

yellow, watchett, greene & blew   20

and drenches oft wth Manna dew

Beds of *Hyacinth* and Roses

where many a Cherub soft reposes. /

Before the starrie threshold of Ioves Courte

my Mansion is, where those immortall shapes   25

           of bright

of bright aereall spiritts live inspheard   ⟨3^v⟩

in regions mylde of Calme and Cerene ayre

Efore the starrie threshold of *Ioves* Court

My mansion is, where those immortall shapes

Of bright aëreall Spirits live insphear'd   10

In Regions mild of calme and serene aire,

amidst the ~~gardens~~ Hespian gardens, ~~on whose bancks~~

~~æternall roses grow & hyacinth~~

bedew'd wth nectar, & celestiall songs   *   *   10
     *yeeld   blow grow ~~blosme~~

æternall roses grow, & hyacinth

& fruits of golden rind, on whose faire tree
                ever
the scalie-harnest ~~waltchfull~~ dragons keeps
    uninchanted
his ~~never charmed~~ eye, & round the verge

& sacred limits of this *happie Isle ~~blissfull~~ *blisfull   15

the jealous ocean that old river winds

his farre-extended armes till wth steepe fall

halfe his wast flood ye wide Atlantique fills

                           (wonder
& halfe the slow unfadom'd ~~poole of styx~~ [|] stygian poole

I ~~doubt me gentle mortalls these may seeme~~ but soft I was not sent to court yor   20

~~strange distances to heare & unknowne climes~~ wth distant worlds, & strange removed clim[e]

yet thence I come and oft frō thence behold   22

5   above the smoke & stirre of this dim, ~~[narrow]~~ spot

---

8 the] e *cancel line poss. apostr.;* Hespian] H *poss. emd; cancellation below could conceal numeral 1.*

12 fruits] s *emd from* e.

14 &] *Wright;* a *in around* Birch, Newton, Warton, Todd; *cf.* a *in BMS* 683.

15 this] s *emd or re-formed;* ~~blissfull~~] *2nd* s *blotted.*

19 unfadom'd] *1st* d *phaps begun as something else;* [ ] *prob. false start cancelled.*

21 clim[e]] *on broken leaf edge;* climes *Birch, Newton, Warton, Todd.*

23 smoke] k *poss. emd or re-formed;* [~~narrow~~]] *Wright.*

above the smoake and stirr of this dim spott 28

Above the smoake and stirre of this dim spot 12

6   wch men call earth, & wth low-thoughted care

8   2 strive to keepe up a fraile & feavourish beeing   25

      ~~beyond the written date of mortall change~~

7   1 confin'd & pester'd in this pinfold heere

9   unmindfull of the crowne that vertue gives

10   after this mortall change to her true servants

      amoungst the enthron'd gods on sainted seates   30

      yet some there be that by due steps aspire

      to lay thire just hands on that golden key

      that *shews the palace of æternity   *ope's

15   to such my errand is, & but for such

      I would not soyle these pure ambrosiall weeds   35

      wth the ranck vapours of this sin-worne mould

         taske

      but to my ₍ₐ₎ ~~buisnesse now.~~ Neptune ~~whose sw~~ay besids the sway

      of every salt flood & each ebbing streame

20   tooke in by lot twixt high, & neather Iove

         all the

impiall ~~the~~ rule ~~& title~~ of ~~each~~ sea-girt Isles   40

28 the] *emd from* y^e, *prob. TMS*^1b.
29 after] a *emd from* t; f *poss. begun as* h.
33 ope's] *poss. TMS*^1d.

37 besids ...] *prob. TMS*^1a *with* taske.
40 Isles] I *begun as* s *or* f.

wch men call earth, and wch low-thoughted Care	Which men call Earth, and with low-thoughted care
Confinde and pestered in this pinfold heere 30	Confin'd, and pester'd in this pin-fold here,

wch men call earth, and wch low-thoughted Care

Confinde and pestered in this pinfold heere   30

strive to keepe vp a fraile & fevourish beeinge

vnmindfull of the Crowne that vertue gives

after this mortall change to her true servants

amongst the enthroned gods, on sainted seats

yet some there be that with due stepps aspire   35

to laye their Iust hands on that goulden keye

that opes the pallace of *Æternitie:*

To such my errand is, and but for such

I would not soile theese pure ambrosiall weedes

wth the ranke vapours of this sin-worne moulde   40

but to my taske; *Neptune* besides the swaye

of everie salte flood, and each ebbinge streame

tooke in by lott, twixt high and neather Ioue

imperiall rule of all the Sea-girt Isles

Which men call Earth, and with low-thoughted care

Confin'd, and pester'd in this pin-fold here,

Strive to keepe up a fraile, and feaverish being   15

Vnmindfull of the crowne that Vertue gives

After this mortall change to her true Servants

Amongst the enthron'd gods on Sainted seats.

Yet some there be that by due steps aspire   19
                                            To

To lay their just hands on that golden key   (2)

That ope's the palace of *Æternity:*

To such my errand is, and but for such

I would not soile these pure ambrosial weeds

With the ranck vapours of this Sin-worne mould.

   But to my task. *Neptune* besides the sway   25

Of every salt Flood, and each ebbing Streame

Tooke in my lot 'twixt high, and neather *Ioue*

Imperial rule of all the Sea-girt Iles

27 my] *horizontal line through* m, *cross above* m, *cross &* by *in left margin, all
written in ink in Pforz.*

that like to rich ~~gemms inlay~~ & various gems inlay

the unadorned bosome of ye deepe

wch he to grace his tributarie gods

25   by course committs to severall goverment

and give them leave to weare thire saphire crowns   45

and weild thire little tridents, but this Isle

the greatest & the best of all ~~his empire~~ the maine

he quarters to his blu-hair'd dieties

30   and all this tract that fronts ye falling sun

a noble peere of mickle trust & power   50

has in his charge wth temper'd aw to guide

an old and haughtie nation proud in armes

where his faire ofspring nurs't in princely lore

35   are comming to attend thire fathers state

and new entrusted scepter. but thire way   55

lies through the perplext paths of this dreare wood

the nodding horror of whose shadie brows

threats the forlorne & wandring passinger

---

47 the maine] *poss. TMS^{2a}.*   56 perplext] *2nd* e *emd, poss. from* i.

BMS		1637	
that like to rich and various gems in laye	45	That like to rich, and various gemms inlay	
the vnadorned bosom of the deepe		The unadorned bosome of the Deepe,	30
wch he to grace his tributarie Gods		Which he to grace his tributarie gods	
by ~~cous~~ Course cōmitts to seu^{r}all goverment		By course commits to severall government	
and gives them leave to weare their saphire Crownes		And gives them leave to weare their Saphire crowns,	
and ~~weild~~ weild their little tridents; but this Isle	50	And weild their little tridents, but this Ile	
the greatest and the best of all the Maine	the $\langle 4^r \rangle$	The greatest, and the best of all the maine	35
he quarters to his blew haired dieties,		He quarters to his blu-hair'd deities,	
and all this tract that fronts the fallinge sunn		And all this tract that fronts the falling Sun	
a noble Peere of mickle trust and power		A noble Peere of mickle trust, and power	
has in his Chardge, wth tempred awe to guyde	55	Has in his charge, with temper'd awe to guide	
an ould and haughty nacoñ, proude in armes		An old, and haughtie Nation proud in Armes:	40
where his faire ofspringe nurst in princely love		Where his faire off-spring nurs't in Princely lore	
are cominge to attend their fathers state		Are comming to attend their Fathers state,	
and newe entrusted scepter, but their waye		And new-entrusted Scepter, but their way	
lies through the perplext paths of this dreare wood,	60	Lies through the perplex't paths of this dreare wood,	
the noddinge horror of whose shadie browes		The nodding horror of whose shadie brows	45
threats the forlorne and wandringe passinger		Threats the forlorne and wandring Passinger.	

57 love] *Top right tail of* v *is lost in a tiny hole in leaf; here, as with* v *elsewhere
(*love 64*), e *starts low & is not connected, whereas in* –re *(where 57,* are 58*)
e *is connected.*

40   and heere thire tender age might suffer perill

but that by quick command from soveraigne Iove   60

I was dispatch't for thire defence, & guard

and listen why, for I will tell you now

what never yet was heard in tale or song

45 from ~~by~~ old or moderne Bard in hall, or bowre

Bacchus, that first from out the purple grape   65

crush't the sweet poyson of mis-used wine

after the Tuscaine mariners transform'd

Coasting the Tyrrhene shore, as ye winds listed   ⟨14⟩

50   on Circe's Island fell, (who knows not Circe

the Daughter of ye sun, whose charmed cup   70

whoever tasted lost his upright shape

& downeward fell into a groveling swine)

thisnymph that gaz'd upon his clustring locks

55   wth ivie be~~e~~ries wreath'd, & his blith youth

had by him ere he parted thence, a son   75

60 but] b *phaps begun as something else;* soveraigne] gn *phaps emd from* ne.   73 this] is *emd from* e.
64 from] *just poss.* TMS^{1d}.   74 be~~e~~ries] *2nd* e *just poss. emd to* r, *as Wright.*

and heere their tender age might suffer perill

but that by quick com̄aund from soveraigne Iove

I was dispatcht, for their defence and guard   65

and listen why, for I will tell you now

what never yet was heard in tale or songe

from old or moderne bard in hall or bowre

   Bacchus that first from out the purple grapes

crusht the sweete poyson of mis-vsed wyne   70

after the *Tuscane* manners transformed

coastinge the *Tyrrhene* shore, as the winds listed

on *Circes* Island fell (whoe knows not *Circe*

the daughter of the *Sunn,* whoes charmed Cup

whoe ever tasted lost his vpright shape   75
    and
and downeward fell into a grovelinge Swyne.)   ⟨4ᵛ⟩

This nimphe that gazed vpon his clustringe locks

wᵗʰ Ivye berries wreath'd, and his blith youth

had by him, ere he parted thence a sonne

And here their tender age might suffer perill

But that by quick command from Soveraigne *Iove*

I was dispatcht for their defence, and guard,

And listen why, for I will tell yee now   50

What never yet was heard in Tale or Song

                             From
From old, or moderne Bard in hall, or bowre.   (3)

   Bacchus that first from out the purple Grape

Crush't the sweet poyson of mis-used Wine

After the *Tuscan* Mariners transform'd   55

Coasting, the *Tyrrhene* shore, as the winds listed,

On *Circes* Iland fell (who knowes not *Circe*

The daughter of the Sun? whose charmed Cup

Whoever tasted lost his upright shape,

And downward fell into a grovling Swine)   60

This Nymph that gaz'd upon his clustring locks

With Ivie berries wreath'd, and his blith youth

Had by him, ere he parted thence, a Son

---

76 *period prob., though high.*

56 Coasting,] *comma deleted by upright stroke in ink in Pforz.*

much like his father, but his mother more

wch therfore she brought up, and nam'd him Comus nam'd　whome

who ripe & frolick of his[ ] full growne age

60　　roaving the Celtick, & Iberian feilds

at last betaks him to this ominous wood　　　　　　　　　　80

& in thick *covert of black shade imbour'd　*
　　　　　　　　might[ie]　　　　shelter
excells his mother at her potent art

offring to every wearie travailer

65　　his orient like liquor in a crystall glasse

to quench the drouth of Phœbus, wch as they tast　　　85
　　　　　fond
(for most doe tast through ˄weake intemperate thirst)

soone as the potions works thire humaine countnance

th' expresse resemblance of o' the gods is chang'd

70　　into some brutish forme of wolfe or beare

or Ounce, or tiger, hog, or bearded goate　　　　　　90

all other pts remaining as before they were

and they, so pfect is thire miserie

77 w^{ch}] *preceded by a small mark not M.'s usual asterisk;* nam'd] *prob.*
TMS^{1b}; whome] *prob. TMS^{1d}.*

78 [ ] *cancelled.*

81 shelter] *TMS^{1d}.*

82 might[ie]] ie *poss.* y; *poss. TMS^{1b}, query connected with 282 revisions.*

83 travailer] t *emd from* p.

89 brutish] ti *emd, poss. from* e.

much like his father, but his mother more,	80	Much like his Father, but his Mother more,	
wch therefore she brought vp and *Comus* nam'd,		Whom therefore she brought up and *Comus* nam'd,	65
whoe ripe and frolick of his full growne age		Who ripe, and frolick of his full growne age	
roavinge the Celtick, and Iberian fields		Roaving the *Celtick,* and *Iberian* fields.	
at last betakes him to this ominous wood,		At last betakes him to this ominous wood,	
and in thick shelter of black shades imbowr'd	85	And in thick shelter of black shades imbowr'd	
excells his mother at her mightie arte,		Excells his Mother at her mightie Art	70
offringe to everie weary traveller		Offring to every wearie Travailer	
his orient liquor in a Christall glasse		His orient liquor in a Chrystall glasse	
to quench the drouth of Phebus, wch as they taste		To quench the drouth of *Phœbus,* which as they tast	
(for most doe tast through fond intemperate thirst)	90	(For most doe tast through fond intemperate thirst)	
soone as the potion workes their humane Countenance		Soone as the Potion works, their humane count'nance	75
th'expresse resemblance of the Gods, is chang'd		Th'expresse resemblance of the gods is chang'd	
into some brutish forme of Wolfe, or Beare,		Into some brutish forme of Wolfe, or Beare	
or ounce, or Tiger, Hogg, or bearded goate,		Or Ounce, or Tiger, Hog, or bearded Goat,	
all other parts remayninge as they were	95	All other parts remaining as they were,	
and they soe ꝑfect is their miserie		And they, so perfect in their miserie,	80

93 into] *no comma.*
94 ounce] o *poss. majuscule.*

80 in] s *written in ink through* n *in Pforz.*

not once p̃ceave thire foule disfigur͜ment

75   but boast themselves more comely then before

& all thire freinds & native home forget   95

to roule wth pleasure in a sensuall stie

therfore when any favour'd of high Iove

chances to passe through this adventůrous glade

80   swift as the sparkle of a gla̶uncing starre

I shoote from heaven to give him safe convoy   100

as now I doe, but first I must put off

these my sky robes spun out of Iris woofe

and take ẙ weeds and liknesse of a swayne

85   that to the service of this house belongs

who wth his soft pipe & smoth dittied song   105

well knows to still the wild winds when they roare

& hush the waving woods, nor of lesse faith

and in this office of his mountaine watch
        the
90   neerest & likliest to ~~give~~ præsent ~~aide~~ ~~chance~~ aide

BMS		1637	
not once ꝑceive their fowle disfigurement		Not once perceive their foule disfigurement,	
but boast themselves more comly then before,		But boast themselves more comely then before	
and all their freinds, and native home forgett		And all their friends; and native home forget	
to rowle wth pleasure in a sensuall stie	100	To roule with pleasure in a sensuall stie.	To (4)
	⟨no catchword⟩		
Therefore when any favour'd of high Iove	⟨5^r⟩	Therefore when any favour'd of high *Iove*	85
chaunces to pass through this advent'rous glade,		Chances to passe through this adventrous glade,	
swift as the sparcle of a glauncinge starre		Swift as the Sparkle of a glancing Starre	
I shoote from heaven, to give him salfe convoy		I shoote from heav'n to giue him safe convoy,	
as nowe I doe: but first I must put off	105	As now I doe: but first I must put off	
these my skye webs, spun out of Iris wooffe,		These my skie robes spun out of *Iris* wooffe,	90
and take the weeds, and liknesse of a Swayne		And take the weeds and likenesse of a Swaine,	
that to the service of this house belongs		That to the service of this house belongs,	
whoe wth his softe pipe, and smooth dittied songe		Who with his soft Pipe, and smooth-dittied Song,	
well knows to still the wild winds when they roare,	110	Well knows to still the wild winds when they roare,	
and hush the wavinge woods, nor of less faith		And hush the waving woods, nor of lesse faith,	95
and in this office of his mountaine watch		And in this office of his Mountaine watch,	
likeliest and neerest to the p^rsent ayde,		Likeliest, and neerest to the present aide	

[f] y^s occasion ~~of this occasion,~~ but I heare the tread   110

               hateful[l]

92   of ~~virgin~~ steps I must be veiwlesse now. ~~Exit~~ goes out

        wth a charming rod & ~~glasse~~ of liquor

Comus enters ₌with his rout all headed like some wild beasts thire

                        come on in

garments some like mens & some like womens they ~~begin~~ a wild &

~~humorous~~ antick fashion

intrant κωμάζοντες.   115

93   Co. The starre that bids ye shepheard fold

           now the top of heav'n doth hold

95   and the gilded carre of day

           his glowing axle doth allay

                     *

           in the steepe ~~Tartessian~~ streame   *Atlantick   120

           & the slope sun his upward beame

           shoots against the ^×northren pole   ^×dusky

110 [f]] *on broken leaf edge;* ~~occasion~~] on *emd.*   114 ~~humorous~~] *1st* u *emd.*
111 hateful[l]] hatefull *Wright;* goes out] *presum. TMS^{1a}.*   120 Atlantick] l *emd.*
112 like] e *Wright; badly formed, query false start for* some. 122 dusky] *& crosses, TMS^{3e}.*
113 on] o *emd, phaps from* i.

of this occasion, but I heare the tread

of hatefull stepps, I must be viewles nowe. /   115

Exit

Comus enters wth a charminge rod in one hand & a

glass of liquor in the other wth him a route of

monsters like men & women but headed like wild beasts

their appell glistringe, they come in makinge a riotous   120

and vnruely noise wth torches in their hands. /

Co: The starr that bids the shepheard fold

now the top of Heaven doeth hold,

and the gilded Carr of daye

his glowinge axle doeth allaye   125

in the steepe *Atlantique* streame
                                                                 and
and the slope sun his vpward beame   ⟨5ᵛ⟩

shoots against the Northerne Pole

Of this occasion. But I heare the tread

Of hatefull steps, I must be viewlesse now.

Comus *enters with a Charming rod in one hand,*   100

his Glasse in the other, with him a rout of

Monsters headed like sundry sorts of wilde Beasts,

but otherwise like Men and Women, their apparell

glistring, they come iu making a riotous and vnru-

ly noise, with Torches in their hands.   105

Comus. The starre that bids the Shepheard fold,

Now the top of heav'n doth hold,

And the gilded Carre of Day

His glowing Axle doth allay,

In the steepe *Atlantik* streame,   110

And the slope Sun his upward beame

Shoots against the duskie Pole,

122 *Co:*] *not in margin.*

102 *Monsters*] *comma poss. in V&A 6591.26.52.12.*
104 *iu*] *n inverted.*

100 pacing toward the other goale

of his chamber in the east

meane while welcome joy & feast   125

midnight shout & revelry

tipsie dance & jollity

105 braid yor locks wth rosie twine

dropping odours, dropping wine

Rigor now is gon to bed   130

[A]dvice & ~~nice~~ [~~l w~~] wth ~~her~~ scrupulous head

Strict age, & sowre severity   **15**

110 wth thire grave saws in slumber lie

wee that are of purer fire

imitate the starrie quire   135

who in thire nightly watchfull spheares

in lead ~~wth~~ swift round the months & yeares

115 the sounds & seas wth all thire finnie drove

128 braid] i *emd from* y.

131 [~~l w~~]] *leaf damaged;* l *poss. majuscule;* quick Law *Birch, Newton, Warton, Todd, but* quick *poss. wrong;* ~~tom~~ *Wright, but space between* ~~nice~~

& [~~tom~~] *greater than needed for* [~~eus~~].

134 are] ar *emd, poss. from unfinished* th.

135 quire] ui *badly formed; query* i *emd from* r.

BMS	1637
pacinge toward the other goale	Pacing toward the other gole
of his Chamber in the East 130	Of his Chamber in the East. Of (5)
meane-while welcome, Ioye & feast,	Meane while welcome Joy, and Feast, 115
midnight shoute, and revelry	Midnight shout, and revelrie,
tipsie daunce and Iollitie,	Tipsie dance, and Jollitie.
braide yor locks wth rosie twine	Braid your Locks with rosie Twine,
droppinge odours, droppinge wine 135	Dropping odours, dropping Wine.
Rigor now is gone to bed,	Rigor now is gone to bed, 120
and advice, wth scrupulous head,	And Advice with scrupulous head,
strict age, and sowre severitie	Strict Age, and sowre Severitie
wth their grave sawes in slumber lye	With their graue Sawes in slumber lie.
Wee that are of purer fire 140	We that are of purer fire,
imitate the starrie quire	Immitate the starrie quire, 125
whoe in their nightly watchfull sphears	Who in their nightly watchfull Spheares,
leade in swift round the months & years,	Lead in swift round the Months and Yeares.
the sounds and seas with all their finnie drove	The Sounds, and Seas with all their finnie drove,

137 advice,] *comma prob.*

now to the moone in wavering morrice move

      *tawnie

and on the ˄~~yellow~~ sands & shelves   *tawnie   140

trip the pert fayries, & the dapper elves.

by dimpled brooke & fountayne brim

120   the wood nimphs deck't wth daysies trim

thire merrie wakes & pastimes keepe

what hath night to doe wth sleepe   145

night has better sweets to prove

Venus now wakes, & wakens Love

125   Come let us our rights begin

tis only daylight that makes sin

wch these dun shades will nere report   150

Haile goddesse of nocturnall sport

Dark-vaild Cotytto, to whome the secret flame

130   of midnight torches burnes, mysterious Dame

that neere art call'd but when the dragon womb

142 brooke] *comma poss.*
152 to whome] *query run together.*

153 burnes] s *inserted, poss. TMS*^3e.

BMS	1637
nowe to the moone in waveringe morrice move, 145	Now to the Moone in wavering Morrice move,
and on the tawny sands and shelves	And on the tawny sands and shelves, 130
trip the pert fairies, and the dapp Ealves	Trip the pert Fairies and the dapper Elves;
by dimpled brooke, and fountaine brim	By dimpled Brooke, and Fountaine brim,
the wood nimphs decte with daisies trim	The Wood-nymphs deckt with daisies trim,
their merry wakes & pastimes keepe 150	Their merry wakes, and pastimes keepe,
what hath night to doe with sleepe	What hath night to doe with sleepe? 135
Night has better sweets to prove	Night hath better sweets to prove,
Venus now wakes, and wakens love,	*Venus* now wakes, and wakens Love.
Come let vs oᵣ rights begyn	Come let us our rights begin
tis only day light that maks sin 155	'Tis onely day-light that makes Sin
wᶜʰ these dun shades will neere report	Which these dun shades will ne're report. 140
haile goddess of nocturnall sport	Haile Goddesse of Nocturnall sport
darke-vayld Cotitto, whome the secret flame	Dark-vaild *Cotytto*, t'whom the secret flame
of mid night torches burne misterious dame	Of mid-night Torches burnes; mysterious Dame
that neere art call'd, but when the dragon woombe 160	That ne're at call'd, but when the Dragon woome

night
⟨6ᵣ⟩

158 *space in the original.*
160 neere] *2nd* e *blotted;* woombe] *2nd* o *emd.*

133 daisies trim] *close, but short final* s *shows words separate.*
143 *Hyphen did not print in BM C.34.d.46, 161.d.72, PM, etc., but clear in Pforz.,
Cambridge, Bright, BM Ashley 1166, etc.*
144 at] r *added above & between* a & t, *caret below,* art *in right margin, all written
in ink in Pforz.*

of Stygian darknesse spitts her thickest gloᵒme *and makes one blot   155

                                                                (& befreind

*~~and makes a blot of nature and throws a blot~~ˏ of all yᵉ aire

clowdie

134   stay thy ~~polisht~~ ebon chaire   wherin thou ~~rid[st]~~ ridst wᵗʰ Hecateˏ

                                        ⊕
                                none

137   of~~ø~~ till all thy dues bee don & ~~nought~~ left out   ~~& favour our close revelrie jocondrie~~

138   ere the blabbing eastreane scout   us thy vow'd preists till utmost end

the nice ['] morne on th'Indian steepe   160

140   from her cabin'd loopehole peepe

and to yᵉ telltale sun discry

our conceal'd sollemnity

Come knit hands, & beate yᵉ ground

144   in ~~wᵗʰ~~ a light ~~& frolick~~ fantastick round   165

the measure (in a wild rude & wanton antick)

155-159 *margin prob. TMS*^{1a}; *M. prob. changed* 156 *to* and throws ... oer ...
    aire, *then after* 159 *or more phaps added* & favour ... jocondrie *with*
    ⊕ *before* & *and* ⊕ *before* till, *then cancelled* & favour ... & ⊕ *before* till,
    wrote 2 lines wherin ... end, *drew a line to insert* wherin *after* chaire,
    emd till *to* of, *then inserted* *and ... blot.

156 blot *(2nd)*] l *emd from* o; of] f *emd, prob. from* er.
160 [`]] *a mark like a hyphen but higher & sloping down right & with spaces*
    before & after wider than usual, or like a grave accent written low.
163 conceal'd] *2nd* c *blotted.*

BMS		1637	
of stigian darknes, spetts her thickest [ ] gloome,		Of Stygian darknesse spets her thickest gloome	145
			And
and makes one blot of all the aire,		And makes one blot of all the aire,	(6)
staye thy cloudie Ebon chaire		Stay thy clowdie *Ebon* chaire,	
wherein thou rid'st with Hecatt' and befriend		Wherein thou rid'st with *Hecat'*, and befriend	
vs thy vow'd preists till vtmost end	165	Vs thy vow'd Priests, till utmost end	
of all thy dues be done, & none left out		Of all thy dues be done, and none left out	150
ere the blabbinge Easterne scoute		Ere the blabbing Easterne scout	
the nice morne on the Indian steepe		The nice Morne on th'*Indian* steepe	
from her Cabin'd loopehole peepe,		From her cabin'd loop hole peepe,	
and to the tell tale sun descrie	170	And to the tel-tale Sun discry	
our Conceal'd solempnitie,		Our conceal'd Solemnity.	155
come knitt hands & beate the ground		Come, knit hands, and beate the ground	
in a light fantastick round. /		In a light fantastick round.	

The measure in a wild, rude, & wanton *Antick*. /   *The Measure.*

161 [ ] *illegible cancellation.*
164 Hecatt'] tt *poss. emd to* t.

155 Our] O *very faint in Bright, but visible from other side of leaf,* & W *super-imprinted on* O *in blacker ink than context.*

145   Comus. Breake off, breake off, I ~~heare~~ feele the different pace

146   of some chast footing neere about this ground

~~some virgin sure benighted in these woods~~

~~for so I can disdinguish by myne art~~   170

147   run to yor shrouds wthin these braks & trees   they all scatter

our number may affright. Some virgin sure

(for so I can distinguish by myne art)

150   benighted in these woods; now to my ~~traines~~ charmes

& to my ~~mothers charmes~~ wilie trains, I shall ere long   175

be well stock't wth as faire a heard as graz'd

about my mother Circe thus I hurle
    dazling
my ~~powder'd~~ spells in to the spungie aire ~~blind~~ *bleare

155   of power to cheate the eye wth *~~sleight~~ illusion
                 lest
and give it false præsentments, ~~else~~ the place   180

and my quaint habits breed astonishment

and put the damse[l]l to suspicious flight

wch must not be, for thats against my course

Co: Breake of, breake of, I feele the different pace	175	Breake off, breake off, I feele the different pace
of some chast footinge, neere about this ground		Of some chast footing neere about this ground, 160
	run	

they all scatter ⟨6ᵛ⟩

run to yoʳ shrouds wᵗʰin these brakes & trees/   Run to your shrouds, within these Brakes, and Trees

our number may affright; some virgin sure   Our number may affright: Some Virgin sure

(for soe I can distingwish by myne arte)   (For so I can distinguish by mine Art)

benighted ~~sure~~ in these woods, now to my Charms   180   Benighted in these woods. Now to my charmes

and to my wilie traynes, I shall ere longe   And to my wilie trains, I shall e're long   165

be well stockt with as fayre a heard as graz'd   Be well stock't with as faire a Heard as graz'd

abouts my mother Circe, thus I hurle   About my Mother *Circe.* Thus I hurle

my dazlinge spells into the spungie aire   My dazling Spells into the spungie aire

of powre to cheate the eye with bleare illusion   185   Of power to cheate the eye with bleare illusion,

and give it false presentments, least the place,   And give it false presentments, lest the place   170

and my quainte habitts breede astonishment   And my queint habits breed astonishment,

and put the damsell to suspitious flight,   And put the Damsel to suspicious flight,

wᶜʰ must not be, for thats against my course,   Which must not be, for that's against my course;

175 *Co:*] *not in margin.*
177 *s.d. slightly below line & cramped.*

160 I under faire prætence of freindly ends

and well-plac't words of glozing courtesie   185

baited wth reasons not unplausible

wind me into the easie hearted man
                    snares
& hugge him into ͜ nets. when once her eye

165 hath met the vertue of this magick dust

I shall appeare some harmelesse villager   190

whome <u>thrift</u> keeps up about his countrie geare /thirst

but heere she comes I fairly step aside

169 & hearken, if I may, her buisnesse heere.

the Ladie enters

170 this way the noise was, if my eare be true   195
              best
my ͜ guide now, me thought it was the sound

of riot, & ill manag'd merriment

BMS		1637	
I vnder fayre p^{r}tence of freindly ends	190	I under faire prætents of friendly ends,	
and well plac't words of gloweinge Curtesie		And wel plac't words of glozing courtesie	175
bayted with reasons not vnplausible		Baited with reasons not unplausible	
winde me into the easie harted man,		Wind me into the easie hearted man,	Wind (7)
and hug him into snares. when once her eye		And hug him into snares; when once her eye	
hath met the vertue of this magick dust	195	Hath met the vertue of this Magick dust,	
I shall appe some harmles villager		I shall appeare some harmlesse Villager	180
whome thrifte keeps vp about his Countrie geare		Whom thrift keepes up about his Country geare	
but heere she comes, I fayrely step aside		But here she comes, I fairly step aside	
and hearken if I may her businesse heere		And hearken, if I may, her buisnesse here.	

The lady enters	200	*The Ladie enters.*	

BMS		1637	
La This waye the noise was, if my eare be true		This way the noise was, if mine eare be true	185
my best guyde nowe, me thought it was the sound		My best guide now, me thought it was the sound	
of riott and ill-manag'd merriment	of ⟨7^r⟩	Of Riot, and ill manag'd Merriment,	

193 harted] e *emd.*
199 *no punctuation.*
201 *La*] *in margin, like all subsequent speech prefixes at beginnings of lines.*

such as the jocond flute or gamesome pipe   when   granges   ⟨16⟩
                                ~~that~~   ~~garners~~ full

174   stirrs up amoungst the loose unletter'd hinds
                    ador[e]   ~~when~~ for thire teeming flocks, &

176   in wanton dance ~~they~~ ₍praise₎ the bounteous Pan   200

& thanke the gods amisse, I should be loath

to meet the rudenesse & swill'd insolence

179   of such late wassailers yet ~~Oh~~ where else ₍shall I informe my unacquainted feete

              mazes   tangled
181   in the blind ₍alleys₎ of ~~these~~ this ₍~~arched~~ wood

my brothers when they saw me wearied out   205

wth this long way resolving heere to lodge

under the spredding favour of these pines

185   stept, as they sed, to the next thicket side

to bring me berries, or such cooling fruit

as the kind hospitable woods provide   210

they left me then, when the gray-hoodded Ev'n

like a sad votarist in palmers weeds

---

198 when] *TMS*^4.

200 ~~ador~~[e]] e *doubtful, poss. unfinished.*

203 ~~Oh~~] O *poss. minuscule.*

204 these] *1st* e *prob. emd from* is.

207 pines] e *virtually Italian, but poss. made as Greek.*

211 hoodded] *2nd* d *emd from* e; Ev'n] E *poss. minuscule, as Wright.*

such as the iocond flute or gamesome pipe	Such as the jocond Flute, or gamesome Pipe
stirrs vp amonge the ~~rude~~ loose vnlettered hindes 205	Stirs up among the loose unleter'd Hinds
when for their teeminge flocks and granges full	When for their teeming Flocks, and granges full 190
in wanton daunce they praise the bounteus *Pan*	In wanton dance they praise the bounteous *Pan,*
and thanke the Gods amisse, I should be loath	And thanke the gods amisse. I should be loath
to meete the rudenes, and swill'd insolence	To meet the rudenesse, and swill'd insolence
of such late wassailers; yet o where els 210	Of such late Wassailers; yet ô where else
shall I ~~acquainte~~ informe my vnacquainted feete	Shall I informe my unacquainted feet 195
in the blinde mazes of this tangled wood,	In the blind mazes of this tangled wood?
my brothers when they sawe me wearied out	My Brothers when they saw me wearied out
with this longe waye, resolvinge heere to lodge	With this long way, resolving here to lodge
vnder the spreadinge favour of these pines, 215	Vnder the spreading favour of these Pines
stept as they s'ed, to the next thickett side	Stept as they se'd to the next Thicket side 200
to bringe me berries, or such coolinge fruite	To bring me Berries, or such cooling fruit
as the kynde hospitable woods provide	As the kind hospitable woods provide.
	They left me then, when the gray-hooded Ev'n
	Like a sad Votarist in Palmers weeds

190   rose from the hindmost weeles of Phœbus ~~chaire~~ waine

but where they are and why they came not back

is now the labour of my thoughts, tiz likliest   215
                wandring
they had ingadg'd thire ~~youthly~~ steps too farre

~~to the soone parting light~~ and envious darknesse ere they could returne

195   had stolne them from me;else O theevish night

why shouldst thou, but for some fellonious end

in thy darke lanterne thus close up the starres   220

that nature hung in heaven & fill'd thire lamps

wth ever lasting oyle to give *~~thire~~ light *due

200   to the misled & lonely travailer

this is ‸place as well as I may guesse

whence even now the tumult of Loud mirth   225

was rife & perfect in my listening eare

yet nought but single darknesse doe I find

205   what might this be? a thousand fantasies

begin to throng into my memorie

---

213 waine] i *inserted.*
216 ingadg'd] *2nd* g *emd.*
218 *query semicolon inserted & for TMS*[3a]*; O] poss. minuscule.*

219 shouldst thou] *poss. run together.*
220 darke] *mark above* e *poss.* l *begun & cancelled.*
224 *caret poss. TMS*[4]*; as (1st)] a begun as something else.*

Rose from the hindmost wheels of *Phœbus* waine.   205

but where they are, and whye they come not back

But where they are, and why they came not back

is now the labour of my thoughts, tis likeliest   220

Is now the labour of my thoughts, 'tis likeliest

They

they had ingaged their wandringe stepps too farr

They had ingag'd their wandring steps too far,   (8)

and envious darknesse ere they could retorne

And envious darknesse, e're they could returne,

had stolne them from me. /

Had stolne them from me, else ô theevish Night   210

Why shouldst thou, but for some fellonious end

In thy darke lanterne thus close up the Stars,

That nature hung in Heav'n, and fill'd their lamps

With everlasting oile to give due light

To the misled, and lonely Travailer.   215

This is the place, as well as I may guesse

Whence even now the tumult of loud Mirth

Was rife, and perfect in my listening eare,

Yet nought but single darknesse doe I find,

What might this be? a thousand fantasies   220

Begin to throng into my memorie

220 *meaningless ink mark after line.*

of calling shaps, & beckning shadows dire   230

and ayrie toungs *that lure night wanderers* that syllable mens nams

on sands, & shoars, & desert wildernesses.

210   these thoughts may startle well, but not astound

the vertuous mind, that ever walks attended

by a strong siding champion conscience ——   235

O welcome pure-eyd Faith, white-handed Hope

_4_   _4_ hov'ring
thou ~~flittering~~ angell girt wth golden wings

*
215   and thou *~~unspotted~~ forme of chastity   unblemish't

216   I see yee visibly, ~~& while I see yee~~

~~this dusky hollow is a paradice~~   240
                                  &
~~& heaven gates ore my head~~ ᴧnow ~~I~~ beleeve
            he
217   that ᴧ the supreme good to' whome all things ill

are but as slavish officers of vengeance

would send a glistring *~~cherub~~ if need were   *guardian

220   to keepe my life, & honour unassaild.   245

was I deceav'd, or did a sable cloud

231 wanderers] erer *emd from* ring; that ... nams] *presum. TMS^{1a}*.
237 hov'ring] *& strangely formed asterisks or crosses, TMS^{4}*.
238 unblemish't] *TMS^{3a}*, le *re-formed or emd.*

241 ~~heaven~~] *mark above 2nd* e *just poss. apostr.*
242 he] *prob. TMS^{1a};* good] d *poss. emd.*
243 are] r *emd, poss. from* s.
246 deceav'd] *1st* e *emd, poss. from or to secretary form.*

Of calling shapes, and beckning shadows dire,

And ayrie tongues, that syllable mens names

On Sands, and Shoars, and desert Wildernesses.

These thoughts may startle well, but not astound   225

The vertuous mind, that ever walks attended

By a strong siding champion Conscience. ———

O welcome pure-ey'd Faith, white-handed Hope

Thou flittering Angel girt with golden wings,

And thou unblemish't forme of Chastitie   230

I see yee visibly, and now beleeve

That he, the Supreme good, t'whom all things ill

Are but as slavish officers of vengeance

Would send a glistring Guardian if need were

To keepe my life, and honour unassail'd.   235

Was I deceiv'd, or did a sable cloud

turne forth her silver lining on the night

I did not erre, there dos a sable cloud

turne forth her silver lining on the night

225   & casts a gleame over this tufted grove   250

[ ]

I cannot hallow to my brothers, but

such noise as I can make to be heard fardest

Ile venter, for my new-enlivńd spirits

229   prompt me & they phapps are not farre hence

Song.   255

230   Sweet Eecho sweetest nymph that liv'st unseene

within thy ayrie *shell   * cell

slow

by *Mæanders margent greene   * slow

nd in the violet-imbroider'd vale

where the love-lorne nightingale   260

235   nightly to thee her sad song mourneth well

250 [ ]] *pen mark, poss. to show that a passage ends with 250; see p. 21.*
251 brothers] *dot near comma prob. meaningless.*
256 sweetest] ee *poss. emd.*

257 cell] *prob.* TMS[1a]; *Dalton (phaps from Birch) & Colman.*
258 greene] gre *poss. emd.*
259 [a]nd] [a] *presum. concealed by paper stuck on to mend the leaf.*

Turne forth her silver lining on the night?

I did not erre, there does a sables cloud

Turne forth her silver lining on the night   239

And

And casts a gleame over this tufted Grove.   (9)

I cannot hollowe to my brothers, but

I cannot hallow to my Brothers, but

such noise as I can make to be heard fardest   225

Such noise as I can make to be heard fardest

I'le venture, for my new enliv'n'd speritts

Ile venter, for my new enliv'nd spirits

prompt me, and they phaꝑs are not farr hence,   ⟨no catchword⟩

Prompt me; and they perhaps are not farre off.

Songe /   ⟨7ᵛ⟩

Song.   245

Sweete Echo, sweetest nymphe that liv'st vnseene

Sweet echo, sweetest Nymph that liv'st unseene

within thy ayrie shell   230

Within thy ayrie shell

by slowe Meanders margent greene

By slow Meander's *margent greene,*

and in the violett imbroderd vale

And in the violet-imbroider'd vale

where the love-torne nightingale

Where the love-lorne Nightingale   250

nightly to thee her sad song mourneth well,

Nightly to thee her sad Song mourneth well.

226 speritts] *no comma.*

233 love-torne] *not quite the scribe's usual* t, *but not his usual* l *either.*

238 sables] *2nd* s *deleted by upright stroke in ink in Pforz.*

Canst thou not tell me of a gentle paire   **17**

that likeʒt thy Narcissus are?

Oh if thou have

hid them in some flowrie cave   265

240   tell me but where

Sweet Queene of parlie, daughter of the spheare

So m̶[—] maist thou be translated to the skies

                *   *
243   [A̶n̶d̶] h̶o̶l̶[d̶——————] *to all heavns harmonies   and give resounding grace

Comus e̶n̶t̶e̶r̶s̶.looks in and speaks   270

244   Co. can any mortall mixture of earths mould

245   breath such divine enchaꭔting ravishment

sure somthing holy lodges in that brest

and wth these raptures moves the vocall aire

to testifie his hidden residence   275

how sweetly did they flote upon the wings

268 So] S *poss. minuscule;* m̶[—]] ̶m̶a̶s̶t̶ *Wright.*
269 *[A̶n̶d̶]] *poss.* TMS^{1a}; h̶o̶l̶[d̶ ...]] *partly obliterated;* h̶o̶l̶d̶ ̶a̶

c̶o̶u̶n̶t̶e̶r̶p̶o̶i̶n̶t̶ *Wright; blot shape poss. not for* [counterpoint];
*] *and ... grace] *poss.* TMS^{1d}.
270 looks ... speaks] *poss.* TMS^{2a}.

Canst thou not tell me of a gentle payre	235
that likest thy *Narcissus* are	
O if thou have	
hid them in some flowrie Cave	
tell me but where. /	
Sweete Queene of parlie, daughter to the spheare	240
soe maystthou be translated to the skyes	
And hould a Counterpointe to all heav'ns harmonies	

Comus looks in & speakes

Co: Can any mortall mixture of Earths mould

breath such divine enchauntinge ravishment   245

sure somethinge holye lodges in that brest

and with these raptures moves the vocall ayre

to testifie his hidden residence

how sweetely did they floate vpon the wings

Canst thou not tell me of a gentle Paire

That likest thy Narcissus *are?*

O if thou have

Hid them in some flowrie Cave,   255

Tell me but where

Sweet Queen of Parlie, Daughter of the Sphære,

So maist thou be translated to the skies,

And give resounding grace to all Heav'ns Harmonies.

Com. Can any mortall mixture of Earths mould   260

Breath such Divine inchanting ravishment?

Sure something holy lodges in that brest,

And with these raptures moves the vocal aire

To testifie his hidden residence;

How sweetly did they float upon the wings   265

250 of silence, through the empty vaulted night

at every fall smoothing the raven downe

of darknesse till she smil'd, I have oft heard ~~sitting~~

        amidst the flowrie-kirtlèd Naiadès

253 my mother Circe wth the Sirens three   potent   280

        culling thire ~~potent~~ hearbs, & balefull druggs

256 who as they sung woùld take the prison'd soule ~~powerfull~~

257 & lap it in Elizium, Scylla ~~would weepe~~ wept m[i]ghty

and ~~and~~ chide~~gh~~er barking waves into attention

and fell Charybdis murmur'd soft applause

260 yet they in pleasing slumber lull'd the sense   285

and in sweet madnesse rob'd it of it selfe

but such a sacred, & home felt delight

such sober certainty of waking blisse

I never heard till now. Ile speake to her

265 and she shall be my queene. Haile forreine wonder 290
     certaine
 whome these rough shades did never breed

280-282 *margin presum. TMS*^{1a}.

280 Naiadès] *superior* e *prob. emd from apostr.;* potent] *prob. TMS*^{1b}.

281 sung] s *begun as something else;* woùld] ld *emd;* take] k *badly formed or emd.*

282 Scylla] y *emd from* i; m[i]ghty] *TMS*^{1b}.

283 and *(1st)*] *poss. TMS*^{2a}; chideg] e *emd to* ing, *then* ing *cancelled.*

284 Charybdis] y *begun as* i; b *emd, phaps from* d.

BMS		1637	
of silence, through the empty vaulted night,	250	Of Silence, through the emptie-vaulted night	
at every fall smoothinge the raven downe		At every fall smoothing the Raven downe	
of darkness till she smil'd, I haue oft heard	of ⟨8ʳ⟩	Of darknesse till she smil'd: I have oft heard	
my mother Circe with the Sirens three		My mother *Circe* with the Sirens three	My (10)
amidst the flowrie-kyrtled *Niades*		Amidst the flowrie-kirtl'd *Naiades*	270
cullinge their potent herbs and balefull druggs	255	Culling their Potent hearbs, and balefull drugs	
whoe when they sung, would take the prisond soule		Who as they sung, would take the prison'd soule	
and lap it in Elisium, Scilla wept		And lap it in *Elysium, Scylla* wept,	
and chid her barkinge waves into attention		And chid her barking waves into attention,	
and fell Caribdis murmurd soft applause		And fell *Charybdis* murmur'd soft applause:	275
yet they in pleasinge slumber lulld the sence	260	Yet they in pleasing slumber lull'd the sense	
and in sweete madnes rob'd it of it selfe,		And in sweet madnesse rob'd it of it selfe,	
but such a sacred and homefelt delight		But such a sacred, and home-felt delight,	
such sober certentie of wakinge bliss		Such sober certainty of waking blisse	
I never heard till now, Ile speake to her		I never heard till now. Ile speake to her	280
and she shalbe my Qweene; Haile forreigne wonder	265	And she shall be my Queene. Haile forreine wonder	
whome certaine these rough shades did never breede		Whom certaine these rough shades did never breed	

260 sence] *1st* e *emd.*

unlesse the goddesse that in rurall shrine

*~~liv'st~~ heere wth Pan or Silvan, by blest song   *dwell'st

forbidding every bleake unkindly fogge

270   to touch the *~~prospering~~ growth of this tall wood   *prosperous   **295**

Ladie Nay gentle shepheard ill is lost that praise

that is addrest to unattending eares

not any boast of skill, but extreme shift

how to regaine my sever'd companie

275   compell'd me to awake the courteous Echo   **300**

to give me answere to ~~give me~~ from her mossie cou^tch

Co. what chance good La. hath bereft you thus

La. dim darknesse, & this leavie labyrinth
                              neere
Co. could that divide you from ~~thire~~ ushering ~~hands~~ guids

280   La. they left me wearie~~d~~ on a grassie terfe[ ]   **305**

Co. by falshood, or discourtesie or why
                              coole
La. to seeke i'th valley some freindly spring

Co. and left yor faire side all unguarded Ladie

293 ~~liv'st~~] v *emd;* song] ng *emd or re-formed; period poss. after* song;   302 bereft] r *emd from* t.
     dwell'st] *prob. TMS*^{1a}.   305 terfe] fe *emd;* [ ]] *phaps comma.*
295 prosperous] *poss. TMS*^{3f}.

BMS	1637
vnless the goddess that in rurall shrine	Vnlesse the Goddesse that in rurall shrine
dwel'st heere with *Pan* or *Silvan,* by blest song	Dwell'st here with *Pan,* or *Silvan,* by blest Song
forbiddinge every bleake vnkindly fogg	Forbidding every bleake unkindly Fog 285
to touch the prosperinge growth of this tall wood 270	To touch the prosperous growth of this tall wood.
La: Nay gentle Shepheard, ill is lost that praise	*La.* Nay gentle Shepherd ill is lost that praise
that is addrest to vnattendinge eares	That is addrest to unattending Eares,
not any boast of skill, but extreame shifte	Not any boast of skill, but extreame shift
how to regayne my severd Companye	How to regaine my sever'd companie 290
Compeld me to awake the Curteus Echo 275	Compell'd me to awake the courteous Echo
to give me answer from her massy Couch	To give me answer from her mossie Couch.
Co: What Chaunce good lady hath bereft you thus? *Co:* what ⟨8ᵛ⟩	*Co.* What chance good Ladie hath bereft you thus?
La: dym darknesse and this leavye laborinth	*La.* Dim darknesse, and this leavie Labyrinth.
Co: Could that devide you from neere vsheringe guydes?	*Co.* Could that divide you from neere-ushering 295
La: they left me weary on a grassie terfe 280	*La.* They left me weary on a grassie terfe. (guides?
Co: by falsehood, or discurtesie, or why?	*Co.* By falshood, or discourtesie, or why?
La: to seeke in the valley some coole freindly springe	*La.* To seeke i'th vally some coole friendly Spring.
Co: and lefte yoʳ fayer side, all vnguarded ladye?	*Co.* And left your faire side all unguarded Ladie?

271 *La:*] *L poss. minuscule.*

La. they were but twaine, & purpos'd quick returne

285 Co. phapps fore stalling night prævented them 310

La. how easie my misfortune is to hit

Co. imports thire losse beside the præsent need

La. no lesse then ~~then~~ if I should my brothers loose.

Co. were they of manly prime, or youthfull blome

290 La. as smooth as Hebe's thire unrazor'd lipps. 315

Co. such tow I saw what tyme the labour'd oxe

in his loose traces from the furrow came

& the swinck't hedger at his supper sate

I saw' em under a greene mantling vine

295 that crawls along the side of yon smal hill. 320

plucking ripe clusters from ye tender shoots

thire port was more then humaine as they stood

I tooke it for a faerie vision

of some gay creatures of the element

300 that in the colours of ye rainbow live 325

& play ith plighted clowds, I was aw-strooke

317 furrow] u *begun as something else.*

La: they were but twaine & purposd quick returne,	
Co: perhaps forestallinge night p^rvented them	285
La: how easie my misfortune is to hit!	
Co: imports their losse, beside the p^rsent neede?	
La: noe lesse then if I should my brothers loose	
Co: were they of manly prime, or youthfull bloome?	
La: as smooth as *Hebes* their vnrazor'd lipps.	290
Co: Two such I sawe, what tyme the labour'd oxe	
in his loose traces from the furrowe came	
and the swink't — hedger at his supper sate,	
I sawe em vnder a greene mantlinge vyne	
that crawles alonge the side of yon smale hill	295
pluckinge ripe clusters from the tender shoots,	
their porte was more then humane as they stood,	
I tooke it for a faerie vision	
of some gaye creatures of the Element	
that in the cooleness of the raynebow live	300
and playe i'th plighted clouds; I was awe-strooke	

La. They were but twain, & purpos'd quick return.	300
	Co.
Co. Perhaps fore-stalling night prævented them.	(11)
La. How easie my misfortune is to hit!	
Co. Imports their losse, beside the præsent need?	
La. No lesse then if I should my brothers lose.	
Co. Were they of manly prime, or youthful bloom?	305
La. As smooth as *Hebe's* their unrazord lips.	
Co. Two such I saw, what time the labour'd Oxe	
In his loose traces from the furrow came,	
And the swink't hedger at his Supper sate;	
I saw them under a greene mantling vine	310
That crawls along the side of yon small hill,	
Plucking ripe clusters from the tender shoots,	
Their port was more then humaine; as they stood,	
I tooke it for a faërie vision	
Of some gay creatures of the element	315
That in the colours of the Rainbow live	
And play i'th plighted clouds, I was aw-strooke,	

305 bloom?] *question mark not in Harvard.*

    & as I past, I worship't, if those you seeke

    it were a journy like the path to heav'n
                      La
    to helpe you find them ~~out~~.   Gentle villager

305   what readiest way would bring me to that place   ⟨18⟩ 330

Co. due west it rises from this shrubbie point

La. to find out that good shepheard I suppose

    in such a scant allowance of starre light

    would overtaske the best land-pilots art
           the
310   w^th^out ˄sure ~~steerage of~~ guesse of well-practiz'd feet   335

Co. I know each lane, & every alley greene

    dingle, or bushie dell of this *wide wood   wild—

    & every ~~bosky~~ ~~bosky~~ bosky bourne from side, to side

    my dayly walks, & ancient ~~neihbour~~ neighbourhood

315   and if yor stray attendance be yet lodg'd
     ed   wthin   [ ]   340
 [o]r shroud˄ w^th^˄in these *limits ~~I shall know~~ I shall know   *shroudie

    ~~ere the larke r[–] se rowse~~ ere morrow wake or the low-roosted Larke

    from her thetch't ~~rowse~~ palate rowse, if otherwise   pallat

---

332 shepheard] *1st* h *emd from* p.   341 [o]r] *on leaf edge.*

334 best] s *re-formed.*   342 r[–] se] *obliterated;* rowse *Wright.*

337 wild] & * & *underline, TMS^4^; hyphen poss. casual mark.*   343 pallat] & *underline, TMS^4^.*

339 neihbour] ei *emd from* ig.

and as I past I worship't: if those you seeke

it were a Iorney like the path to heav'n

helpe you finde them; *La:* gentle villager

what readiest waye would bringe me to that place? 305

Co: due west it rises from this shrubbie pointe,

La: to finde out that good shepheard I suppose

in such a scant allowance of starr light

would overtaske the best land pilots arte

wthout the sure guesse of well practiz'd feete; 310

Co: I knowe each lane, and every Alley greene,

dingle, or bushie dell, of this wide wood,

and everie boskie bourne from side to side

my daylie walks and antient neighbourhood

and if yor straye attendance, be yet lodg'd 315

or shroud wthin these lymitts, I shall know

ere morrowe wake, or the lowe rooster larke

from her thatcht palat rowse, if otherwise

to
⟨9ʳ⟩

And as I past, I worshipt; if those you seeke

It were a journy like the path to heav'n

To helpe you find them. *La.* Gentle villager 320

What readiest way would bring me to that place?

Co. Due west it rises from this shrubbie point.

La. To find out that good shepheard I suppose

In such a scant allowance of starre light

Would overtask the best land-pilots art 325

Without the sure guesse of well-practiz'd feet.

Co. I know each lane, and every alley greene

Dingle, or bushie dell of this wild wood,

And every boskie bourne from side to side

My daylie walks and ancient neighbourhood, 330

And if your stray attendance be yet lodg'd

Or shroud within these limits, I shall know

Ere morrow wake, or the low-roosted larke

From her thach't palate rowse, if otherwise

Ere
(12)

304 to *omitted.*

I can conduct you Ladie to a low

320   but loyall cottage, where you may be safe   345

till furder quest ~~be made~~ La. Shepheard I take thy word

& trust thy honest offer'd courtesie

wch oft is sooner found in lowly sheds

with & smoakie rafters, then in tapstrie halls

325   & courts of princes ~~were~~ ^h^where it first was nam'd   350

& ~~is prætended yet~~ yet is most prætended. in a place
           2   1

lesse warranted then this ~~I cannot be~~ or lesse secure

I cannot be, that I should feare to change it
                   my
eye ~~eye~~ me blest providence, & square ‸this tryall

330   to my proportion'd strength, shepheard lead on. Exeunt   355

the tow brothers enter

1 bro. unmuffle ye faint starres, & thou faire ~~N~~moone

332   that ~~wont'st~~ wont'st to love the travailers benizon

---

344 Ladie] L *poss. minuscule.*
350 princes] ce *emd.*
351 ~~is~~] *poss. emd.*
353 change] *large Greek ∈ poss. begun as Italian.*

354 ~~eye~~] y *emd;* providence] *1st* e *poss. Italian.*
355 shepheard] *1st* h *emd from* p; Exeunt] t *emd.*
358 ~~wont'st~~] *1st* t *emd from* d.

BMS		1637	
I can conduct you ladie, to a lowe,		I can conduct you Ladie to a low	335
but loyall cottage, where you may be safe	320	But loyall cottage, where you may be safe	
till furder quest; *La:* Shepheard I take thy word		Till further quest'. *La.* Shepheard I take thy word,	
and trust thy honest offer'd Curtesie		And trust thy honest offer'd courtesie,	
wch ofte is sooner found in lowly sheds		Which oft is sooner found in lowly sheds	
with smoakie rafters, then in tap'strie halls		With smoakie rafters, then in tapstrie halls,	340
and Courts of princes, where it first was nam'd	325	And courts of Princes, where it first was nam'd,	
and yet is most p^rtended, in a place ~~lesse w~~		And yet is most prætended: in a place	
lesse warrented then this, or lesse secure		Lesse warranted then this, or lesse secure	
I cannott be, that I should feare to change it		I cannot be, that I should feare to change it,	
Eye my blest ꝑvidence, and square my tryall		Eye me blest Providence, and square my triall	345
to my ꝑportion'd streingth; shepheard leade on.	330	To my proportion'd strength. Shepheard lead on. –	
	The		

The two brothers 〈9ᵛ〉	*The two Brothers.*

El: bro Vnmuffle yee fainte starrs, and thou faier moone	*Eld. bro.* Vnmuffle yee faint stars, and thou fair moon
that wonst to love the travailers benizon	That wontst to love the travailers benizon

332 Vnmuffle] 1 *poss. emd.*

stoope thy pale visage through an amber cloud

and disinherit Chaos, that raignes heere   360

335   in double night of darknesse & of shades.

or if yor influence be quite dam'd up

wth black usurping mists, some gentle taper

though a rush candle from the wicker hole

of some clay habitation visit us   365
             thy
340   wth ^a long levell'd rule of streaming light

and thou shalt be our starre of Arcadie

or Tyrian Cynosure. 2 bro. or if our eyes

be barr'd that happinesse, might wee but heare
             thire
the folded flocks pen'd in ^watled ~~e[osat]~~ cotes   370

345   or sound of pastorall reed wth oaten stopps

or ~~wistle~~ whistle from ye lodge, or village cock

count the night watches to his featherie dames

BMS		1637	
stoope thy pale visadge through an amber cloude		Stoope thy pale visage through an amber cloud	350
and disinherit Chaos, that raignes heere	335	And disinherit *Chaos,* that raigns here	
in double night of darkness, and of shades		In double night of darknesse, and of shades;	
or if yor influence be quite damm'd vp		Or if your influence be quite damm'd up	
wth black vsurpinge mists, some gentle taper		With black usurping mists, some gentle taper	
though a rushe candle, from the wicker hole		Though a rush candle from the wicker hole	355
of some claye habitacoñ visite vs	340	Of some clay habitation visit us	
wth thy long levell'd rule of streaming light		With thy long levell'd rule of streaming light	
and thou shalt be o^r starr of Arcady		And thou shalt be our starre of *Arcadie*	
or Tirian Cynosure: *2 bro:* or if o^r eyes		Or *Tyrian* Cynosure. *2 Bro.* Or if our eyes	
be barr'd that happines might wee but heare		Be barr'd that happinesse, might we but heare	360
the folded flocks pen'd in their watled cotes	345	The folded flocks pen'd in their watled cotes,	
or sound of pastorall reede with oaten stopps		Or sound of pastoral reed with oaten stops,	
or whistle from the lodge, or village Cock		Or whistle from the Lodge, or village cock	
count the night watches to his featherie dames		Count the night watches to his featherie Dames,	Count (13)

336 double] u *emd, phaps from* o.

t'would be some solace yet, some little cheering

    this ~~sad~~ close

349 in ˌ~~lone~~ˌ dungeon of innumerous bowes.   375

         x

ead the   but oh that haplesse vergin our lost sister

                 wander   (amoungst rude burrs & thistles

per over   where may she ˌnow, whether betake her ~~phapps some cold hard banke~~

gainst   from the chill dew ~~in this dead solitude ˌsuˌrrounding wilde.~~

           perhaps some cold bank is

[n] ste[a]d of ~~phapps some cold banck [e] is~~ her boulster now   (fraught wth sad feares

[   ]s do-   or 'gainst the rugged barke of some broad elme   380

wne

happs sōe   ~~she~~ leans her t~~houghtfull head musing at our unkindnesse~~ unpillow'd head ~~frau~~

          what if

old banke is   ~~or else~~ in wild amazment, and affright

          ~~so fares as did forsaken Proserpine~~

                ~~rowling~~

——   ~~when the big ˌwallowing flakes of pitchie clowds~~

          ~~& darknesse woˌnd her in.~~ 1 ~~Bro[.] Peace brother peace~~   385

375 close] *poss. TMS^3e.*

376-378 [r]ead the [pa]per over [a]gainst] *on broken leaf edge; prob.*
     TMS^3e; see 456-470 margin, reconstructed at 386-402.

376 *cross presum. TMS^3d;* vergin] *e inserted or poss. emd from* i.

379 ~~some~~] s *poss. majuscule.*

379-382 *margin* [in] ste[a]d of [   ]s do-wne [p]happs sōe [c]old banke is]
     on broken leaf edge; poss. TMS^2b; ste[a]d] a *poss.* e; [   ]s] *prob. 4*
     letters before s, *badly written & obscured by cancel lines; query* [lean]s,

or [a] *query* [æ] *(cf. præsumption 464); Shawcross suggests always,*
but descender in [y] *is cancel line, though cf. cancelled* w *in* ~~swoord~~
526; sōe] *tittle poss. cancelled.*

379 *above* perhaps ... bank is] *TMS^4.*

382 ~~else~~] *lost Birch, Newton, Warton, Todd;* what if] *prob. TMS^4.*

383-385 *cancel lines poss. TMS^3e.*

384 *margin lines presum. TMS^3e.*

385 ~~Bro[.]~~] *period poss. colon or cancel stroke.*

t'would be some solace yet, some little cheeringe	
in this lone dungeon of inumerous bows,	350
but O that haples virgin o^r lost sister	
where may she wander nowe? whether betake her	
from the chill dewe, amongst rude burrs & thistles	
̣phaps some could banke is her boulster nowe,	
or gainst the rugged barke of some broade Elme	355
leanes her vnpillow'd head fraught wth sad feares	
or els in wild amazement and affright,	
soe fares as did forsaken *Proserpine*	soe ⟨10^r⟩
when the bigg rowling flakes of pitchie clouds	
and darkness wound her in: *El bro:* peace brother peace	360

T'would be some solace yet, some little chearing   365

In this close dungeon of innumerous bowes.

⟨Reconstructed '[pa]per over [a]gainst'⟩ ⟨19a⟩ 386

350 bu[t O that haplesse virgin our lost sister]

wh[ere may she wander now, whether betake her]

fr[om the chill dew amoungst rude burrs & thistles]

[phapps some cold banke is her boulster now] 390

o[r gainst the rugged barke of some broad elme]

355 l[eans her unpillow'd head fraught wth sad feares]

w[hat if in wild amazment, & affright]

or [while we speake w^thin the direfull graspe]

o[f salvage hunger or of salvage heate] 395

1 [bro. peace brother be not over exquisit]

360 t[o cast the fashion of uncertaine evills]

[wch grant they be so while they rest unknowne]
                                his
[what need a man forestall ~~the~~ date of greife]

[and run to meet what he would most avoid] 400

[or if they be but false alarms of feare]
                                such
365 [how bitter is ~~this~~ selfe delusion] 402

386-402 *TMS^{3d} reconstructed; cf. 456-470 margin.*

386 [ ]] *see 456.*

398 [w^ch] which *Todd.*

399 ~~the~~] *Newton, Warton, Todd; emd TMS^{3d}.*

402 ~~this~~] *Newton, Warton, Todd; emd TMS^{3d}.*

But ô that haplesse virgin our lost sister

Where may she wander now, whether betake her

From the chill dew, amongst rude burs and thistles?

Perhaps some cold banke is her boulster now   370

Or 'gainst the rugged barke of some broad Elme

Leans her unpillow'd head fraught with sad fears.

What if in wild amazement, and affright

Or while we speake within the direfull graspe

Of Savage hunger, or of Savage heat?   375

   Eld: bro. Peace brother, be not over exquisite

To cast the fashion of uncertaine evils,

For grant they be so, while they rest unknowne

What need a man forestall his date of griefe

And run to meet what he would most avoid?   380

Or if they be but false alarms of Feare

How bitter is such selfe-delusion?

366   I doe not thinke my sister so to seeke   403

or so unprincipl'd in vertues booke

and the sweet peace y^t goodnesse bosomes ever   405
                        want
369   as that the single ʌof light & noise (not beeing in danger, as I trust she is n

371   could stirre the s[tabl] e [co]nstant mood of her calme thoughts

& put them into misbecomming plight

Vertue could ad all her see to doe what vertue would   **19**

by her owne radiant light though sun & moone   410

375   were in the flat sea sunke: and wisdom's selfe

oft seeks to solitarie sweet retire oft seeks to sweet retired solitude

where wth her best nurse Contemplation

she plum'es her feathers, & lets grow her wings

that in the various bustle of resort   415

380   were all to ruffl'd, and sometymes impair'd
                        owne
       he that has light w^thin his ʌcleere brest

---

406 n[ot)]] [ot)] *presum. concealed by scrap stuck on to mend the leaf.*

407 s[tabl]e] *Birch, Newton, Warton, Todd;* steadie *Wright;* [co]nstant] *smudged.*

408 misbecomming] o *emd.*

409 Vertue] V *poss. minuscule.*

412 oft ... solitude] *prob.* TMS^{1d}.

414 plum'es] e *strongly Italian; just poss. emd from* s *contextually for* TMS^{1a}.

416 were] we *emd from* a.

BMS	1637
I doe not thinke my sister soe to seeke 361	I doe not thinke my sister so to seeke
or soe vnprincipl'd in vertues booke,	Or so unprincipl'd in vertues book
and the sweete peace that goodness bosoms ever	And the sweet peace that goodnesse bosoms ever 385
as that the single want of light and noise	As that the single want of light, and noise
(not beinge in danger, as I hope she is not) 365	(Not being in danger, as I trust she is not)
could stirr the constant mood of her calme thoughts	Could stir the constant mood of her calme thoughts
and put them into misbecominge plight	And put them into mis-becomming plight.
vertue could see to doe what vertue would	Vertue could see to doe what vertue would 390
by her owne radiant light, though sun & moone	By her owne radiant light, though Sun and Moon
were in the flatt sea sunke, and wisdoms selfe 370	Were in the flat Sea sunck, and Wisdoms selfe
of seeks to sweete retired solitude	Oft seeks to sweet retired Solitude
where, wᵗʰ her best nurse contemplacō	Where with her best nurse Contemplation
she plumes her feathers, and letts grow her wings	She plumes her feathers, and lets grow her wings 395
that in the various bustle of resorte,	That in the various bustle of resort That (14)
were all to ruffl'd and sometyms impayr'd 375	Were all to ruffl'd, and sometimes impair'd.
he that has light within his owne cleere brest	He that has light within his owne cleere brest

may sit i'th center, and enjoy bright day

but he that hides a darke soule, & foule thoughts

~~walks in black~~ ~~vapours, though the noontyde brand~~ benighted walks under y^e   420
                                          midday sun

385   ~~blaze in the summer solstice~~[ ] 2 Bro. tis most true himselfe is his owne
                                                      dungeon

that musing meditation most affects

the pensive secrecie of desert cell

                                  and/
farre from the che^erfull haunt of men ~~or~~/heards

and sits as safe as in a senate house   425

                                      weeds
390   for who would rob a Hermit of his ~~beads~~ g^owne ~~beads~~
               few   or   beads
his^ books, his ~~hairie gowne~~, or maple dish

or doe his gray hairs any violence

but beautie like the faire Hesperian tree

laden wth blooming gold had need the guard   430

395   of dragon watch wth uninchaunted eye

                                         u
to save her blossoms & defend her ~~frite~~ fruite

from ye rash hand of bold incontinence.

418 i'th] *apostr. partly concealed by* t, *phaps cancelled; query comma inserted.*
420-421 benighted ... dungeon] *poss.* TMS^3c.

421 [ ]] *cancellation; period (Wright) just possible.*
424 and] *prob.* TMS^3a; *stroke presum.* TMS^3a.

BMS	1637
may sit i'th Center, and enioye bright daye	May sit i'th center, and enjoy bright day,
but he that hides a darke sowle, & foule thoughts	But he that hides a darke soule, and foule thoughts　400
walks in black vapours, though the noone tyde brand	Benighted walks under the mid-day Sun,
blaze in the summer solstice. *2 bro:* tis most true　380	Himselfe is his owne dungeon.
	2. Bro. 'Tis most true
that musinge meditacon̄ most affects	That musing meditation most affects
the pensive secrecie of desert Cell	The Pensive secrecie of desert cell　405
farr from the cheerefull haunte of men or heards,	Farre from the cheerefull haunt of men, and heards,
̣and sitts as safe as in a senate house	And sits as safe as in a Senat house
for whoe would robb an hermitt of his weeds,　385	For who would rob an Hermit of his weeds
his few bookes, or his beads, or maple dishe	His few books, or his beades, or maple dish,
or doe his graye haiers any violence?	Or doe his gray hairs any violence?　410
but bewtie like the fayre hesperian tree	But beautie like the faire Hesperian tree
laden with bloominge gould, had neede the guard	Laden with blooming gold, had need the guard
of dragon watch with vninchaunted eye　390	Of dragon watch with uninchanted eye
to save her blossoms, and defend her fruite,	To save her blossoms, and defend her fruit
from the rashe hand of bold Incontinence,	From the rash hand of bold Incontinence.　415

and
⟨10ᵛ⟩

you may as well spread out the unsun'd heapes

of misers treasure by an outlaws den   435

400   and tell me it is safe, as bid me ~~thinke~~ hope

danger will winke on opportunity

and let a single helplesse mayden passe

uninjur'd ~~th~~ in this ~~vast, & hideous wild~~ wide surrounding wast.

of night, or lonlinesse it recks not me   440
                                 2 1

405   I feare the dread events that dog them both

lest some ill greeting touch attempt the pson

of our unowned sister. 1 Bro: I doe not brother

inferre, as if I thought my sisters state

409   secure, w^{th}out all doubt or question, no   445
                                 r

~~beshew me but I would~~ I could be willing though now i'th darke to trie
         encounter
a tough ~~passado~~ wth the shaggiest ruffian

that lurks by hedge or lane of this dead circuit

to have her by my side, though I were sure

she might be free from perill where she is   450

439 wide ... wast] *prob. TMS^{1a}.*

440 lonlinesse] *2nd 1 phaps begun as something else; numerals presum.*
    TMS^{1a}.

443 1 Bro] 1 *emd or re-formed.*

445 no] *period just poss.*

you may aswell spreade out the vnsum'd heapes	You may as well spread out the unsun'd heaps
of misers treasures by an outlawes den,	Of misers treasure by an outlaws den
and tell me it is safe, as bid me hope 395	And tell me it is safe, as bid me hope
dainger will winke at opportunitie	Danger will winke on opportunitie
and she a single helpeles mayden passe	And let a single helplesse mayden passe 420
vniniur'd in this wide surroundinge wast	Vninjur'd in this wild surrounding wast.
of night or lonelinesse, it recks me not	Of night, or lonelynesse it recks me not
I feare the dread events that dog them both 400	I feare the dred events that dog them both,
lest some ill greetinge touch attempt the ꝑson	Lest some ill greeting touch attempt the person
of our vn owned sister. *El bro:* I doe not brother	Of our unowned sister. 425
	Eld. Bro. I doe not brother
inferr as if I thought my sisters state	Inferre, as if I thought my sisters state
secure, wth out all doubt or question, no;	Secure without all doubt, or controversie: Secure (15)
I could be willinge though now i'th darke to trie 405	
a tough encounter, with the shaggiest ruffian	
that lurks by hedge or lane, ofthis dead circuit	
to have her by my side, though I were suer	
she might be free from ꝑill where she is, she ⟨11^r⟩	

410   but where an equall poise of ~~hopes~~ & ~~feares~~

dos arbitrate the event my nature is

that I incline to hope, rather then feare

and gladly banish squint ~~suspition~~ suspicion

          2   1

my sister is not so defencelesse left   455

415   [ ]   as you imagine brother she has a hidden strength

        bu   wch you remember not 2 bro. what hidden strenth

        wh   unlesse the strength of heavèn, if you meane that

        fr   1 bro. I meane that too, but yet a hidden stre^{g}nth

      [p]   w^{ch}, if heaven gave it, may be term'd her owne   460

420   o   tis chastitie, my brother, chastitie

       l   she that has that is clad in compleate steele   (keene

422   up   —————and like a quiverd nymph wth arrows

     w   ~~& may (on any needfull accident~~

             ~~don~~   ~~in~~

    ~~may be it not [d   ] in pride or wilfull tempting) præsumption)~~

    or   trace

423   may ˄walke ~~through~~ huge forrests, & unharbour'd heaths   465

---

453 incline] *1st i emd, prob. from e; rather] 1st r emd or re-formed.*
454 *numerals presum. TMS^{1a};* 1 *emd or re-formed.*
456-470 *margin letters TMS^{3d} down torn butt of* '[pa]per over [a]gainst', *reconstructed at 386-402.*

456 [ ]] *indecipherable mark; query cross (cf. 376 margin), or start of version of 375;* she] s *re-formed.*
458 heavèn] *apostr. above e; e poss. cancelled; comma poss. inserted.*
463 w] *imperfect; and like ... keene] TMS^{1a}.*
464 *margin* or] r *imperfect.*

but where an equall poise of hope, & feare	410
does arbitrate th'event, my nature is	
that I encline to hope, rather then feare,	
and gladly banish squint suspition,	
my sister is not soe defencelesse left	
as you immagine brother, she has a hidden strength	415
wch you remember not, *2 bro:* what hidden strength?	

vnless the strength of heav'n, if you meane that?

El: bro I meane that too: but yet a hidden strength

wch if heaven gave it, may be tearm'd her owne,

tis Chastitie, my brother Chastitie   420

she that has that is clad in compleate steele,

and like a quiver'd nimphe with arrowes keene,

may trace huge forrests, and vnharbour'd heaths

Yet where an equall poise of hope, and feare

Does arbitrate th'event, my nature is   430

That I encline to hope, rather then feare

And gladly banish squint suspicion.

My sister is not so defencelesse left

As you imagine, she has a hidden strength

Which you remember not.   435

    2. Bro. What hidden strength

Vnlesse the strength of heav'n, if meane that?

    Eld. Bro. I meane that too, but yet a hidden strength

Which if heav'n gave it, may be term'd her owne:

'Tis chastitie, my brother, chastitie: 440

She that has that, is clad in compleat steele,

And like a quiver'd nymph with arrowes keene

May trace huge forrests, and unharbour'd heaths

---

415 strength] th *emd, prob. from* ht.

437 meane] you *written in ink above & after* meane *& caret below in Pforz.*

o   infamous hills, & ~~þe~~ sandie perilous wilds

                   rays

425   l   where through the sacred ~~aw~~* of chastitie *rays

    t   no salvage feirce, bandite, or mountaneere

[w] will ~~shall~~ dare to soile her virgin puritie

[w]   yea even where very desolation dwells   470

429   by grots, and cavern's shag'd wth horrid shads

      ~~& yawning denns where glaring monsters house~~

430   she may passe on wth unblensh't ~~majestie~~ majestie

      bee it not don in pride or in præsumption

      ~~Nay more~~ Some say   ⟨20⟩

      ~~Some say~~ ‸‸no evill thing that walks by night   475

      in fog, or fire, by lake, or moorie fen

          * meager

~~wrin[e]l'd~~ Blue [ ] ‸~~wrinckled~~ hagge, or stubborne unlayd Ghost

435   that breaks his magick chains at curfew tyme

      no goblin, or swart faerie of the mine

         hurtfull

      has‸power ~~o'er~~ true virginity   480

      doe yee beleeve me yet, or shall I call

468 t] *imperfect;* no] n *poss. emd;* salvage] l *poss. inserted.*

469-470 [w]] [w]] *only remnants of left strokes visible.*

469 virgin] *1st* i *poss. emd from* e.

472 *cancel line* TMS^3e.

473 majestie] TMS^3e.

475 *above* Some say] *poss.* TMS^3e.

477 [ ] *poss. hyphen cancelled;* ~~wrinckled~~] k *poss. emd.*

480 o'er] *poss.* over *(Wright), emd to* o'er, *then to* o'er *(*o'er *Wright in transcript,* ore *in note); emd poss.* TMS^1b.

BMS		1637	
infamous hills, and sandie perrilous wildes,		Infamous hills, and sandie perillous wilds	
where through the sacred rayes of Chastitie	425	Where through the sacred rays of chastitie	445
noe salvage, feirce, bandite, or mountaneere		No savage fierce, bandite, or mountaneete	
will dare to soile her virgin puritie,		Will dare to soyle her virgin puritie	
yea even where, very desolacoñ dwells		Yea there, where very desolation dwells	
by grots, & caverns sh[ag] shag'd wth horrid shades		By grots, and caverns shag'd with horrid shades	
and yawninge denns, where glaringe monsters house	430		
she may pass on wth vnblensh't maiestie		She may passe on with unblench't majestie	450
be it not done in pride or ˄in p^rsumption		Be it not done in pride, or in presumption.	
naye more noe evill thinge that walks by night		Some say no evill thing that walks by night	
in fogg or fire, by lake or moorish Fen,	in ⟨11^v⟩	In fog, or fire, by lake, or moorish fen	
blew meagar hag, or stubborne vnlayed ghost	435	Blew meager hag, or stubborne unlayd ghost	
that breaks his magick chaines at Curfew tyme		That breaks his magicke chaines at curfeu time	455
noe goblinge, or swarte fayrie of the mine		No goblin, or swart Faërie of the mine	
has hurtefull power ore true virginitie,		Has hurtfull power ore true virginity.	
doe you beleeve me yet, or shall I call		Doe yee beleeve me yet, or shall I call	

444 Infamous] *small mark above* a *in Pforz. poss. acute accent written in ink.*
(Small marks, clearly in paper, after 547 *&* 613 *resemble grave accents but are lighter & smaller than* 444.)

antiquity from the old schooles of Greece

440   to testifie the arms of chastitie

441   hence had the huntresse Dian her dred bow

                    ——faire silver-shafted Q. for ever chast

443   wherwith she tam'd the brinded lionesse   485

     & spotted mountayne pard, but set at naught

445   the frivolous bolt of Cupid, gods & men

     fear'd her sterne frowne, & she was Q. o'th woods

     what was that snakie-headed Gorgon sheild (unconquer'd

                                *~~unvanquish~~'t

     that wise Minerva wore, *æternall virgin   490

     ~~freezind~~ wherwith she freez'd her foes to congeal'd stone

450   but rigid looks of chast austerity

     & noble grace that dash't brute violence and blank aw

                              ~~of bright rays~~

     wth suddaine adoration ~~of her purenesse~~

485 faire ... chast] *TMS*[1d]; lionesse] l *poss. majuscule.*   490 ~~unvanquish~~'t] *prob. TMS*[1a].

489 unconquer'd] *prob. TMS*[1a].   494 w^th] w *re-formed or phaps* i *inserted.*

BMS		1637	
antiquitie from the ould schooles of Greece	440	Antiquity from the old schools of Greece	459
			To
to testifie the armes of Chastitie,		To testifie the armes of Chastitie?	(16)
hence had the huntress *Dian* her dread bow		Hence had the huntresse *Dian* her dred bow	
faire silver shafter Qweene, for ever chast		Faire silver-shafted Queene for ever chast	
wherewith she tam'd the brinded Lyonesse		Wherewith we tam'd the brinded lionesse	
and spotted mountaine Pard, but sett at nought	445	And spotted mountaine pard, but set at nought	
the frivolous bolt of Cupid, Gods and men		The frivolous bolt of *Cupid,* gods and men	465
feard her sterne frowne, & she was Qweene o'th' woods		Fear'd her sterne frowne, & she was queen oth' woods.	
what was that snakie headed Gorgon sheild,		What was that snakie headed *Gorgon* sheild	
the wise *Minerva* wore, vnconquer'd virgin		That wise *Minerva* wore, unconquer'd virgin	
wherewith she freezed her foes to congeald stone?	450	Wherewith she freez'd her foes to congeal'd stone?	
but rigid lookes of chast awsteritie		But rigid looks of Chast austeritie	470
and noble grace that dasht brute violence		And noble grace that dash't brute violence	
with sudden adoracon, and blanke awe		With sudden adoration, and blancke aw.	

463 we] *deleted by horizontal line, caret below & before,* she *above, all written in*
ink *in Pforz.*

        So deare to heaven is sainctly chastitie   495
                is found
        that when ~~it finds~~ a soule ˄sincerely so
                             (guilt

455   a thousand liveried angells lackey her
                  ————driving farre off each thing of sin &

457   and in cleere dreame & sollemne vision
                that
        tell her of things no grosse eare can heare

        till oft converse wth heavnly habitants   500

460   ~~begins~~ to cast a beame on th' outward shape

        the unpolluted temple of the mind

        and turnes ~~by~~ it by degrees to the souls essence

        till all be made immortall. but when lust

        by unchast looks, loose gestures, & foule talke   505
                leud &*
465   & most by ˄~~the lascivious~~ act of sin   lavish

        lets in defilement to ye inward parts

        the soule grows clotted by contagion

        imbodies, and imbrutes till she loose quite
                        2 1

495 sainctly] s *emd or re-formed;* chastitie] h *begun as something else.*
496 found] fo *emd.*
497 angells] *mark above* e *like circumflex accent, prob. meaningless or misplaced caret for* 496.
498 driving ... guilt] *TMS*[1d]*;* &] *emd, poss. from* or.
501 begins] s *cancelled; phaps TMS*[3f].

503 turnes ~~by~~] s *phaps inserted.*
506 &*] lavish] & *presum. cancel line, TMS*[3e].
508 the] h *phaps emd from* il.
509 imbodies ... imbrutes] *prefixes detached, as often in M.'s handwriting; cf.* 580, 744, 867, *etc.; ct.* 559, 560.

BMS		1637	
soe deere to heav'n is sainctly Chastitie		So deare to heav'n is saintly chastitie	
that when a sowle is found cinceerely soe	455	That when a soule is found sincerely so,	
a thousand liveried Angells, lackey her		A thousand liveried angels lackie her	475
drivinge farr of, each thing of sin, & guilte		Driving farre off each thing of sinne, and guilt,	
and in cleer dreame and solemne vision		And in cleere dreame, and solemne vision	
tell ~~of~~ her of things that noe grosse eare can heare		Tell her of things that no grosse eare can heare,	
till oft converse with hevenly habitants	till ⟨12ʳ⟩	Till oft converse with heav'nly habitants	
begins to cast a beame on th' outward shape	461	Begin to cast a beame on th' outward shape	480
the vnpolluted temple of the mynde		The unpolluted temple of the mind	
and turnes it by degrees to the souls essence		And turnes it by degrees to the souls essence	
till all be made immortall, but when lust		Till all bee made immortall; but when lust	
by vnchast lookes, loose gesturs, and foule talke	465	By unchast looks, loose gestures, and foule talke	
and most by lewde lascivious act of sin		But most by leud, and lavish act of sin	485
letts in defilement to the inward ptes,		Lets in defilement to the inward parts,	
the soule growes clotted by contagion,		The soule growes clotted by contagion,	
imbodies, and imbruts till she quite loose		Imbodies, and imbrutes, till she quite loose	

the divine propertie of her first beeing   510

470   such are those thick & gloomie shadows dampe

oft seene in charnel vaults, & ~~monume~~sepulchers

hovering, & sitting by a new made grave

as loath to leave the bodie that it lov'd

& link't it selfe by carnall sensualtie   515

475   to a degenerate, & degraded state.
                                                      (phy
2 Bro. how charming is divine philoso ~~Hallow within~~

not harsh, & crabbed as dull fooles suppose

but musicall as is Apollo's lute

and a p̷petuall feast of nectar'd sweets   520
                                              (I hear~~d~~ᵉ
480   where no crude surfeit reigns. 1 Brother. list ~~bro.~~ list, ~~me thought~~

some farre-of hallow breake the silent aire
                                              hallow farre off
2 Bro. mee thought so too, what should it be. 1 Bro. for certaine

either ~~either~~ some one like us night founder'd heere

511-514 *margin fine line in unidentified pen.*   522 of] *Wright, but poss.* off, *though pen splitting in context;* off] *1st* f
516 to] t *emd.*   *faint, but 2 horizontal strokes, not 1 as in* of; hallow *(1st)*] llo *emd.*
                                                                    523 should] 1d *emd from* d *or re-formed.*

the divine ppertie of her first beeinge,   470

such are those thick, & gloomie shadowes dampe

oft seene in Charnell vaults, and sepulchers,

hoveringe and sittinge by a new [ ] made grave

as loath to leave the bodye that it loved

and linc'kt it selfe by carnall sensualitie   475

to a degenerate, and degraded state. /

2 bro: How charminge is divine philosophie

not harshe and crabbed as dull fooles suppose

but musicall as is Appolloes lute

and perpetuall feast of Nectard sweets   480

where noe crude surfeit raignes, *El: bro:* list, list, I heare

some farr of hollowe breake the silent ayre

2 bro: me thought soe too what should it be, *el: b:* for certaine

either some one like vs night founderd heere

The divine propertie of her first being.

Such are those thick, and gloomie shadows damp   490

Oft seene in Charnell vaults, and Sepulchers

Hovering, and sitting by a new made grave

As loath to leave the body that it lov'd,

And link't it selfe by carnall sensualitie

To a degenerate and degraded state.   495

   2 Bro. How charming is divine Philosophie!

Not harsh, and crabbed as dull fools suppose,

But musicall as is *Apollo's* lute,

And a perpetuall feast of nectar'd sweets

Where no crude surfet raigns. *El:bro.* List, list I heare   500

Some farre off hallow breake the silent aire.

   2 Bro. Me thought so too, what should it be?

   Eld: bro. For certaine

Either some one like us night founder'd here,

Hovering,
(17)

484   or else some neighbour woodman, or at worst   525

                            hedge

some roaving some ~~curl'd~~ man of y^e ~~swoord~~ calling to his fellows

    robber   2 Bro. heav'n keepe my sister. ~~yet~~ agen, agen & neere.

              ~~1 Bro.~~ best draw, & stand upon our guard. 1 Bro. Ile hallow

488   if he be freindly he comes well, if not

          ~~scratch~~   ———————~~a just defence~~ is a

he may cha^unce ~~had best looke to his forehead, heere be brambles~~   530

489   defence is a good cause & heav'n be for us

             he hallows ~~hallo~~ the guardian Dæmon hallows agen & enters 531

           in the habit of shepheard

                                  you

490   that hallow, I should know, what are speake

                          iron

Come not ~~too neere~~, you fall on ^pointed stakes else

             Dæ. what voice is that? my yong lord? speake agen   535

             2 Bro: oh. brother tis my fathers shepheard sure

             1 Broth. Thyrsis? whose artfull streines have oft delay'd   **21**

495   the huddling brooke to heare his madrigall

             and sweetned every muskrose of the ~~valley~~ dale

---

526-527 some ... robber] *& cancel lines, TMS^1b.*

526 hedge] *poss. TMS^1b*; curl'd] *just poss.* curlèd.

529-530 *M. phaps 1st wrote* if he be ... if not / had best looke ... brambles
    & s.d. To revise, he struck out 2nd line & began a new line a just defence
    is a, *inserted by a line beginning under* ell *in* well. *Then he cancelled*
    these words & added in left margin he may cha^unce scratch *& restored*

his forehead *by underlining. Finally, he cancelled this attempt & wrote*
defence is ... be for us *in the space above s.d., poss. for TMS^1b.*

529 ~~defence~~] d *minuscule.*

530 forehead,] *comma poss. semicolon, or period as Wright.*

532 shepheard] *1st* h *prob. emd from* p.

534 iron] *poss. TMS^1b*; o *poss. conceals caret for* 533.

537 Thyrsis] y *emd from* i.

BMS		1637	
or els some neyghbour woodman, or at worst,	485	Or else some neighbour wood man, or at worst	505
	some		
some roavinge robber, callinge to his fellowes;	⟨12ᵛ⟩	Some roaving robber calling to his fellows.	
2 bro heav'n keepe my sister: agen, agen, & neere		*2 Bro.* Heav'n keepe my sister, agen agen and neere,	
best drawe, & stand vpon oʳ guard, *el: bro:* Ile hallowe		Best draw, and stand upon our guard.	
		Eld: bro. Ile hallow,	
if he be freindly he comes well, if not		If he be friendly he comes well, if not	510
defence is a good Cause, and heav'n be for vs	490	Defence is a good cause, and Heav'n be for us.	
he hallowes and is answered, the guardian dæmon		*The attendant Spirit habited like a shepheard.*	
comes in habited like a shepheard. /			
El: bro: That hallowe I should knowe, what are yoᵘ speake,		That hallow I should know, what are you, speake,	
come not too neere, you fall on Iron stakes els		Come not too neere, you fall on iron stakes else.	
Dæ: What voice is that? my young Lord? speake agen.	495	*Spir.* What voice is that, my yong Lord? speak agen.	515
2 bro: O brother tis my fathers shepheard sure		*2 Bro.* O brother 'tis my father Shepheard sure.	
el: b: Thirsis? whose art full streynes haue oft delayed		*Eld: bro. Thyrsis?* whose artfull strains have oft de-	
the hudlinge brooke to heere his madrigall		The huddling brook to heare his madrigale, (layd	
and sweetned every muskerose ofthe dale,		And sweeten'd every muskrose of the dale,	

516 father] s *written in ink after* r *in Pforz.*

how cam'st thou heere good shepheard, hath any ramme   540
    from his   fold   or
slip't ~~leapt ore~~ ˄the˄ <u>penne</u> ˄young ~~ki~~ kid lost his damme

or straggling weather[ ] ~~hath~~ the pen't ~~flock~~ forsook?

500   how couldst thou find this darke sequestềrd nooke

Dæ. O my lov'd maisters heire, & his next joy

I came not heere on such a triviall toy   545

as a stray'd ewe, or to p̃sue the stealth

of pilfering wolfe, not all the fleecie wealth

505   that doth enrich these downs is worth a thought

to this my errand, & the care it brought

but oh my virgin Ladie where is she   550

how chance she is not in yor companie

1 Bro. to tell thee sadly shepheard; w^thout blame

510   or our neglect wee lost her as wee came

Sheph. ay me unhappie! then my fears are true

1 bro. what feares, good *~~shep~~. preethee breifly shew Thyrsis   555

     Dæ. ~~Shep~~. Ile tell you. Tis not vaine or fabulous

---

541 the] e *emd from* is; fold] *poss.* TMS^1b; kid] k *emd, or poss. majuscule.*   547 wealth] w *badly formed;* a *emd.*
542 [ ]] *poss. cancelled comma.*   556 fabulous] *1st* u *emd from* o.

how camst heere good shepheard, hath any ram	500
slipt from the fould, or young kyd lost his dam	
or straglinge weather the pent flock forsooke	
how couldst thou finde this darke sequesterd nooke?	
De̢: O my Lov'd masters heire, and his next Ioye	
I came not heere on such a triviall toye	505
as a strayed Ewe, or to pursue the stealth	
of pilferinge wolfe, not all the fleecie wealth	
that doeth enrich these downes is worth a thought	
to this my errand and the Care it brought. /	
but O my virgin lady where is she	510
	howe
howe chaunce she is not in yoʳ Companie?	⟨13ʳ⟩
el: bro: To tell thee sadly shepheard, wᵗʰout blame	
or our neglect wee lost her as wee came,	
De̢: Ay me vnhappie then my feares are true./	
el: bro: what feares, good *Thirsis* pʳthee briefly shewe	515
De̢: Ile tell you, tis not vayne, or fabulous,	

How cam'st thou here good Swaine, hath any ram	520
Slip't from the fold, or yong kid lost his dam,	
Or straggling weather the pen't flock forsook,	
How couldst thou find this darke sequester'd nook?	How
	(18)
Spir. O my lov'd masters heire, and his next joy	
I came not here on such a triviall toy	525
As a strayd Ewe, or to pursue the stealth	
Of pilfering wolfe, not all the fleecie wealth	
That doth enrich these downs is worth a thought	
To this my errand, and the care it brought.	
But ô my virgin Ladie where is she,	530
How chance she is not in your companie?	
Eld:bro. To tell thee sadly shepheard, without blame	
Or our neglect, wee lost her as wee came.	
Spir. Aye me unhappie then my fears are true.	
Eld:bro. What fears good *Thyrsis?* prethee briefly	535
Spir. Ile tell you, 'tis not vaine, or fabulous (shew.	

(though so esteem'd by shallow ignorance)

515   what the sage poets, taught by th' heav'nly Muse

storied of old in high immortall verse

of dire chimæra's and inchaunted Isles   560

518   & rifted rocks whose entrance leads to hell.

———for such there be, but unbeleife is blind

520   wthin the navill of this hideous wood

immur'd in cipresse shades a sorcerer dwells

of Bacchus & of circe borne, great Comus

      nt
deepe ~~lear enur'd~~ in all his mothers witcheries   565

skill'd and heere to every thirstie wanderer

525   by sly enticement gives his banefull cup

wth many murmurs mixt, whose pleasing poison

the visage quite transforms of him y^t drinks

       * *   *
and the inglorious likenesse of a beast   ~~makes~~   570

557 esteem'd] *1st* e *emd from* o *or just poss. from Italian* e.   563 shades] e *emd, prob. from* s.
558 *comma poss. inserted.*   570 the] e, *rather large, cuts an apostr., prob. to cancel it.*
562 for such ... blind] *poss. TMS*^{1d}.

BMS		1637	
(though soe esteem'd by shallowe ignorance)		(Though so esteem'd by shallow ignorance)	
what the sage poets, taught by th- heav'nly muse		What the sage Poëts taught by th'heav'nly Muse	
storied of old in high immortall verse		Storied of old in high immortall verse	
of dire *Chimeras*, and enchaunted Isles	520	Of dire *Chimera's* and inchanted Iles	540
and rifted rocks, whose entrance leads to hell		And rifted rocks whose entrance leads to hell,	
for such there be, but vnbeliefe is blinde,		For such there be, but unbeliefe is blind.	
within the navill of this hidious wood		Within the navill of this hideous wood	
immured in Cipress shades a sorserer dwells		Immur'd in cypresse shades a Sorcerer dwells	
of Bacchus and of Circe borne, greate *Comus*	525	Of *Bacchus,* and of *Circe* borne, great *Comus,*	545
deepe skild in all his mothers witcheries		Deepe skill'd in all his mothers witcheries,	
and heere to everie thirstie wanderer		And here to every thirstie wanderer	
by slye enticem^t gives his banefull Cup		By slie enticement gives his banefull cup	
with many murmurs mixt, whose pleasinge poyson		With many murmurs mixt, whose pleasing poison	
the visage quite transformes of him that drinkes	530	The visage quite transforms of him that drinks,	550
and the inglorious likeness of a beast		And the inglorious likenesse of a beast	

518 *hyphen poss. start of* h, *though hyphens often faint in the original; no*
    apostr.
523 *indented.*

fixes insteed, unmoulding reasons mintage

[ ]

530 characterd in the face this have I learn [']t

        hillie   crofts

[t]ending my flocks hard by i'th ˄ ~~pastur'd˄lawn~~ [']s

that ~~brows~~ this bottome glade whence night by night

he & his monstrous rout are heard to howle   575

like stabl'd wolvs, or tigers at thire prey

535 doing abhorred rites to Hecate

in thire obscured haunts of inmost bowers

Yet have ~~they~~ they many baits, & ~~gil~~ guilefull spells

to̊ inveigle & invite th' unwarie ~~spell~~ sense   580

of them y^t passe unweeting by the way.

540 this evening late by then the chewing flocks

had tane thire supper on the savourie herbe

of knot grasse dew besprent, and were in fold

I sate me downe to watch, upon a banke   585

---

572 [ ]] *small mark above* e & r *poss. apostr. (cf.* sequesterd 543*), prob.*
    meaningless.

573 [t]ending] [t] *heavily thickened, poss. emd;* ~~lawn['] s~~ *conjectural*
    apostr. poss. cancelled.

577 Hecate] H *emd.*

579 Yet] Y *emd, prob. from* th*;* they] e *emd, poss. from* at.

580 *prefixes* in in un *detached; cf.* 509 *n.;* sense] *2nd* s *emd from* c.

BMS		1637	
fixes insteed, vnmouldinge reasons mintage		Fixes instead, unmoulding reasons mintage	
charactred in the face, This have I learnt		Character'd in the face; this have I learn't	
tendinge my flocks, hard by i'th hillie ~~flocks~~ Crofts		Tending my flocks hard by i'th hilly crofts	554
that browe this bottome glade, whence night by night	that ⟨13ᵛ⟩	That brow this bottome glade, whence night by night	That (19)
he and his monstrous route are heard to howle	536	He and his monstrous rout are heard to howle	
like stabled wolves, or tigers at their preyᵉ		Like stabl'd wolves, or tigers at their prey	
doeinge abhorred rites to *Heccate*		Doing abhorred rites to *Hecate*	
in their obscured haunts of inmost bowers,		In their obscured haunts of inmost bowres.	
yet have they many baites and guylefull spells	540	Yet have they many baits, and guilefull spells	560
to invegle, and invite the vnwarie sence		T'inveigle, and invite th'unwarie sense	
of them that passe vnweetinge by the waye,		Of them that passe unweeting by the way.	
this eveninge late, by then the chewinge flocks		This evening late by then the chewing flocks	
had tane their supper on the savorie herbe		Had ta'ne their supper on the savourie herbe	
of knot grasse dew-besprent and were in fold,	545	Of Knot-grass dew-besprent, and were in fold	565
I sate me downe to watch vpon a banke		I sate me downe to watch upon a bank	

with ivie canopied, & interwove   blowing
          blowing   *
545   wth ˌs[ucklin]g* honiesuckle, & began   *flaunting flaunting

547   2 to meditate my rurall minstrelsie

546   1 wrapt in a pleasing fit of melancholy

                                              a
548   till fancie had her fill, but ereˌthe close   590

        the wonted roare was up amidst the woods

550   and fill'd the aire wth barbarous dissonance

                              d
        at wch I ceaseᵈ, & listenˌthem awhile

        till an unusuall stop of suddaine silence

        gave respit to the drousie flighted steeds   595

        that draw the litter of close-curtain'd sleepe   *
                *still[—]ft[—] *   *sweet soft
555   At last a softˌ& sollemne breathing sound
              a   **slow
        rose likeˌthe soft steame ofˌdistill'd ꝑfumes   slow *rich

586 canopied,] *mark above comma presum. meaningless.*
587 s[ucklin]g] suckling *Wright ('difficult to read'); presum.* s[ucklin]g,
     then blowing *(above),* flaunting, blowing *(margin),* TMS^1a; *then* blowing
     cancelled & flaunting *added for* TMS^2a.
591 up] u *begun as something else.*
593 ceaseᵈ] *apostr. above* d; s *prob. emd; phaps* cease (*cf.* listen), *then* d
     added, e *deleted, apostr. inserted.*
595 flighted] l *emd from* r *with unusual open loop (but cf.* julep *787), prob.*

TMS^1a; frighted *BMS, 1637, 1645, 1673;* flighted *Peck, Peck ms., Dalton*
(1759, not 1738, poss. from Peck, as Todd said in Comus *(1798)), Newton,*
Warton, Todd; ct. r *prob. emd from* l *in* brandish't *691; see L. Abercrom-*
bie, 'Drowsie Frighted Steeds', Proceedings of the Leeds Philosophical
and Literary Society, Literary and Historical Section, II, Part I (Leeds
1928), pp. 1-5.
597 soft] *poss.* TMS^3e.
598 soft] *poss.* softe, *as Wright;* a] **slow] *slow] rich] *poss.* TMS^3e.

BMS	1637
with Ivie Cannopied and interwove	With ivie canopied, and interwove
with flauntinge hony sucle, and began	With flaunting hony-suckle, and began
wrapt in a pleasinge fitt of melencholy	Wrapt in a pleasing fit of melancholy
to meditate my rurall minstrelsie 550	To meditate my rural minstrelsie 570
till fansie had her fill, but ere a close	Till fancie had her fill, but ere a close
the wonted roare was vp amidst the woods	The wonted roare was up amidst the woods,
and filld the aire with barbarous dissonance	And filld the aire with barbarous dissonance
at wch I ceast, and listned them a while	At which I ceas't, and listen'd them a while
till an vnvsuall stop of suddaine silence 555	Till an unusuall stop of sudden silence 575
gave respite to the drowsie frighted steeds	Gave respit to the drowsie frighted steeds
that drawe the litter of close-curtain'd sleepe	That draw the litter of close-curtain'd sleepe.
at last a sweete, and solemne breathinge sound	At last a soft, and solemne breathing sound
rose like the softe steame of distill'd p̃fumes	Rose like a steame of rich distill'd Perfumes

573 barbarous] barboruus *BM C.34.d.46.*

and stole upon the aire, that even silence

[ ]

was tooke e're she was ware, & wish't she might   600

deny her nature & be never more

         so

560   still to be‸displac't. I was all eare

and tooke in streins that might create a soule   ⟨22⟩

under the ribbs of Death. but oh ere long

too well I might p̣ceave it was ye voice   605

of my most honour'd Ladie yor deare sister

565   amaz'd I stood, harrow'd wth greife & feare

and O poore haplesse nightingale thought I

how sweet thou sing'st, how neere the deadly snare

then downe the lawnes I ran wth headlong hast   610

through paths & turnings often trod by day

570   till guided by myne eare I found the place

where that damn'd wisard hid in sly disguise

(for so by certaine signes I knew) had met

---

600 e're] *small apostr. poss. inserted;* [ ]] *indecipherable pen marks, 1st poss. apostr. inserted between* g & h *in* might; *several meaningless marks in area* 595-600.

603 might] m *begun as* t.
609 sing'st] *apostr. above descender of* g.

and stole vpon the aire, that even silence   560

was tooke ere she was ware, & wisht she might

deny her nature and be never more
                                                               still
still to be soe displac't, I was all eare   ⟨14ʳ⟩

and tooke in th̶ streines, that might create a sowle

vnder the ribbs of death. but O ere long   565

two well I might p̟ceive, it was the voice

of my most honor'd lady, yoʳ deere sister

amaz'd I stood, harrow'd with greife, & feare,

and O poore hapless nightingale thought I

how sweete thou singst, how neere the deadly snare, 570

then downe the lawnes I ran, wᵗʰ headlonge hast

through paths and turnings, often trod by daye,

till guyded by myne eare, I found the place

where that damn'd wizard hid in slye disguise

(for soe by certaine signes I knowe) had met   575

And stole upon the aire, that even Silence   580

Was tooke e're she was ware, and wish't she might

Deny her nature, and be never more

Still to be so displac't. I was all eare,

And took in strains that might create a soule

Vnder the ribs of Death, but ô ere long   585

Too well I did perceive it was the voice
                                                               Of
Of my most honour'd Lady your deare sister.   (20)

Amaz'd I stood, harrow'd with griefe and feare,

And ô poore haplesse nightingale thought I

How sweet thou sing'st, how neere the deadly snare! 590

Then downe the lawns I ran with headlong hast

Through paths, and turnings often trod by day

Till guided by mine eare I found the place

Where that dam'd wisard hid in slie disguise

(For so by certain signs I knew) had met   595

565 the] e emd from r.
571 comma faint but prob.

583 Still] S italic BM C.34.d.46, V&A 6591.26.52.12.

alreadie ere my best speed could prævent 615
    aidlesse
the ~~helplesse~~ innocent Ladie his wisht prey ~~who tooke him~~

575   ~~who gen~~ who gently askt if he had seene such tow

supposing him some neighbour villager

longer I durst not stay, but soone I gues't

yee were the tow she meant, & wth that I sprung 620

into swift flight till I had found you heere

580   ~~and this~~ but furder know I not. 2 Bro. O night & shades

how are yee joyn'd wth hell in triple knot

against th' unarmed weakenesse of one virgin

alone, & helplesse, is this the confidence 625

you gave me brother? 1 Bro. yes: and keepe it still

585   leane on it safely not a piod

shall be unsaid for me, against the threats

of malice, or of sorcerie, or that power

wch erring men call chance this I hold firme 630

vertue may be assayl'd but never hurt

590   surpris'd by unjust force, but not enthrall'd ~~and~~

629 that] at *poss. emd.*   632 enthrall'd] d *re-formed or poss. added.*

BMS	1637

alreadie eare my best speede could p^rvent

the aideless innocent ladie his wisht prey

whoe gently askt if he had seene such two,

supposinge him some neighbour villager,

longer I durst not stay, but soone I guest   580

yee were the two she meant, wth that I sprung

into swift flight, till I had found you heere

but furder know I not; *2: bro* O night & shades

how are you ioyn'd with hell in triple knott

against the vnarmed weaknes of one virgin   585

alone, and helpeless, Is this the confidence?

you gave me brother? *el: bro:* yes & keepe it still

leane on it salfly, not a period

shalbe vnsai'd for me, against the threats

                        of

of malice, or of Sorcerie, or that powre   ⟨14^v⟩

wch erringe men call chaunce this I hould firme   591

virtue may be assail'd but never hurte

surpris'd by vniust force, but not enthrall'd,

593 surpris'd] *2nd s re-formed & apostr. inserted.*

Alreadie, ere my best speed could prævent

The aidlesse innocent Ladie his wish't prey,

Who gently ask't if he had seene such two

Supposing him some neighbour villager;

Longer I durst not stay, but soone I guess't   600

Yee were the two she mean't, with that I sprung

Into swift flight till I had found you here,

But farther know I not. *2 Bro.* O night and shades

How are yee joyn'd with hell in triple knot

Against th'unarmed weaknesse of one virgin   605

Alone, and helplesse! is this the confidence

You gave me brother? *Eld:bro.* Yes, and keep it still,

Leane on it safely, not a period

Shall be unsaid for me; against the threats

Of malice or of sorcerie, or that power   610

Which erring men call Chance, this I hold firme,

Vertue may be assail'd, but never hurt,

Surpriz'd by unjust force, but not enthrall'd,

596 Alreadie,] *Comma did not print in Pforz. & BM C.34.d.46, but clear in Berg, PM, BM C.12.g.34, Ashley 1166, etc.*

Yea even that wch mischeife ment most harme

sha[l]l in the happie triall prove most glory

but evill on it selfe shall back recoyle   635

~~till all to place~~ & mixe no more wth goodnesse, when at last

595 gather'd like scum & setled to it s̉elfe

it shall be in æternall restlesse change

selfe fed, & selfe consum'd if this faile

the pillar'd firmament is rottennesse   640

and earths base built on stubble. but Come lets on

600 against th' opposing will & arme of heav'n

may never this just swoord be lifted up.

but for y^t damn'd magician, let him be girt

wth all the greisly legions that troope   645

under the sootie flag of Acheron
       all
605 harpyes & Hydra's or ͜ the monstrous Buggs

twixt Africa & Inde. Ile find him out

---

633 Yea] Y *poss. minuscule.*
634 sha[l]l] *damaged leaf.*
635 selfe] *comma just poss.*
637 scum &] *space in original equals about 2 letters in context;* s̉elfe].
  apostr. prob., phaps between s & e.
639 consum'd if] *space in original equals* less *above it in* 638.

641 base] *query dots before & after, higher than periods but not more so*
  than period after stubble, *poss. meaningless.*
642 th' opposing] *phaps* th'opposing.
645 the greisly] *run together.*
647 Hydra's] d *re-formed;* Buggs] B *phaps re-formed or begun as something*
  else; s *re-formed.*

yea even that wch mischiefe meant most harme	Yea even that which mischiefe meant most harme,
shall in the happie triall prove most glorie, 595	Shall in the happie triall prove most glorie. 615
but evill on it selfe shall back recoyle	But evill on it selfe shall backe recoyle
and mixe noe more with goodnesse, when at last	And mixe no more with goodnesse, when at last
gather'd like scum, and setl'd to it selfe	Gather'd like scum, and setl'd to it selfe
it shalbe in eternall restless change	It shall bee in eternall restlesse change
selfe fed, and selfe consum'd, if this fayle 600	Selfe fed, and selfe consum'd, if this faile 620
the pillard firmament is rottennesse	The pillar'd firmament is rottennesse,
and earth's base built on stubble. but come lets on:	And earths base built on stubble. But come let's on.
against the opposinge will, and arme of heav'n	Against th'opposing will and arme of heav'n
may this iust sword be lifted vp,	May never this just sword be lifted up,
but for that damn'd magitian, let him be girt 605	But for that damn'd magician, let him be girt 625
with all the grisley legions that troope	With all the greisly legions that troope
vnder the sootie flagg of Acheron,	Vnder the sootie flag of *Acheron,*
Harpies, & Hidraes, or all the monstrous buggs	*Harpyies* and *Hydra's,* or all the monstrous bugs
twixt Africa, and Inde, I'le finde him out	'Twixt *Africa,* and *Inde,* Ile find him out

In the BMS column, line 604 has "neu^r" written above "may" with a caret.

The 1637 column shows "It" and "(21)" alongside the line "It shall bee in eternall restlesse change".

604 neu^r] *ink lighter than context.*

and force him to ~~release his new got prey~~ restore his purchase back

or drag him by the curls & cleave his scalpe   650

downe to the ~~hipps~~ †[——] hips. Dæ. alas good ventrous youth

610   I love thy courage yet & bold emprise

                               swoord

*swoord but heere thy ~~swo*steele~~ can doe thee ~~little stead~~ ~~small availe~~

farre other arms & other weapons must

be those that quell the might of hellish charms   655

                                  *

he wth his bare wand can ~~unquilt~~ thy joynts *unthred

                    all thy

615   & crumble ~~every~~ sinews. ⅂ Bro. why preethee shep.

how durst thou then thy selfe approach so neere

as to make this relation. Dæ. care, & utmost shifts

how to secure the ladie from surprisal   660

brought to my mynd a certaine shepheard lad

620   of small regard to see to yet well skill'd

in every vertuous plant, & healing herbe

---

649 him] i *emd;* ~~new-got~~] *poss. hyphen;* restore ... back] *TMS*^{2a}.   651 downe] d *emd or re-formed;* †[——] ~~lowest~~ *Wright.*

650 curls] s *emd, poss. from* es.

BMS	1637
and force him to restore his purchase back 610	And force him to restore his purchase backe 630
or drag him by the Curles, and cleave his scalpe	Or drag him by the curles, and cleave his scalpe
downe to the hipps, *Dem:* Alas good ventrous youth	Downe to the hipps.
	Spir. Alas good ventrous youth,
I love the Courage yet, and bold emprise,	I love thy courage yet, and bold Emprise,
but heere thy sword can doe thee little stead	But here thy sword can doe thee little stead, 635
farr other armes, and other weopons must 615	Farre other arms, and other weapons must
be those that quell the might of hellish Charmes, be ⟨15ʳ⟩	Be those that quell the might of hellish charms,
he with his bare wand can vnthred thy ioynts	He with his bare wand can unthred thy joynts
and crumble all thy sinewes, *El: bro:* why pre'thee shepheard	And crumble all thy sinewes.
	Eld. Bro. Why prethee shepheard 640
how durst thou then approach soe neere,	How durst thou then thy selfe approach so nëere
as to make this relacon; *Dem:* Care, & vtmost shifts 620	As to máke this relation?
	Spir. Care and utmost shifts
how to secure the lady from surprisall,	How to secure the Ladie from surprisall
brought to my mynd a certaine shepheard lad	Brought to my mind a certaine shepheard lad 645
of smale regard to see to, yet well skill'd	Of small regard to see to, yet well skill'd
in every verteus plant, and healinge herbe	In every vertuous plant, and healing herbe

614 stead] a *emd from* e, *or vice versa.*

641 thou then] *run together.*

that spreds her verdant leafe to th' morning ray

he lov'd me well, & oft would beg me sing   665

wch when I did he on the tender grasse

625   would sit and hearken even to extasie   23

& in requitall ope his le^atherne scrip

& shew me simples of a thousand ~~hews~~ names

telling thire strange & vigorous faculties   670

amoūgst the rest a small unsightly root

630   but of divine effect he culld me out

the leafe was darkish & had prickles on it

but in an other countrie as he said

bore a bright golden flowre, but not in this soile   675

unknowne & like esteem'd & the dull swayne

635   treads on it dayly wth his clouted shoo<u>ne &</u> yet more med'cinall ˰then that is it ~~anci~~
           it

638   he call'd ˰Hæmon^{y̆} & gave it me   ~~ent~~ Moly, ˰that ~~Mercury~~ wch to wise ulysse[s]
           gave   (Hermes once)

---

668 letherne] *a phaps TMS*^{3f}.
669 names] *TMS*^{2a}.
677-678 *margin* & yet ... gave ... once] *presum. TMS*^{1a}.
677 med'cinall] *apostr. above* c; *that*] a *prob. emd from* e.

678 Hæmony] æ *badly formed, almost* a; y *emd or re-formed; cross above*
y *phaps cancelled tittle or accent;* ent] n *emd or re-formed;* Mercury]
2nd r *phaps emd from* s; ulysse[s]] s *on broken leaf edge.*

that spreades her verdant leafe to th'morninge ray, 625	That spreds her verdant leafe to th'morning ray,
he lov'd me well, and oft would begg me singe,	He lov'd me well, and oft would beg me sing,
wch when I did, he on the tender grasse	Which when I did, he on the tender grasse 650
would sit, and hearken even to extasie	Would sit, and hearken even to extasie, Would (22)
and in requitall open his letherne scrip,	And in requitall ope his leather'n scrip,
and shew me simples of a thousand names 630	And shew me simples of a thousand names
tellinge their strange, and vigorous faculties,	Telling their strange, and vigorous faculties,
amongst the rest, a smale vnsightly roote	Amongst the rest a small unsightly root, 655
but of divine effect, he cull'd me out	But of divine effect, he cull'd me out;
the leafe was darkish, and had prickles on it,	The leafe was darkish, and had prickles on it,
	But in another Countrie, as he said,
	Bore a bright golden flowre, but not in this soyle:
	Vnknowne, and like esteem'd, and the dull swayne 660
	Treads on it dayly with his clouted shoone,
	And yet more med'cinall is it then that *Moly*
	That *Hermes* once to wise *Vlysses* gave,
he call'd it *Hẹmony*, and gaue it me 635	He call'd it *Hæmony*, and gave it me

627 I] *emd from* he.
635 gaue] u *phaps* v *blotted.*

& bad me keepe it as of soveraine use

640   gainst all enchauntments, mildew blast, or dampe   680

or gastly Furies apparition

I purs't it up, but little reckoning made

till now that this extremity compell'd

but now I find it true, for by this meanes

645   I knew the fowle enchanter though disguis'd   685

enter'd the very limetwigs of his spells

and yet came off, if you have this about you
      * ~~when on the way~~   *
(as I will give you ~~as wee goe~~) you may   when we goe.
         cers
boldly assault ~~h~~y^{e}necromant~~ik~~ hall

650   where if he be wth ~~suddaine violence~~ dauntless hardyhood   690

& brandish't ~~blades~~ rush on him, breake his glasse
    shed
and ‸powre the lushious ~~potion~~ liquor on the ground

~~but~~and sease his wand. though he & his curs't crew

feirce signe of battaile make & menace high

680 blast] l *emd, phaps from 1st stroke of* a.
681 Furies] e *emd or re-formed.*
689 ~~h~~y^e] y^e *emd from* is.
690 hardyhood] y *emd from* i, *or less prob. vice versa;* hardyhood *Wright.*

691 brandish't] r *emd, prob. from* l.
692 the *(2nd)*] h *emd or re-formed.*
693 but] *poss.* TMS^{2a}.
694 make] *comma poss., or meaningless mark.*

and bad me keepe it as of soveraigne vse

gainst all enchauntm^{ts}, mildew blast, or dampe,

or gastlie furies apparition,

I purst it vp, but little reckoninge made

till now that this extremitie compell'd,   640

but now I finde it true, for by this meanes

I knew the fowle Enchaunter, though disguis'd

entered the very lymetwiggs of his spells

and yet came off, if you have this about you

(as I will give you when wee goe) you may   645

boldly assaulte the Negromancers hall,

where if he be, with dauntlesse hardy-hood

and brandisht blade rushe on him, breake his glasse

and shed the lussious liquor on the ground,

but cease his wand, though he and his curst crew   650

fierce signe of battaile make, and menace high

I knew
⟨15ᵛ⟩

And bad me keepe it as of soveraine use   665

'Gainst all inchantments, mildew blast, or damp

Or gastly furies apparition;

I purs't it up, but little reck'ning made

Till now that this extremity compell'd,

But now I find it true, for by this means   670

I knew the foule inchanter though disguis'd,

Enter'd the very limetwigs of his spells,

And yet came off, if you have this about you

(As I will give you when wee goe) you may

Boldly assault the necromancers hall,   675

Where if he be, with dauntlesse hardihood

And brandish't blade rush on him, breake his glasse,

And shed the lushious liquor on the ground

But sease his wand, though he and his curst crew

Feirce signe of battaile make, and menace high,   680

655   or like the sons of Vulcan vomit smoake   695

           yet they will soone retire if he but shrinke
                 2   1   (before us

657   1 Bro. Thyrsis lead on apace I follow thee

                                    and some good angell beare a sheild

           ~~& good heaven cast his best regard upon us~~   Ex

           the scene [ch]a changes to a stately pallace set out wth all manner
                   tables spred wth all dainties
           of deliciousness.$_\wedge$ Comus is discover'd wth his rabble. & the Ladie set in   700

           an inchanted chaire   She offers to rise

---

695   Vulcan] V *poss. minuscule;* vomit] *small slanted mark above* v *prob.*
      meaningless.
697   and some ... before us] *TMS*^{2a}.

698   us] *period poss.*
700   set] s *emd, poss. from* p.

or like the sonns of *Vulcan* vomitt smoake

yet will they soone retire, if he but shrinke.

El: bro Thirsis leade on apace, I followe thee

and some good Angell beare a shield before vs.   655

The *Sceane* changes to a stately pallace set out w^{th}all mann^{r}

manner of delitiousness, tables spred with all dainties

Comus appes wth his rabble, and the lady set in an

inchauntedchayre, to whome he offers his glasse

wch she puts by, and goes about to rise./   660

Or like the sons of *Vulcan* vomit smoake,

Yet will they soone retire, if he but shrinke.

Eld:
    Eld. Bro. Thyrsis lead on apace Ile follow thee,   (23)

And some good angell beare a sheild before us.

The Scene Changes to a stately palace set out with all   685

manner of deliciousnesse, soft musicke, tables spred

with all dainties. Comus *appeares with his rabble,*

and the Ladie set in an inchanted chaire to whom he

offers his glasse, which she puts by, and goes about

to rise.   690

656 mann^{r}] *ink fainter than context.*

682 shrinke.] *no period in Pforz., PM, BM C.34.d.46, etc., but clear in Bright.*
685 *Changes ... all*] *Conges ... all man- BM C.34.d.46, V&A 6591.26.52.12.*
686 *manner*] *ner BM C.34.d.46, V&A 6591.26.52.12; deliciousnesse*] *u inverted in Hunt.*

659   Co. nay Ladie sit, if I but wave this wand   La: foole ~~thou art over proud~~ doe not boas

                                         thou canst not touch the freedome of my mind

660   yor nerves are all chain'd up in alablaster wth all thy charmes although this corporall rind

                     or   thou hast immanacl'd while heavn sees good

    and you a statue, ~~fixt~~, as Daphne was   Co. why are you vext Ladie, why doe y^u frow

662   root-bound, that fled Apollo. ~~why doe ye frow~~ne   705

667   ~~heere fro~~ heere dwell no frowns$_\wedge$^{n}or anger, from these gates

        sorrow flies farre. see here be all the pleasures

                          ~~invent~~

    that ~~youth & fancie~~ fancie can$_\wedge$ ~~beget~~ on youthfull thoughts

                *fresh

670   when the$_\wedge$ ~~briske~~ blood ~~return~~ grows lively & returnes   *fresh

671   brisk as the ~~Aprills~~ budds in primrose season   710

                                 that wch follows heere is in the

                               ⟨pasted leafe begins ~~poore ladie~~   739⟩

                               ⟨and first behold this &c.   740⟩

702–704 La: foole ... frow[n]] *poss.* TMS^{2a}; *see p. 7.*   *phaps begun as* s *or* f; tu *written through an asterisk;* fresh *(margin)*]

702 boas[t]] s *on leaf edge;* boast *Wright.*   *dot after & above presum. meaningless.*

704 was] *comma faintly poss.;* are] e *emd from* t *in odd form, phaps*   710, 739–740 *margin* that wch follows ... behold this &c.] *in original all one*

    secretary; frow[n]] w *on broken leaf edge;* frow *Wright.*   *marginal note, in this edition broken & repeated; prob.* TMS^{2a}, TMS^{3b};

708 on] o *emd to* i, *then underlined with* ~~beget~~ *to be restored.*   *see p. 7.*

709 ~~return~~] n *abandoned after 1st stroke & word cancelled;* returnes] t   710 ~~Aprills~~] A *phaps re-formed.*

Co: Nay ladye sit, if I but wave this wand	*Comus.* Nay Ladie sit; if I but wave this wand,
your nerves a̶l are all chain'd vp in alablaster	Your nervs are all chain'd up in alablaster,
and you a statue, or as Daphne was	And you a statue; or as *Daphne* was
roote bound, that fled Apollo. *La:* foole doe not boast	Root bound that fled *Apollo.*
	La. Foole doe not boast, 695
thou canst not touch the freedome of my mynde 665	Thou canst not touch the freedome of my mind
with all thy charmes, although this corporall rind	With all thy charms, although this corporall rind
thou hast immanacl'd, while heav'n sees good,	Thou hast immanacl'd, while heav'n sees good.
Co: Whye are you vext ladie, why doe you frowne	*Co.* Why are you vext Ladie, why doe you frowne?
heere dwell noe frownes, nor anger, from these gates	Here dwell no frowns, nor anger, from these gates 700
sorrowe flies farr, see heere be all the pleasures 670	Sorrow flies farre: see here be all the pleasurs
that fancie can begett on youthfull thoughts	That fancie can beget on youthfull thoughts
when the fresh blood grows lively, and returnes	When the fresh blood grows lively, and returns
briske as the Aprill budds in primrose season.	Brisk as the *April* buds in primrose season.

heere ⟨16ʳ⟩

697 With all] *run together.*
701 be all] *run together.*

⟨'pasted leafe'⟩ | why should you be so cruell to yor ⟨**22a**⟩ 711

selfe, and to those daintie lims

672 and first behold this cordiall julep heere | wch nature lent for gentle

y^t flams & dances in his crystall bounds | usage, and soft delicacie, but

674 wth spirits of baulme, & fragrant syrops mixt | you invert the cov'nants of her 715

νηπενθὲς not that Nepenthes wch the wife of Thone | trust, and harshly deale like an

in Ægypt gave to Ioveborne Helena | ill borrower wth that wch you

is of such power to stirre up joy as this | receav'd on other terms scorning

678 to life so freindly or so coole to thirst | the unexempt condition by wch all

~~poore ladie thou hast need of some refreshing~~ mortall frailtie must subsist 720

have
688 that ˌhast bin tir'd all day wthout repast | refreshment after toile, ease

have but
& timely rest ˌ~~hast~~ wanted, ~~heere~~ faire virgin | after paine, that have bin

690 this will restore all soone. La. t'will not false traitor tir'd &c.

711-738 *the pasted leaf* ⟨*p. 22a*⟩ *referred to in marginal note* 739 *in original
& inserted here in this edition; see p. 9.*
711-723 *margin* why should ... tir'd &c.] *& line from* refreshing *(720) to*
why *(711), pasted leaf (b),* TMS^{3c}.
713-738 and first behold ... men &c.] *pasted leaf (a), prob.* TMS^{3b}.
714 delicacie] *1st* c *emd, phaps from* r.
715 baulme] e *Italian.*
716 Thone] e *Italian.*

717 borne] e *Italian.*
719 freindly] *comma just poss.;* or] *Dalton, Newton, Peck ms.; and Birch,
Warton, Todd, prob. in error.*
720 some] e *Italian; cancel line* TMS^{3c} *with pasted leaf (b).*
721 have] *& cancel line & caret,* TMS^{3c}.
722 have] but] *& cancel lines & carets,* TMS^{3c}; wanted] n *re-formed.*
723 soone] e *Italian.*

and first behould this cordiall Iulep heere

that flames, and dances in his christall bounds,   675

with spiritts of baulme, and fragrant sirrops mixt;

Not that Nepenthes wch the wife of *Thone*

in Egipt gave to Iove-borne *Hellena*

is of such power to stirre vp Ioye as this

to life, soe freindly, or soe coole too thirst,   680

poore ladie thou hast neede of some refreshinge

that hast been tired aldaye without repast,

a timely rest hast wanted. *h*eere fayre Virgin

And first behold this cordial julep here   705

That flames, and dances in his crystall bounds

With spirits of balme, and fragrant syrops mixt.

Not that *Nepenthes* which the wife of *Thone*

In *Ægypt* gave to *Iove*-borne *Helena*

Is of such power to stirre up joy as this,   710

To life so friendly, or so coole to thirst.

Why should you be so cruell to your selfe,

And to those daintie limms which nature lent   And (24)

For gentle usage, and soft delicacie?

But you invert the cov'nants of her trust,   715

And harshly deale like an ill borrower

With that which you receiv'd on other termes,

Scorning the unexempt condition,

By which all mortall frailty must subsist,

Refreshment after toile, ease after paine,   720

That have been tir'd all day without repast,

And timely rest have wanted, but faire virgin

This will restore all soone.

676 *semicolon prob. since stroke of* t *goes beyond the dot; cf.* 684.

t'will not restore the truth & honestie

that thou hast banisht from thy toungue wth lies   725

was this the cottage & the safe abode

thou toldst me of? what grim aspects are these

695   these ougly headed monsters? mercie guard me!

Hence wth thy ~~hel brewd opiate foule brud~~ brewd enchauntments foule deceaver

hast thou betrayd my credulous innocence   730

wth visor'd falshood & base forgeries

and wouldst thou seeke againe to trap me heere

700   wth lickerish baites fit to ensnare a brute?

were it a draft for Iuno when she banquets

I would not taste thy treasonous offer, none   735

but such as are good men can give good things

704   and that wch is not good is not delicious to a well govern'd, & wise appetite

706   Co. O foolishnesse of men &c.   738

728 headed] *apostr. poss. above 2nd* e.
729 *M. poss. left half line* Hence ... opiate *in pasted leaf (a) (query hyphen after* hel*), cancelled* hel brewd opiate *(cancel line in less dense ink, phaps like that of some words in 713-719), added* foule brud *& cancelled both words (ink reluctant in* e *& in line through* brud, *though line darker than through* hel ... opiate*), then added* brewd ... deceaver, *presum.* TMS^{3b}.

733 baites] it *emd*, i *poss. inserted.*
734 when] e *in odd form, poss. secretary.*
735 taste] e *Italian;* none] e *Italian.*
737 appetite] *2nd* e *Italian.*
738 men] *period poss.*

this will restore all soone; *La:* t'will not false traytor

twill not restore the trueth and honestie   685

that thou hast banisht from thy ~~thoughts~~ tongue wth lies,

was this the Cottage, and the safe aboade

thou touldst me of? what grim aspects are these?

these ougley headed Monsters? Mercie guard me,

hence with thy brewd enchauntm^{ts}, fowle deceaver   690

were it a drafte for Iuno, when she banquetts

I would not taste thy treasonous offer, none

but such as are good men, can give good things

and that wch is not good, is not delitious

to a well govern'd and wise appetite,   695
                                                             Co:

La. T'will not false traitor,

T'will not restore the truth and honestie   725

That thou hast banish't from thy tongue with lies,

Was this the cottage, and the safe abode

Thou told'st me of? what grim aspects are these,

These ougly-headed monsters? Mercie guard me!

Hence with thy brewd inchantments foule deceiver,   730

Hast thou betray'd my credulous innocence

With visor'd falshood, and base forgerie,

And wouldst thou seek againe to trap me here

With lickerish baits fit to ensnare a brute?

Were it a draft for *Iuno* when she banquets   735

I would not tast thy treasonous offer; none

But such as are good men can give good things,

And that which is not good, is not delicious

To a wel-govern'd and wise appetite.

---

693 things] *no comma.*

⟨**23 continued**⟩

⟨that wch follows heere is in the 710⟩

706 Co. Oh foolishnesse of men! that lend thire eares

                739

         pasted leafe begins ~~poore ladie~~

    to those budge doctors of the stoick ~~gowne~~ furre   740

        and first behold this &c.

    and fetch thire precepts from the Cynick tub   741

    praising the leane, & sallow abstinence

710   wherfore did nature powre her bounties forth

    wth such a full, & unwithdrawing hand

    covering the earth wth odours, ~~& w^th~~ fruits, & flocks 745

 thronging ~~cramming~~ the seas wth spawne innumerable

             but all to please & sate the curious taste

    ~~the feilds wth cattell & the aire wth fowle~~⌋

715   and set to worke millions of spinning worms

    that in thire greene shops weave the smooth haird silke

   to a~~dorne~~ deck

  [—] ˄to ~~deck~~˄ her sons, and that no corner might   750

    be vacant of her plentie in her owne loynes

    she hutch't thĕ all-worship't ore & precious gemms

720   to store her children wth. if all the world

    should in a pet of temperance feed on ~~pulse~~ fetches pulse

739-740 *margin prob. TMS^2a emd. for TMS^3b; see p. 10.*

740 doctors] d *emd or re-formed.*

741 Cynick] C *emd from* c.

744 unwithdrawing] *prefixes somewhat detached; cf. 509 n.*

746 [t]hronging] h *on broken leaf fold;* spawne] p *emd or re-formed.*

749 smooth] h *poss. emd from* e; smooth haird] *poss. run together.*

754 in] i *emd from* b[ ].

Co: O foolishnes of men, that lend their eares	⟨16ᵛ⟩	*Co.* O foolishnesse of men! that lend their eares	740

Co: O foolishnes of men, that lend their eares ⟨16ᵛ⟩

to those budge doctors of the Stoick ~~furr~~ furr

and fetch their pʳcepts from the Cinick tub

praisinge the leane, and shallow abstinence.

wherefore did nature power her bounties furth   700

with such a full, and vnwithdraweinge hand,

coveringe the earth with odours, fruits and flocks

throngeinge the seas with spawne innumerable

but all to please, and sate the Curious tast,

and set to worke millions of spinninge wormes   705

that in their greene shopps, weave the smoote-haired silke

to deck her sonns, and that noe corner might

be vacant of her plentie, in her owne loynes

she hutch't th'all worshipt oare, and pretious gems

to store her childeren with, if all the world   710

should in a pet of temperance, feede on pulse

Co. O foolishnesse of men! that lend their eares   740

To those budge doctors of the *Stoick* furre,

And fetch their præcepts from the *Cynick* tub,

Praising the leane, and sallow Abstinence.

Wherefore did Nature powre her bounties forth   744
                                                  With
                                                  (25)

With such a full and unwithdrawing hand,

Covering the earth with odours, fruits, and flocks

Thronging the seas with spawne innumerable

But all to please, and sate the curious tast?

And set to work millions of spinning worms,

That in their green shops weave the smooth-hair'd silk   750

To deck her Sons, and that no corner might

Be vacant of her plentie, in her owne loyns

She hutch't th'all worshipt ore, and precious gems

To store her children with; if all the world

Should in a pet of temperance feed on Pulse,   755

---

697 Stoick] S *poss. minuscule;* ~~furr~~] *2nd* r *phaps emd from* e.
698 Cinick] *phaps italic style intended.*

drinke the cleere streame, & nothing weare but freise   755

th' all giver would be' unthank't would be unprais'd

not halfe his riches knowne, & yet dispis'd

725   and wee should serve him as a grudging maister
                 [ ] like   as a penurious niggard of his wea[lth]
727   & live g̶ ͫ as ͫ natures bastards not her sons   759

who would be quite surcharg'd wth her owne waight   (dark't wth plumes   ⟨**24**⟩

729   and strangl'd wth her wast fertilitie _____th' earth cumber'd & the wing'd aire

731   the heards would over multitude thire Lords
                                            sea   swell
732   t̶h̶e̶ ̶s̶e̶a̶ ̶o̶r̶e̶f̶r̶a̶u̶g̶h̶t̶ the [o̶]r̶e orefraught would h̶e̶a̶v̶e̶ ̶h̶e̶r̶ ̶w̶a̶t̶e̶r̶s̶ ̶u̶p̶

a̶b̶o̶v̶e̶ ̶t̶h̶e̶ ̶s̶h̶o̶a̶r̶e̶,̶ and th' unsought diamonds

                                                                    deepe
w̶o̶u̶l̶d̶ ̶s̶o̶ ̶b̶e̶ ̶s̶t̶u̶d̶d̶e̶ ̶t̶h̶e̶ ̶c̶e̶n̶t̶e̶r̶ ̶w̶^th̶ ̶t̶h̶i̶r̶e̶ ̶s̶t̶a̶r̶r̶e̶l̶i̶g̶h̶t̶ would   765

733   w̶e̶r̶e̶ ̶t̶h̶e̶y̶ ̶n̶o̶t̶ ̶t̶a̶k̶e̶n̶ t̶hence that they below   \a̶n̶d̶ ͫ so emblaze the forhead of y^e
                                    light   and so bestudde wth starres y^t they below
735   would grow enur'd to d̶a̶y̶ & come at last

758 as a ... wea[lth]]] *presum. TMS^1a*.
759 liveg] e *emd from* in, *as Wright;* [ ]] f̶o̶r̶ *Wright.*
760 waight] a *poss. begun as* h; dark't] t *emd from* e & *apostr. inserted.*
766 a̶n̶d̶] nd *emd;* emblaze] *1st* e *emd;* M. *prob. wrote* 763-766, *then*

cancelled were ... thence *in 766 & added 2 marginal lines, then revised*
763 & 764 *to make one Alexandrine, cancelled* 765 *& emended* and *to*
would *in 766; phaps now rather than earlier he wrote* and so bestudde ...
below, *forgetting to cancel the duplicated remainder of* 766.

drinke the cleere streame, and nothinge weare but freeze

th'allgiver would be vnthank't, would be vnprais'd

not halfe his riches knowne, and yet despis'd

and wee should serve him as a grudgeinge Master,   715

as a penurious niggard of his wealth

and live like natures bastards, not her sonns,

whoe would be quite surcharg'd wth her owne waite

and strangl'd with her wast fertillitie,

th'earth cumberd, and the wing'd ayre dark'd wth plumes   720

the heards would over multitude their Lords

the sea orefraught would swell, and th'vnsaught diamonds

                                                          would
would soe emblaze with starrs, that they belowe   ⟨17^{r}⟩

would growe enur'd to light, and come at last

Drink the clear streame, and nothing weare but Freize,

Th'all-giver would be unthank't, would be unprais'd,

Not halfe his riches known, and yet despis'd,

And we should serve him as a grudging master,

As a penurious niggard of his wealth,   760

And live like Natures bastards, not her sons,

Who would be quite surcharg'd with her own weight,

And strangl'd with her wast fertilitie;   (plumes,

Th'earth cumber'd, and the wing'd aire dark't with

The heards would over-inultitude their Lords,   765

The sea ore-fraught would swell, and th'unsought dia-

Would so emblaze the forehead of the Deep,   (monds

And so bestudde with stars that they below

Would grow inur'd to light, and come at last

718 surcharg'd] g *emd from* d; 'd *poss. added.*

762 weight,] *omitted in Harvard.*

to gaze upon the sun wth shamelesse browes.

            nor ~~and~~

list Ladie be not coy, ~~nor~~ be not cozen'd

with that same vaunted name virginity   770

beautie is natures coine must not be hoorded

740   but must be curr nt, & the good therof

consists in mutuall & partaken blisse

unsavoury in th' enjoyment of it selfe

if you let slip tyme like (an) neglected rose   775

it withers on the stalke ~~& fades away~~ wth languish't head

745   beautie is natures brag & must be shewne

in courts, at feasts, on high sollemnities

where most may wonder at the workmanship.

it is for homely features to keepe home   780

                ~~from~~

they had thire name thence, coarse ~~beetle bro brows~~ complexions

750   and cheeks of sorrie graine will serve to ply

the sample, or to teize the huswifes wooll

768 browes.] *mark above* r *prob. meaningless; period prob.*

769 Ladie] L *poss. minuscule.*

770 with] w *abnormally formed, or begun as something else;* vaunted] u *emd from* n.

772 current] a *poss. TMS*^{3f}.

774 enjoyment] e *emd from* i.

775 an] *circle & marginal cross prob. TMS*^{3c}, *not TMS*⁴.

776 wth ... head] *presum. TMS*^{1a}, *not TMS*^{3f}.

778 on] o *emd, phaps from undotted* i; sollemnities] ti *emd from* es.

779 workmanship] manship *presum. TMS*^{1a}, *not TMS*^{3f}

781 complexions] *presum. TMS*^{1a}, *not TMS*^{3f}

to gase vpon the sunn with shameles browes.   725

To gaze upon the Sun with shameless brows.   770

List Ladie be not coy, and be not cosen'd

With that same vaunted name Virginitie,

Beautie is natures coine, must not be hoorded,

But must be currant, and the good thereof

Consists in mutuall and partaken blisse,   775

Vnsavourie in th'injoyment of it selfe

If you let slip time, like a neglected rose   If
(26)

It withers on the stalke with languish't head.

Beautie is natures brag, and must be showne

In courts, at feasts, and high solemnities   780

Where most may wonder at the workmanship;

It is for homely features to keepe home,

They had their name thence; course complexions

And cheeks of sorrie graine will serve to ply

The sampler, and to teize the huswifes wooll.   785

what need a ve[r]meil tinctur'd lip for that   ~~hence wth thy hel bru'd liquor lest I~~

love-darting eyes, or tresses like the morne   ~~th[row] i[t] against ye gr[ound] were it a draft~~

there was a nother meaning in these guifts   &c 786

     & be advis'd, you are but young yet

755   thinke what, ~~& looke upon this cord[ia] ll julep   [ ]~~

673   ~~that flames & dances in his ch crystall bounds~~

~~wth spirits of balme & fragrant syrops mixt~~

675   ~~not that nepenthes wch the wife of Thôn~~   790

~~in Ægypt gave to Iove borne Helena~~

~~is of such power to stirre up joy as this~~

678   ~~to life freindly so, or so coole to thirst~~

        2   1

~~poore ladie thou hast need of some refreshing~~

688   ~~that hast bin tir'd all day w^thout repast~~   795

~~& timely rest hast wanted heere sweet Ladie faire [-] virgin~~

690   ~~this will restore all soone La stand back false traitor~~

663   ~~thou can'st not touch the freedome of my mynd~~

784-786 *margin just poss. TMS*^2b.

784 ve[r]meil] r *prob. emd from* i; veirmeil *just poss.*

785 ~~throw it against ye ground~~ *Wright.*

786 there] t *emd.*

787-808 *cancel lines prob. TMS*^2b.

787 & be advis'd ... young yet] *query TMS*^3f; you] ou *emd from* ee; *caret poss. doubled;* julep] l *prob. re-formed.*

792 ~~power~~] er *poss.* r.

795 ~~repast~~] *comma poss.*

What need a vermeil-tinctur'd lip for that   786

Love-darting eyes, or tresses like the Morne

There was another meaning in these gifts?

Thinke what, and be adviz'd, you are but yong yet.

wth all thy charmes although this corporall rind

665   thou hast immanacl'd, while heaven sees good   800

693   was this the cottage, & the safe abode   (m[—]ie gua[r]d me

        me of?   ougly   what grim aspects are these?

[t]hou toldst amoung'st these [-] musl'd monsters, mercie guard me these ougly headed monsters

        how have I bin betrai'd

697   O my simplicity what sights are these? wth darke disguises   bruage

whether deluded   & soothing flatteries

698   and soothing lies, & soothing flatteries. hence wth thy teacherous kindnesse

        falshood

        thou man of lies & falshood fraud, if thou give me it   bru'd sorcerie 805

        it

701   I throw on the ground, were it a draft for Iuno

        should reject

        I hate it from thy hands treasonous offer, none

703   but such as are good men can give good things

756   La. I had not thought to have unlock^t my lips

        in this unhallowd aire, but that this juggler   810

        would thinke to charme my judgement as my̅e eyes

        obtruding false rules pranck't in reasons garbe

760   I hate when vice can boult her arguments

801-805 m[—]ie gua[r]d me *(margin)*] what grim aspects are these?] these ...
monsters *(margin)*] w^th ... disguises] bruage] whether deluded] hence
w^th ... kindnesse] bru'd sorcerie] *just poss. TMS^2b*.

801 m[—]ie] mercie *Wright*.

802 [t]hou] t *on leaf edge;* [-]] h *Wright;* these ... monsters *(margin)*]
begins between aspects & guard.

804 flatteries.] *period poss. comma.*

811 my̅e] e & *tittle poss. TMS^3f*.

812 obtruding] o *emd, poss. from* e, *or badly formed.*

813 boult] u *deleted, poss. TMS^3f*.

La: I had not thought to have vnlockt my lipps	*La.* I had not thought to have unlockt my lips 790
in this vnhallowed ayre, but that this Iugler	In this unhallow'd aire, but that this Jugler
would thinke to charme my Iudgement, as my eyes	Would thinke to charme my judgement, as mine eyes
obtrudinge false rules prank't in reasons garbe.	Obtruding false rules pranckt in reasons garbe.
I hate when vice can boult her arguments 730	I hate when vice can bolt her arguments

and vertue has no tongue to check her pride
      not
impostor doe_∧charge most innocent nature   815
      would
as if she_∧~~ment~~ her children should be riotous

wth her abundance, she good cateresse

765   ~~inte~~[n]ds means her provision only to the good

that live according to her sober laws

and holie dictate of spare temperance   820

if every just man that now pines wth want

had but a moderate & beseeming share

770   of that wch lewdly-pamperd Luxurie   **25**

now heapes upon some few wth vast excesse

natures full blessings would be well dispens't   825

in unsupfluous eeven proportion

and she no whit encumberd wth her store

775   and then the giver would be better thankt

his praise due paid, for swinish gluttonie

ne're looks to heav'n amidst his gorgeous feast   830

816-817 riotous ... abundance] *blurred by a catching pen.*   826 in] n *poss. re-formed.*
817 wth] h *re-formed;* cateresse] c *re-formed.*   828 the] e *re-formed;* would] w *re-formed.*

BMS	1637
and vertue has noe tongue to check her pride.	And vertue has no tongue to check her pride: 795
Imposter, doe not ~~thinke~~ charge most innocent nature	Impostor doe not charge most innocent nature
as if she would her children should be riotous	As if she would her children should be riotous
with her abundance, she good Chateresse	With her abundance, she good cateresse
means her p̱vision onely to the good, 735	Means her provision only to the good
that live accordinge to her sober lawes,	That live according to her sober laws 800
and holy dictate of spare temperance.	And holy dictate of spare Temperance,
If every Iust man that now pynes with want	If every just man that now pines with want
had but a moderate and beseeminge share	Had but a moderate, and beseeming share
of that wch leudly-pamper'd luxurie 740	Of that which lewdy-pamper'd Luxurie
now heap's vpon some fewe, with vast excesse	Now heaps upon some few with vast excesse, 805
natures full blessinge, would be well dispenst	Natures full blessings would be well dispenc't
in vnsup̱flous even proportion,	In unsuperfluous even proportion,
and she noe whit encomberd with her store:	And she no whit encomber'd with her store,
and then the giver would be better thank't 745	And then the giver would be better thank't, And (27)
his praise due payed, for swinish gluttonie	His praise due paid, for swinish gluttony 810
neere looks to heav'n, amidst his gorgeous feasts	Ne're looks to heav'n amidst his gorgeous feast,

732 *comma faint & small.*

but wth besotted base ingratitude no more   831

779   cramms & blasphems his feeder. Co. Come ~~y'are too morall~~

831 besotted] *emd from* a sottish.

but wth beesotted base ingratitude   748

crams, and blaspheames his feeder, *Co:* Come, noe more

                                           this

But with besotted base ingratitude

Cramms, and blasphemes his feeder. Shall I goe on?

Or have I said enough? to him that dares

Arme his profane tongue with reproachfull words   815

Against the Sun-clad power of Chastitie

Faine would I something say, yet to what end?

Thou hast nor Eare, nor Soule to apprehend

The sublime notion, and high mysterie

That must be utter'd to unfold the sage   820

And serious doctrine of Virginitie,

And thou art worthy that thou shouldst not know

More hapinesse then this thy præsent lot.

Enjoy your deere Wit, and gay Rhetorick

That hath so well beene taught her dazling fence,   825

Thou art not fit to heare thy selfe convinc't;

Yet should I trie, the uncontrouled worth

Of this pure cause would kindle my rap't spirits

To such a flame of sacred vehemence,

815 reproachfull] *scored through in ink with cross over* e, & contemptu *with cross over* c *written in ink in right margin, shorn, in Pforz.*

807 ~~your morall stuffe~~   ~~tilted~~
    ~~this is meere morall stuffe the very lees~~ this meere moral bable, & direct
                                    ∧

810 ~~& setlings of a melancholy blood~~   against the canon laws of our foundation
                                    I must not suffer this, yet t[i]s but the lees
    but this will cure all streite, one sip of this   and setlings of a melancholy blood   835

    will bath the drooping spirits in delight
              ye blisse
813 beyond of dreames. be wise & tast.
          ∧

833-834 *underlines poss. TMS²ᵃ*.   834-835 *margin* I must not ... blood] *poss. TMS²ᵃ*; t[i]s ti *prob. emd from*
                                                     it.

That dumb things would be mov'd to sympathize,   830

And the brute Earth would lend her nerves, and shake,

Till all thy magick structures rear'd so high

Were shatter'd into heaps ore thy false head.

   Co. She fables not, I feele that I doe feare

Her words set off by some superior power;   835

And though not mortall, yet a cold shuddring dew

Dips me all o're, as when the wrath of *Iove*

Speaks thunder, and the chaines of *Erebus*

To some of *Saturns* crew. I must dissemble,

And try her yet more strongly. Come; no more,   840

this is meere morrall babble, and direct   ⟨17ᵛ⟩

This is meere morall babble, and direct'   This (28)

against the Canon lawes of our foundacoñ   751

Against the canon laws of our foundation,

I must not suffer this; yet tis but the lees

I must not suffer this, yet 'tis but the lees

and setlinge of a mellancholy bloud,

And setlings of a melancholy blood;

But this will cure all streite, one sip of this

But this will cure all streight, one sip of this   845

will bath the droopinge spiritts in delight   755

Will bathe the drooping spirits in delight

beyond the blisse of dreames. be wise, and tast;

Beyond the blisse of dreams. Be wise, and tast. —

756 *semicolon prob.*

the brothers rush in strike his glasse downe the ~~monsters~~ shapes make

as though they would resist but are all driven in. Dæmon enter wth them

814   Dæ. what have you let the false enchaunter ~~spasse~~ scape?   840

815   oh yee mistooke, yee should have snatch't his wand

                                  rod
       & bound him fast; w^thout his ₍~~art~~ revers't

and backward mutters of dissevering power

wee cannot free the La. that ~~remaines~~ heere sits

in stonie fetters fixt & motionlesse.   845

820   yet stay, be not disturb'd, now I bethinke me
    some other meanes I have
       ~~there is another way~~ that may be us'd

wch once of Melibæus old I learn't

the soothest shepheard that ere pip't on plaines

there is a gentle nymph not farre from hence   850

825   that wth moist curbe swaies the smooth severne streame

---

840 *From here, & especially from 886, the pen deteriorated.*
844 La.] L *poss. minuscule.*

846 yet] y *emd, poss. from* s.
847 meanes] ea *emd, poss. from* od; have] e *re-formed.*

The brothers rushe in with swords drawne, wrest his glasse

of liquor out of his hand, and breake it against the ground

his rowte make signe of resistance, but are all driven in,

the *Demon* is to come in with the brothers. / 760

De: What have yee left the false Inchaunter scape?

O yee mistooke, yee should have snatcht his wand,

and bound him fast, without his rod reverst

and backward mutters of disseveringe power

wee cannot free the lady that sitts heere 765

in stonie fetters fixt, and motionlesse.

yet staye, be not disturb'd, nowe I bethinke me

some other meanes I haue that may be vsed

wch once of Millebeus old I learnt

the soothest shepheard that ere pipt on playnes 770

　There is a gentle *Nimphe* not farr from hence

that wth moist Curbe, swayes the smoote seaverne streame,

The brothers rush in with swords drawne, wrest his

glasse out of his hand, and breake it against the

ground; his rout make signe of resistance, but are 850

all driven in; the attendant Spirit comes in.

Spir. What, have you let the false enchanter scape?

O yee mistooke, yee should have snatcht his wand

And bound him fast; without his rod revers't,

And backward mutters of dissevering power 855

Wee cannot free the Ladie that sits here

In stonie fetters fixt, and motionlesse;

Yet stay, be not disturb'd, now I bethinke me,

Some other meanes I have which may be us'd,

Which once of *Melibæus* old I learnt 860

The soothest shepheard that ere pipe't on plains.

　There is a gentle nymph not farre from hence

That with moist curb sways the smooth Severn stream,

767　staye,] *comma poss. semicolon.*
770　playnes] s *poss. added.*
771　*indented.*

Sabrina is her name a virgin ~~goddesse chast~~ pure

whilome she was the Daughter of Locrine

that had the scepter from his father Brute

she guiltlesse damsell flying the mad psuite   855

830   of her enraged stepdame Guendolen

commended her faire innocence to the fl[ou] d*streame floud

that stayd her flight wth his crosse flowing course

the waternymphs that in the bottome playd
     pearled   & ~~carie take~~ took
held up thire ∧white wrists ~~to receave~~ ∧her in   860
      straite
835   bearing ~~and bore~~ her ∧to aged Nereus hall

who piteous of her woes, rear'd her lanck head

and gave her to his daughters to imbath

in nectar'd lavers strew'd wth Asphodil

and through the porch & inlet of each sence   865

840   dropt in ambrosiall oyles till she reviv'd

and underwent a quick immortall change

made goddesse of the river, still she retaines

---

853 Daughter] D *poss. minuscule.*
857 ~~streame~~ floud] *poss.* TMS^1b*; asterisk poss. cancelled cross.*
860 pearled] & ... took] *just poss.* TMS^1b*.*

864 Asphodil] A *emd from* a, i *from* e.
866 dropt] d *emd from* p; reviv'd] d *emd from* e.
867 underwent] *prefix detached; cf.* 509 n.

BMS	1637
Sabrina is her name, a virgin pure,	*Sabrina* is her name, a virgin pure,
whilome she was the daughter of Locrine	Whilome shee was the daughter of *Locrine,* 865
whoe had the scepter from his fathe Brute. 775	That had the scepter from his father *Brute.*
she guiltless dam'sell, flyinge the mad psuite	She guiltlesse damsell flying the mad pursuit
of her enraged stepdame, *Gwendolen*	Of her enraged stepdam *Guendolen*
commended her faire innocense to the floud,	Commended her faire innocence to the flood
that stayed her flight with his Crosse floweinge course,	That stay'd her flight with his crosse-flowing course, 870
the water nimphs that in the bottom played 780	The water Nymphs that in the bottome playd
held vp their peackled wrists, and tooke her in	Held up their pearled wrists and tooke her in,
bearinge her straite to aged *Nereus* hall	Bearing her straite to aged *Nereus* hall
whoe piteous of her woes, reard her lanke head	Who piteous of her woes reatd her lanke head,
and gave her to his daughters to imbath	And gave her to his daughters to imbathe 875
in nectar'd lavers, strewd with Asphodill 785	In nectar'd lavers strewd with asphodil,
and through the portch and inlet of each sence	And through the porch, and inlet of each sense
dropt in abrosiall oyles, till she revived	Dropt in ambrosial oyles till she reviv'd,
and vnderwent a quick immortal change	And underwent a quicke, immortall change
made goddess of the River. still she retaines	Made goddesse of the river; still she retaines 880

Marginal notes in BMS column: of her ⟨18ʳ⟩ (beside lines 777–778); The (29) (beside lines 780–781).

774 Locrine] e *blotted, phaps emd from* a.
776 dam'sell] *apostr. doubtful.*
777 *comma faint.*
785 Asphodill] i *prob. emd from* e.

her ma^{i}den gentlenesse, and oft at ~~eeve~~

visits the heards along the twilight me^{a}dows   870

845   helping all urchin blasts, & ill luck signes

846   that the shrewd medling Elfe delights to ~~leave~~ makes

    and often takes our cattell ~~w~~ wth strange pinches

847   which she wth precious viold liquors heales

    for wch the shepheads at thire festivals   875

                  *rustick

    carroll her goodnesse loud in ~~lovely~~ layes

850   and throw sweet garland wreaths into her streame

           pinks &

    of pancies ˄& of ~~bonnie~~ * daffadils * *gaudie

    and as the old swaine sed, she can unlock

                         thaw the

the ~~each~~ clasping cha^{r}me & ~~secret holding spell~~ ˄melt ~~each~~ nu͞ming spell   880

    if she be right invok't in warbled song

855   for maidenhood she loves & will be swift

        aide

    to ˄a virgin such as was her selfe

      *

  * ~~in honourd vertues cause,~~ this will I trie *in hard distressed need

              power

858   and adde the ~~power~~ [ca]ll of some ~~strong~~ verse * adjuring   885

---

870 visits] *1st* s *phaps re-formed;* ts *poss. emd from* st.
874 liquors] s *re-formed.*
875 shepheads] *1st* h *emd, prob. from* p.

876 ~~lovely~~] o *badly formed or poss. emd (Birch, Warton, Todd) from*
     undotted i.
880 the] thaw ... spell] *poss. TMS*^{1d}.
884 in ... need] *poss. TMS*^{1d}.

BMS		1637	
her maiden gentleness, and ofte at Eve	790	Her maiden gentlenesse, and oft at eve	
visitts the heards alonge the twilight meadowes		Visits the heards along the twilight meadows,	
helpinge all vrchin blasts, and ill luck signes		Helping all urchin blasts, and ill lucke signes	
that the shrewd medlinge Elfe delights to make,		That the shrewd medling elfe delights to make,	
		Which she with precious viold liquors heales.	885
for wch the shepheards at their festivalls		For which the shepheards at their festivalls	
Carroll her goodnes loud in rustick layes	795	Carroll her goodnesse lowd in rusticke layes,	
and throwe sweete garland wreaths into her streame		And throw sweet garland wreaths into her streame	
of pancies, pinkes, and guady daffadils.		Of pancies, pinks, and gaudie daffadills.	
and, as the owld swayne said, she can vnlock		And, as the old Swaine said, she can unlocke	890
the claspinge Charme, and thawe the numminge spell		The clasping charme, and thaw the numming spell,	
if she be right invok'd in warbled songe:	800	If she be right invok't in warbled Song,	
for maydenhood she loves, and wilbe swifte		For maidenhood she loves, and will be swift	
to ayde a Virgin such as was her selfe	to ayde ⟨18^v⟩	To aid a virgin such as was her selfe	
(in hard besettinge neede) this will I trie		In hard besetting need, this will I trie	895
and add the power of some adiuringe verse. /		And adde the power of some adjuring verse.	

791 alonge] l *emd, poss. from* g.
804 *period prob.*

Song   ⟨26⟩

859   Sabrina faire

860   listen ~~virgin~~ where thou ~~sitst~~ art sitting

          under the glassie coole translucent wave

              in twisted braids of lillies knitting   890

          the loose ~~taine~~ traine of thy amber-dropping haire

              listen for deare honours sake

865   Goddesse of the silver lake

              listen and save

          Listen and appeare to us   to be said   895

886-1039 *basic text TMS^1c; exceptions noted.*   893 Goddesse] *1st e Italian.*
886 *From here the pen was sometimes very thick & more & more scratchy.*   894 listen] *e poss. re-formed.*
887 Sabrina] n *poss. emd.*   895 Listen] L *poss. in margin, as Wright;* to be said] *presum. TMS^1c; cf.*
889 under] r *poss. re-formed.*   the end 1039.
890 braids] a *emd or blotted.*

songe. /   805   *Song.*

Sabrina faire   *Sabrina faire*

   listen where thou art sittinge   *Listen where thou art sitting*

vnder the glassie, coole, transelucent wave   *Vnder the glassie, coole, translucent wave,*   900

   in twisted braides of lillies knitting   *In twisted braids of lillies knitting*

                                                                                                                 The
the loose traine of thy Amber-droppinge haire;   810   *The loose traine of thy amber-dropping haire,*   (30)

   listen for deere honors sake   *Listen for deare honours sake*

   Goddess of the silver lake   *Goddesse of the silver lake*

      listen & save. /   *Listen and save.*   905

   The verse to singe or not.

listen and appe to vs   815   Listen and appeare to us   906

814 singe] i *emd, phaps from* a.

868   in name of great Oceanus   by th'earthshaking neptunes mace   896
                                  and Tethys grave majestick pace

875   by Leucothea's lovely hands
                                  by hoarie Nereus ~~wrin[cl]ed~~ wrincled looke

         & her son that rules the strands
                                  and the Carpathian wizards hooke

         by Thetis tinsel-slipper'd feet
                                  by Scaly Tritons winding shell

878   and the songs of Sirens sweet   and old sooth-saying Glaucus spell   900

         by dead Parthenope's deare tomb   by leucotheas &c

         and faire Ligéas golden combe

         wherw^th she sits on diamond rocks

         sleeking her soft alluring locks   by all the nymphs that nightly dance

885   rise rise & heave thy rosie head   upon thy streams wth wilie glance   905

896-901 by th'earth ... leucotheas &c] *TMS^2a*.   900 Glaucus] *dot after s phaps unfinished aspostr.*
896 Oceanus] *comma just poss.*   904-905 by all ... glance] *presum. TMS^1c*.
898 ~~wrin[cl]ed~~] cl *emd.*   905 glance] g *emd, poss. from* s, *or re-formed.*
899 Thetis] T *emd from* t.

BMS	1637
in name of greate Oceanus,	In name of great *Oceanus,*
by th'earth-shakinge Neptunes mace,	By th'earth shaking *Neptun's* mace
and Tethis grave maiestick pace,	And *Tethys* grave majesticke pace,
el br: by hoarie *Nereus* wrincled looke,	By hoarie *Nereus* wrincled looke, 910
and the Carpathian wizards hooke, 820	And the *Carpathian* wisards hooke,
2 bro: by scalie Tritons windinge shell,	By scalie *Tritons* winding shell.
and ould sooth-sayinge Glaucus spell,	And old sooth saying *Glaucus* spell,
el br: by Lewcotheas lovely hands,	By *Leucothea's* lovely hands,
and her sonne that rules the strands,	And her son that rules the strands, 915
2 br: by T̶e̶[h̶] Thetis tinsel-slipperd feete, 825	By *Thetis* tinsel-flipper'd feet;
and the songs of sirens sweete,	And the songs of *Sirens* sweet,
el br: by dead *Par*thenopes deare tombe,	By dead *Parthenope's* deare tomb,
and fayer Ligeas golden Combe, and ⟨19ʳ⟩	And faire *Ligea's* golden comb,
wherewith she sitts on diamond rocks,	Wherewith she sits on diamond rocks 920
sleekinge her soft allueringe locks, 830	Sleeking her soft alluring locks,
De͜: By all the Nimphes of nightly daunce,	By all the *Nymphs* that nightly dance
vpon thy streames with wilie glaunce,	Vpon thy streams with wilie glance,

823 Lewcotheas] w *poss. in italic style.*
825 T̶e̶[h̶] *cancelled after h half finished.*
827 Parthenopes] *ar prob. in italic style.*

908 th'earth] *Apostr. did not print in Pforz., BM C.34.d.46, C.12.g.34, etc., but clear in PM & faint in V&A 6591.26.52.3.*

from thy corall-paven bed   906

and bridle in thy headlong wave

till thou our summons answerd have

889   Listen & save

Sabrina rises attended wth the water nymphs   910

        Sings

890   By the rushie-fringed banck

            where grows the willow, & the osier danck

        my sliding chariot stayes

        thick set wth Agat, and the azurne sheene   915

            of ~~turquis~~ turkis blew, & ~~emrald~~ emrauld greene

895   ~~that my rich wheeles inlayes~~ that in the channell straies

        Whilst from off the waters fleet

        thus I set my printlesse feet

906 paven] n *emd from* d.   918 Whilst] W *re-formed.*

rise, rise, and heave thy rosie head,		Rise, rise and heave thy rosie head
from thy Corall paven bed,		From thy coral-paven bed,	925
and bridle in thy headlonge wave,	835	And bridle in thy headlong wave
till thou o^r summons answered have,		Till thou our summons answerd have.

Listen & save.

Listen and save.

Sabrina rises attended by the water nimphes
and singes. /

Sabrina rises attended by water Nimphes and sings.

By the rushie fringed banke   840

    where growes the willow, and the Osier danke

       my slydinge Charriott stayes,

Thick sett with Agate, and the Azur'd sheene

Of Turkiss blew, and Emerald greene

       that in the Channell strayes,   845

Whilst from of the waters fleete

thus I rest my printles feete

By the rushie fringed banke,   930

    Where growes the willow and the osier dancke

       My sliding chariot stayes,

         Thicke set with agat, and the azurne sheene   *Thick*
                                                                                                                                           (31)

Of turkkis blew, and Emrould greene

       That in the channell strayes,   935

Whilst from off the waters fleet

Thus I set my printlesse feet

839 *period faint.*
843 with] i *prob. begun as* a.
844 Turkiss] *1st* s *prob. emd from* e *&* 2nd s *added.*

ore the couslips velvet head   920
                              not
            that bends␣as I tread

900   Gentle swaine at thy ~~behe~~request

            I am heere

Dæ. Goddesse deere

            wee implore thy powerfull hand   925

            to undoe the ~~mag~~ charmed band

905   of true virgin heere distres't

            through the force, & through the wile

            of unblest enchanter vile.

Sa. Shepheard tis my office best   930

            to helpe ensnared chastitie

910   ~~vertuous~~ Brightest ladie looke on me

            thus I sprinckle on thy b᷍est

            drops that from my fountaine pure

            I have kept of precious cure   935

            thrice upon thy fingers tip

925 powerfull] w *phaps emd or re-formed.*
929 vile.] *period prob.*
930 Shepheard] S *poss. minuscule.*

932 Brightest] B *emd from* b, *or poss.* b *intended, emd from* i.
936 thrice] hr *emd, prob. from* ri.

BMS		1637	
ore the Couslips head		*Ore the cowslips velvet head,*	
that bends not as I tread		*That bends not as I tread,*	
gentle swayne at thy request	850	*Gentle swaine at thy request*	940
I am heere		*I am here.*	
	Dẹ:		
De: Goddess deere	⟨19ᵛ⟩	*Spir.* Goddesse deare	
Wee ymplore thy powerfull hand		Wee implore thy powerfull hand	
to vndoe the Charmed band		To undoe the charmed band	
of true virgin heere distrest	855	Of true virgin here distrest,	945
through the force, and through the wile		Through the force, and through the wile	
of vnblest inchaunters vile.		Of unblest inchanter vile.	
Sab: Shepheard tis my office best		*Sab.* Shepheard tis my office best	
to helpe ensnared Chastitie,		To helpe insnared chastitie;	
brightest lady looke on me,	860	Brightest Ladie looke on me,	950
thus I sprincle on this brest		Thus I sprinckle on thy brest	
drops that from my fountayne pure		Drops that from my fountaine pure	
I have kept of pretious Cure,		I have kept of precious cure,	
thrice vpon thy fingers tip,		Thrice upon thy fingers tip,	

915   thrice upon thy rubied lip.

next this marble venom'd seate

smear'd wth gumms of glutenous heate

                                    Sabrina descends   940

I touch wth chast palmes moist & cold

now the spell hath lost his hold ——— the ladie rises out

920   and I must hast ere morning howre   of her seate

To waite in Amphitrites ~~in her~~ bowre

Dæ   Virgin daughter of Locrine

sprung of old Anchises line   945
                        brimmed
may thy ₍crystall₎ waves for this   27

925   thire full tribute never misse

from a thousand petty rills
                        the
that tumble downe ~~from~~ snowie hills

summer drouth, or singed aire   950

never scorch thy tresses faire

937 thrice] h *emd from* r.
939 Sabrina descends] *poss.* TMS^{1d}.
941-942 the ladie ... seate] *presum.* TMS^{1c}.

943 in *(1st)*] i *emd from* o.
944 Virgin] V *poss. minuscule;* r *emd or re-formed.*

BMS		1637	
thrice vpon thy rubied lip,	865	Thrice upon thy rubied lip,	955
next this marble venom'd seate		Next this marble venom'd seate	
smeard with gum̄s of gluttenous heate		Smear'd with gummes of glutenous heate	
I touch with chast palmes, moist, & could		I touch with chast palmes moist and cold,	
now the spell hath lost his hold		Now the spell hath lost his hold.	
and I must hast, ere morninge howre	870	And I must hast ere morning houre	960
to waite in Amphitrites bower		To waite in *Amphitrite's* bowre.	

Sabrina descends and

the lady rises out

			Sabrina
		Sabrina descends and the Ladie rises out	(32)

of her seate.

De: Virgin daughter of Locrine	*of he seate. /*	*Spir.* Virgin, daughter of *Locrine*	
sprung of owld Anchises lyne,	875	Sprung of old *Anchises* line	965
may thy brimmed waves for this		May thy brimmed waves for this	
their full tribute never misse		Their full tribute never misse	
from a thousand pettie rills		From a thousand pettie rills,	
that tumble downe the snowie hills		That tumble downe the snowie hills:	
Summer, drouth, or singed aire	summer ⟨20ʳ⟩	Summer drouth, or singed aire	970
never scortch thy tresses fayer	881	Never scorch thy tresses faire,	

930   nor wet Octobers torrent flood

thy molten crystall fill wth mud

may thy billowes roule a shore

the beryll & ye golden ore   955

may thy lofty head be crownd

935   wth many a towre, & terrace round

and heere & there thy bancks upon

wth groves of mirrhe, & cinnamon.   Song ends

Come Ladie while heav'n lends us grace   960

let us fly this cursed place

940   lest the sorcerer us intice

wth some other new device

not a wast or needlesse sound

till wee come to holyer ground   965

I shall be yor faithfull guide

945   through this gloomie covert wide

952 Octobers] O *poss. minuscule.*
953 mud] u *emd.*
956 crownd] c *secretary form.*

960 Come] C *thickly written, phaps in margin, as Wright.*
964 sound] o *poss. re-formed.*

nor wett Octobers torrent floud	Nor wet Octobers torrent flood
thy molten Cristall fill with mud	Thy molten crystall fill with mudde,
may thy billowes rowle a shoare	May thy billowes rowle a shoare
the beryll and the goulden Oare 885	The beryll, and the golden ore, 975
may thy loftie head be Crownd	May thy loftie head be crown'd
with many a towre, and terrace round	With many a tower, and terrasse round,
and heere and there thy bankes vpon	And here and there thy banks upon
with groves of mirhe and Cynamon.	With groves of myrrhe, and cinnamon.

songe ends. /   890

sister
el: br: Come ~~lady will~~ while heav'n lends vs grace   Come Ladie while heaven lends us grace,   980

let vs fly this cursed place	Let us fly this cursed place,
least the Sorcerer vs intice	Lest the sorcerer us intice
wth some other newe device,	With some other new device.
not a wast, or needles sound 895	Not a wast, or needlesse sound
till wee come to holier ground	Till we come to holyer ground, 985
De: I shalbe yor faithfull guide	I shall be your faithfull guide
through this gloomie Covert wide,	Through this gloomie covert wide,

891 sister] *in scribe's hand above line.*

and not many furlongs thence

is yor fathers residence

                 met
where this night are ~~come~~ in state   970

many a freind to gratulate

950   his wish't præsence, & beside

all the swayns that neere abide

wth Iiggs & rurall dance resort

wee shall catch them at thire sport   975

and our suddaine comming there

955   will double all thire mirth & cheere

                                             *grow
come let us hast the starres *are high

957   But night ~~raignes~~ sitts monarch yet in the mid skie   Exeunt.

the scene changes and then is præsented Ludlow towne   980

& the præsidents castle then enter countrie dances & such

like gambols &c.
          at
Af~~te~~ those sports the Dæmon wth ye 2 bro. & the Ladie enter

the Dæmon sings

970 this] s *re-formed.*
971 gratulate] l *split pen, prob. not* ll.
977 che~~e~~re] *2nd* e *poss. cancelled for TMS*^{3f}.

978 grow] *1645, 1673.*
980 scene] *2nd* e *Italian;* towne] e *Italian.*
983 at] *poss. TMS*^{3b}.

and not many furlongs thence	
is yor fathers residence,	900
where this night are met in state	
many a freiṇd to gratulate	
his wisht p^rsence, and beside	
all the swaynes that neere abide	
with Iiggs, and rurall daunce resorte	with ⟨20^v⟩
wee shall catch them at this sporte,	906
and our suddaine Cominge there	
will double all their mirth, and cheere,	
el br: come let vs hast the starrs are high	
but night sitts Monarch, yet in the mid skye	910

The sceane changes then is p^rsented Ludlow towne
and the Presidents Castle, then come in Countrie
daunces, and the like &c, towards the end of those
sports the demon with the 2 brothers and the
ladye come in. the spiritt singes. /   915

And not many furlongs thence	
Is your Fathers residence,	
Where this night are met in state	990
Many a freind to gratulate	
His wish't presence, and beside	His (33)
All the Swains that there abide,	
With Iiggs, and rurall dance resort,	
Wee shall catch them at their sport,	995
And our suddaine comming there	
Will double all their mirth, and chere,	
Come let us hast the starrs are high	
But night sits monarch yet in the mid skie.	

The Scene changes presenting Ludlow towne and the   1000
Presidents Castle, then come in Countrie dancers, af-
ter them the attendant Spirit with the two Brothers
and the Ladie.

                Song.

958 Back shepheards back enough yor play   985

    till next sunshine Holyday

960 heere be wth out duck or nod

    other trippings to be trod such neate
    <s>nimbler</s>   such neate
f l[*]ighter of <s>speedier</s> toes<s>ng</s>, & <s>courtly</s> ₍guise of lighter toes, & such court guise
       *[first]
    <s>such</s> as <s>Hermes</s> did ₍[*]devise   Mercury *first 990

    wth the mincing Dryades

965 on the lawns, & on the leas

    Noble Lord & Ladie bright   2 song.

    I have brought yee new delight

    heere behold so goodly growne   995

    three faire branches of yor owne

970 Heav'n hath timely try'd thire youth

           * patience
    thire faith, thire *<u>patience</u>, & thire truth <s>temperance</s>

985 shepheards] *1st* he *emd, prob. from* ph.
989 [o]f] f *on leaf edge, of Wright;* toes<s>ng</s>] s *emd from* i; [o]f lighter] of
  lighter ... guise] *scratch & flood pen, presum. TMS^{1c}.*

990 [first]] *badly written, poss. deleted;* Mercury] *first] *presum. TMS^{1c}.*
993 2 song] *scratch pen, presum. TMS^{1c}.*
998 patience *(2nd)*] <s>temperance</s>] *scratch pen, presum. TMS^{1c}.*

Back shepheards, back, enough yor playe

till next sunshine holy daye

heere be without duck, or nod

other trippings to be trod

of lighter toes, and such court guise 920

as Mercurie did first devise

with the mincinge Driades

on the lawnes, and on the leas

2 songe p^rsents them to their father & mother./

Noble Lord and Lady bright 925

I have brought yee new delight

heere behould soe goodly growne

three fayer branches of yor owne

three
⟨21^r⟩

Heav'n hath timely tri'd their youth

their faith their patience, and their truth 930

Spir. *Back shepheards, back enough your play,* 1005

Till next Sun-shine holiday,

Here be without duck or nod,

Other trippings to be trod

Of lighter toes, and such Court guise

As Mercury *did first devise* 1010

With the mincing Dryades

On the lawns, and on the leas.

This second Song præsents them

to their father and mother.

Noble Lord, and Lady bright, 1015

I have brought yee new delight,

Here behold so goodly growne.

Three faire branches of your owne,

Heav'n hath timely tri'd their youth,

Their faith, their patience, and their truth, 1020

And

and sent them heere through hard assayes

w^th ~~to~~ a crowne of deathlesse ~~bays~~ praise   1000

to triumph in victorious dance   ⟨28⟩

975   ore sensuall folly, & intemperance

they dance.   the dances all ended

the Dæmon sings. or sayes

976   To the Ocean now I fly   1005

and those happie climes that lie

where day never shuts his eye

979   up in the *~~plaine~~ feilds of the skie   *broad

farre beyond ye earths end

          low   1010

where the welkin ~~cleere~~ doth bend

980   ther I suck the liquid aire

all amidst the gardens faire
          Hesperus   ~~neeces~~
of ~~Atlas~~ & his ~~daughters~~ three

999 through] *1st* h *phaps emd from* r.
1000 w^th] praise] *both prob. same scratch pen, presum. TMS^{1c}*; deathlesse]
          d *poss. majuscule.*
1003-1038 *long diagonal cancel lines TMS^{3a}.*

1004 sings] *flooding pen TMS^{1c};* or sayes] *scratch pen, presum. TMS^{1c}.*
1008 broad] *scratch pen, presum. TMS^{1c}.*
1010 ~~cleere~~] c *emd, poss. from* l.

and sent them heere through hard assaies

wth a Crowne of death lesse praise

to triumphe in victorious daunce

ore sensuall folly and Intemperance

They daunce, the daunces all ended the   935

Dæmon singes or sayes. /

⟨**With TMS 1005-1026 cf. BMS 4-23**⟩

And sent them here through hard assays   (34)

With a crowne of deathlesse Praise,

To triumph in victorious dance

Ore sensuall Folly, and Intemperance.

The dances ended, the Spirit Epilogizes.   1025

934 ore] r *emd.*

1021 assays] assaye *PM.*

983   that sing about the golden tree

988   there æternall summer dwells   1015

       and west winds wth musky wing

990   about the ~~myrtle~~* alleys fling   *cedar'ne

    nard   balmy

~~balme~~ . ~~balme~~, & casia's ~~fragrant~~ smells

       Iris there wth ~~garnish~~'t bow   *~~garish~~ humid

       waters the odorous banks y^t blow   1020

       flowers of more mingled hew

           purfl'd

995   then her ~~watchet~~ scarfe can shew

       yellow, watchet, greene, & blew

996   and drenches oft wth manna dew

998   beds of Hyacinth, & roses   1025

999   where many a cherub soft reposes

         taske   smoothly

1012   now my ~~message well~~ is don   *~~buisnesse~~

          2 1

       I can fly, or I can run

                 earths

       quickly to the ~~earths~~ greene end

         [2]   1

1017 cedar'ne] *scratch pen, presum. TMS*^{*1c*}.

1018 nard] *scratch pen, presum. TMS*^{*1c*}.

1019 ~~garnish~~'t] g & s *poss. emd or re-formed;* humid] *scratch pen, presum.*
    TMS^{*1c*}.

1027 *caret poss. blot; numeral 2 deleted.*

1029 earths] *& numerals, TMS*^{*3a*}.

Now my taske is smoothly done   937

I can flye or I can run

quickly to the earths greene end

1015 where the bow'd welkin slow doth bend 1030

and from thence can soare as soone

to the corners of ye moone

mortalls that would follow me

love vertue she alone is free

1020 she can teach yee how to clime 1035

higher then the sphærie chime

or if vertue feeble were

                         stoope

heaven it selfe would bow to her.   Exit

        the end.   Finis[.]

      The Dæmon sings or says   **29** 1040

976 To the Ocean now I fly,

and those happie climes that lie

where day never shuts his eye

1037 vertue] *1st* e *badly formed.*
1039 Finis[.]] *phaps TMS^2b.*

1040-1089 *very regularly written & spaced, TMS^3a.*
1042 happie] e *badly formed Italian.*

where the bow'd welkin slow doeth bend,   940

and from thence can soare as soone

to the Corners of the Moone

Mortalls that would follow me

love vertue, she alone is free

she can teach you how to clyme   945

higher then the sphearie chime

or if vertue feeble were

Heven it selfe would stoope to her

       Finis   949

Spir. To the Ocean now I flie,   1026

   And those happie climes that lie

   Where day never shuts his eye,

up in the broad feilds of ye skie:

980   there I suck the liquid aire   1045

all amidst the gardens faire

of Hespus & his daughters three

           that sing about the golden tree.

~~where grows the right borne gold~~ upon his native tree.

along the crisped shades and bowrs

985   revells the spruce and jocond Spring   1050

the Graces and the rosie-bosom'd Howrs

thither all thire bounties bring

that there eternall Summer dwells

& west winds wth muskie wing

990   about the cedar'ne alleys fling   1055

Nard & Cassia's baulmie smells

Iris there wth humid bow

waters the odorous banks that blow

flowers of more mingled hew

995   then her purfl'd scarfe can shew   1060

1048 that sing ... tree] & *cancel line, prob.* TMS^{3a}; borne] e *Italian.*   1060 scarfe] e *Italian.*
1049 shades] e *emd from* s.

Vp in the broad fields of the skie:

There I suck the liquid ayre   1030

All amidst the gardens faire

Of *Hesperus,* and his daughters three

That sing about the golden tree,

Along the crisped shades, and bowres

Revells the spruce and jocond Spring,   1035

The Graces, and the rosie-bosom'd Howres

Thither all their bounties bring,

That there æternall Summer dwells

And west winds, with muskie wing

About the cedar'n alleys fling   1040

Nard, and *Cassia's* balmie smells.

Iris there with humid bow

Waters the odorous banks that blow

Flowers of more mingled hew

Then her purfl'd scarfe can shew,   1045

~~yellow, watchet, greene, & blew~~

Elysian

996 & drenches w^th ~~Sabæan~~ dew

(list mortals if yor eares be true)

998 beds of hyacinth & roses

where young Adonis oft reposes

1000 waxing well of his deepe wound   1065

in slumber soft, & on the ground

sadly sits th' Assyrian Queene

but farre above in spangled sheene

celestiall Cupid her fam'd son advanc't

1005 holds his deare Psyche sweet entranc't   1070

after her wandring labours long

till free consent the gods among

make her his eternall Bride

and from her faire unspotted side

1010 tow blissfull twins are to be borne   1075

Youth & Ioy: so Ioue hath sworne

1061 ~~greene~~] *3rd* e *Italian.*   1067 Queene] *3rd* e *Italian.*
1062 Elysian] *& cross & cancel line, TMS³ᶜ;* (list ... true)] *prob. TMS³ᵃ.*   1073 Bride] B *poss. emd from* b.
1065 deepe] *3rd* e *Italian.*

And drenches with *Elysian* dew

(List mortalls, if your eares be true)

Beds of *Hyacinth,* and roses)

Where young *Adonis* oft reposes,

Waxing well of his deepe wound   1050

In slumber soft, and on the ground

Sadly sits th'*Assyrian* Queene;   Sadly
                                                                   (35)

But farre above in spangled sheene

Celestiall *Cupid* her fam'd Son advanc't,

Holds his deare *Psyche* sweet intranc't   1055

After her wandring labours long,

Till free consent the gods among

Make her his æternall Bride,

And from her faire unspotted side

Two blissfull twins are to be borne,   1060

Youth, and Ioy; so *Iove* hath sworne.

But now my taske is smoothly don

I can fly, or I can run

quickly to the greene earths end

1015 where the bow'd welkin slow doth bend 1080

& from thence can soare as soone

to the corners of the Moone.

mortalls that would follow me

love vertue she alone is free

1020 she can teach yee how to clime 1085

higher then the sphearie chime

or if vertue feeble were

heaven it selfe would stoope to her.

The end. 1089

But now my taske is smoothly done,

I can fly, or I can run

Quickly to the greene earths end,

Where the bow'd welkin slow doth bend,   1065

And from thence can soare as soone

To the corners of the Moone.

  Mortalls that would follow me,

Love vertue, she alone is free,

She can teach yee how to clime   1070

Higher then the Sphærie chime;

Or if vertue feeble were

Heav'n it selfe would stoope to her.

The principall persons in this Maske; *were*

| The Lord BRACLY, | } | The Lady ALICE | 1075 |
| Mr. THOMAS EGERTON, | } | EGERTON. | |

The End.   1077

APPENDICES

I *Words of Songs in Music Manuscripts*

BM Add. Ms. 53723

⟨fol.⟩ 37⟨ʳ⟩ *Henry Lawes*
the 5 songes followinge, were sett for A Maske
presented at Ludlo Castle, before yᵉ Earle of Bridgwater
Lord president, of yᵉ Marches. October. 1634.

⟨1⟩

from yᵉ Heau'ns, now I flye,
and those happye Clymes yᵗ lye,
wher daye never shuts his Eye,
vp in the Broad feilds of the skye;
there I suck yᵉ Liquid Ayre,   5
all amidst the garden faire,
wᵗʰ(ᵒᶠ) Hesperus & his daughters three,
that singe about the Golden Tree;
Iris there wᵗʰ Humid Bow,
waters the odrous banks yᵗ blow   10

BM Add. Ms. 11518

⟨fol.⟩ Five Songs Set for a Mask presented at Ludlo Castle,
before the Earl of Bridgewater Lord President of the Marches.
October 1634

⟨1⟩

From the Heav'ns now I fly,
and those happy Climes that lie
where day never shuts his Eye
up in the broad Fields of the Sky
There I suck yᵉ liquid Air   5
all amidst the Garden fair
of Hesperus & his daughters three
that sing about the golden Tree;
Iris there with humid Bow
waters the od'rous Banks that blow   10

Foliation, which is that of the original, is inserted before the first word of each page. Heading in 3 lines ending at 'Maske', 'Bridgwater', '1634.' Song numbers introduced by editor. In the original, words & lines of verse are spaced to follow the music; here words are divided & lines of verse are arranged as in TMS, & lines of verse are numbered in each song. Capital S partly regularized.

Marches] *repeated below in another hand.*
⟨1⟩3 shuts] u *emd.*
4 *semicolon uncertain.*

Heading in 2 lines ending 'Earl of', '1634'. Song numbers in original except ⟨1⟩. In the original, words & lines of verse are spaced to follow the music; here words are divided & lines of verse are arranged as in TMS, and lines of verse are numbered in each song.

flowers of more Mingled hew,
then her purflde scarfe can shew,
Beds of Hyecinths & roses,
wher many å Cherub softe reposes./

Flowers of more mingled Hew
than her purfled scarfe can shew
Beds of Hyacinths & Roses
where many 'a Cherub soft reposes.

⟨37ᵛ⟩ *Henry Lawes*

⟨2⟩

Sweet Eccho, sweetest Nimphe that liu'st vnseene,
wth in thye Airye shell,
by slow Meanders Margent greene
& in thy violet Embroiderd vale,
wher the Loue-lorne Nightingale,   5
nightly to thee, her sad songe mourneth well,

Canst thou not tell me of a gentle payre,
y^t likest thy Narssisus are,
O if thou haue
hid them in some flowrye Cave,   10
tell me but where,
sweet Queen of parly, daughter of ye Sp^h ære;
soe maiest thou be Transplanted to ye skies,
And hold A Counterpoint to All Heau'ns Harmonies./

2

Sweet Echo sweetest Nymph that liv'st unseen
within thy Airy shell
by slow Meanders margent green
& in thy violet embroiderd Vale
where the Love lorn Nightingale   5
nightly to thee her sad song mourneth well

Canst thou not tell me of a gentle Pair
that likest thy Narcissus are
O if thou have
hid them in some flowry Cave   10
tell me but where
sweet Queen of Pity Daughter of the Sphere
so may'st thou be Transplanted to the Skyes
& hold a Counterpoint to all Heav'ns Harmonies

38⟨ʳ⟩ *Henry Lawes*

⟨3⟩

Sabrina, Sabrina fayre,
listne where thou Art Sittinge,

3

Sabrina Sabrina fair
Listen where thou art sitting

⟨2⟩1 that] a *emd.*
4 vale,] *comma uncertain.*
12 parly] r *emd.*

vnder the glassye coole Translucent waue,

   in Twisted brades of lillyes knittinge

the Loose Trayne of thy Amber-droppinge haire;   5

   Listne for deer Honors sake

   Goddess of the silver Lake,

     listne, listne & save.

         ⟨4⟩

Back shepperds Backe Enough yor playe

till ye next sunshine Hollidaye,

Heer be wthout [—] or nod,

Other trippings to be trod,   [duck]

of lighter Toes & such Court ⟨38ᵛ⟩ guise,   5

as Mercurye did first devise,

wth ye mincinge Dryades,

Or'e the Lawnes & or̃e the Leas

     2^d part

Noble Lord and Ladye Bright,

I haue brought yee new delight;   10

heer behold soe goodly Growne,

three faire branches of yor Owne

Heauñ hath Tymely tryde their youth;

their faith, their patience, & their Truth,

And sent them heer Through hard Assayes,   15

wth a Crowne of deathles praise,

to Triumph in victorious daunce,

Or̃e sensuall Follye and Intemperance.

---

under ye glassy cool translucent wave

   in twisted braids of Lillys knitting

the loose Train of thy Amber dropping Hair;   5

   Listen for dear Honours sake

   Goddess of the silver Lake

    Listen Listen and Save.

         4

Back shepherds Back enough your Play

till the next sunshine Holiday

Here be without Duck or Nod

other trippings to be trod

of lighter Toes & such Court Guise   5

as Mercury did first devise

wth ye mincing Dryades

o're the Lawns & o're the Leas

     2^d part

Noble Lord & Lady bright

I have brought you new delight   10

Here behold so goodly grown

three fair Branches of your own

Heav'n hath timely try'd their Youth

their Faith their Patience & their Truth

and sent them here thro' hard Assays   15

with a Crown of Deathless Praise

to triumph in victorious Dance

o're sensual Folly and Intemperance

⟨3⟩8 save.] *no slash.*

⟨4⟩10 yee] *1st* e *curiously formed, phaps emd from* o.

18 Intemperance.] *no slash.*

39⟨ᴿ⟩ Henry Lawes

⟨5⟩

Now my taske is smoothly done
I can flye or I can run,
Quicklye to the Earthes green End,
where the Bowde welkin slow doth bend,
& from thence can Soare as soone   5
to the Corners of the Moone;
Mortals that would follow me,
loue vertue, she alone is free,
she can teach yoᵘ how to Clyme
Higher then the sphærye chyme;   10
Or if vertue feeble were,
Heaun̓ it selfe would stoop to her./

5

Now my task is smoothly done
I can fly or I can run
quickly to the Earths green end
where the bow'd Welkin slow doth bend
and from thence can soar as soon   5
to the corners of the Moon
Mortals that would follow me
love Virtue she alone is free
she can teach you how to climb
higher than the sphæry chime   10
or if Virtue feeble were
Heav'n its Self would stoop to Her.

                    Henry Lawes.

II *Reconstructed Text of* [MS^1]

The contents and text of [MS^1], a hypothetical fair copy of 'A maske' probably written by Milton in 1634, are reconstructed here by conjecture on the principles explained in the Introduction. In accord with these, the prologue is omitted, certain speeches are assigned to the Demon rather than to the brothers, and passages are omitted that are omitted in BMS, though I am not equally certain of all of them. No list of actors is included, since although the resemblances in content and layout of the lists in BMS and *1637* suggest a common source, that source could have been an addition by Lawes for [MS^2], even if the spelling of 'Brackley' varies.

The spelling of [MS^1] is problematical. Despite BMS and *1637*, we can probably count on Milton to have preserved his own spelling in words that he uses often in 'A maske' and always spells the same way in TMS (e.g., 'thire', 'then' for than) and only slightly less probably in words that he uses several times without varying (e.g., 'amoungst', 'maister', 'therfore', 'tow' for two, etc.); such spelling I have retained or supplied. Milton spelled, however, and may have pronounced, inconsistently, sometimes for euphony or to rhyme, sometimes for recreation, sometimes from nonchalance (e.g., 'cheere' and 'chere', 'ne're' and 'neere', 'spheare' and 'sphære'). To regularize his spelling is to mislead, except in that small and developing core of words that he can be shown to have spelled in one way only; each case of each word must be considered on its own evidence. The spelling of [MS^1] is most probably indicated by agreement between the three texts, then by agreement between TMS and BMS against *1637*, and next by agreement between BMS and *1637* against TMS. Of diminished authority is agreement between TMS and *1637* against BMS, because *1637* may have used a revision for [MS^3]. In all cases the authority of BMS and *1637* is virtually negligible where either uses a spelling habitual to itself, even if that is a Miltonic variant, and sometimes both BMS and *1637* may have arrived at the one reading against TMS by their individual habits. When in doubt, which is often, I have tended to retreat to the spelling in TMS, even where BMS and *1637* agree against TMS in a Miltonic variant that each could have attained by its own proven bent, and almost always where all three texts disagree. This conservative procedure may suppress an occasional spelling in [MS^1] where Milton varied from TMS, but it cannot introduce any un-Miltonic reading. One seeks always to be able to explain how a reading in BMS or *1637* could have come from the hypothetical reading in [MS^1]; occasionally, a unique reading in BMS which is also a known Miltonic variant may indicate that that variant was in [MS^1], provided it does not involve a normal spelling habit of BMS; unique readings in *1637* in a similar category I tend to assume were probably derived from [MS^3]. In short, it is not possible to be certain that [MS^1] was spelled everywhere precisely as in this reconstruction, but much of it probably was, and elsewhere I trust that the reconstruction does not wander beyond what Milton was likely to have written in 1634.

Similar considerations apply in punctuation, but here the evidence is slighter and the conclusions correspondingly even less secure. In TMS Milton punctuated very lightly indeed, using very few stops, either within or at the ends of lines, even to close periods; he does appear to have included some medial punctuation to obviate ambiguity, and indifferently he allowed a comma before 'and' or '&' or 'or', though he was inconsistent. The scribe of BMS was wayward, omitting, including, changing, or adding stops, especially commas, but maintaining a fairly light punctuation. The punctuation in *1637* is heavier than in the other versions, especially in the use of periods and commas at the ends of lines. Possibly, some stops in *1637* reproduce or derive from revisions made by Milton for [MS^3]; certainly some were introduced by the compositor, inconsistently and not always correctly. Milton's periods have sometimes been broken into shorter sentences, often with full stops, and other stops have been introduced, especially in what may be called formula situations such as the comma before a conjunction (as sometimes in TMS) and with phrases and adverbial clauses. I have been suspicious of agreements between BMS and *1637* at the ends of lines, and even within, where a formula situation was involved that could have provoked both scribe and compositor independently to make the same emendation. In each case I have attempted to allow for general tendencies of BMS and *1637* and for the trend apparent in the local context. Sometimes BMS and *1637* both omit punctuation that is in TMS; in so doing, they may follow [MS^1], since even if each omits stops elsewhere, the tendency of both is to add, though BMS may sometimes have added a light and *1637* a heavier stop, and hence the chances are small that both independently omitted the same stop. Several passages in BMS and lines in *1637* suggest that [MS^1] was lightly punctuated in the manner of TMS but perhaps with a few stops more, especially within lines, to alleviate uncertainty. Its punctuation may have been a shade heavier than in this reconstruction if this is read without the more conjectural marks that are placed in square brackets, and a shade lighter than if this is read with them. In this edition of [MS^1] the brackets signify conjectural possibilities, whereas in the accompanying editions of TMS and BMS the brackets contain conjectural probabilities. The heavier punctuation acknowledges evidence from the congruence of BMS and *1637*; the lighter reflects Milton's habits in TMS. The two are in some conflict, unless they can be reconciled by the assumption that Milton sometimes punctuated a little more heavily in a copy [MS^1] to be read by others than he did in TMS for himself, as indeed he allowed the heavier punctuation in later printed editions.

Initial speech prefixes are all located in margins, though in [MS^1] some may have been in the text as in TMS. Indentations of lines, especially in songs, may reflect those in the original. The numbers of *lines of print* in this first edition of [MS^1] are shown down the right-hand margins, and they may be the numbers of lines of writing in the original. For reference the standard numbers of *lines of verse* in *1645* are printed in **bold** down the left-hand margins.

A maske[.]

The first scene discovers a wild wood,
then a Guardian spirit[,] or Dæmon descends or enters[.]

Before the starrie threshold of Ioves Court
my mansion is, where those im̄ortall shapes
of bright aereall spirits live insphear'd
in regions mild of calme & serene aire
5   above the smoake & stirre of this dim spot
wch men call earth, & wth low-thoughted care
confin'd & pester'd in this pinfold heere   10
strive to keepe up a fraile & feavourish beeing
unmindfull of the crowne that vertue gives
10   after this mortall change to her true servants
amoungst the enthron'd gods on sainted seats
yet some there be that by due steps aspire
to lay thire just hands on that golden key
that ope's the palace of Æternity:
15   to such my errand is, & but for such
I would not soile these pure ambrosiall weeds
wth the ranck vapours of this sin-worne mould   20
but to my taske. Neptune besides the sway
of every salt flood[,] & each ebbing streame
20   tooke in by lot twixt high[,] & neather Iove
impiall rule of all the Sea-girt Isles
that like to rich & various gems inlay
the unadorned bosome of ye deepe
wch he to grace his tributarie gods
25   by course committs to severall goverment
and gives them leave to weare thire saphire crowns
and weild thire little tridents, but this Isle   30
the greatest & the best of all the maine

he quarters to hïs blu-hair'd dieties

30 and all this tract that fronts ye falling sun

a noble peere of mickle trust & power

has in his charge [,] wth temper'd aw to guide

an old and haughtie nation proud in armes

where his faire ofspringe nurs't in princely lore

35 are comming to attend thire fathers state

and new entrusted scepter, but thire way

lies through the perplext paths of this dreare wood   40

the nodding horror of whose shadie brows

threats the forlorne & wandring passinger

40 and heere thire tender age might suffer perill

but that by quick command from soveraigne Iove

I was dispatcht for thire defence, & guard

and listen why, for I will tell you now

what never yet was heard in tale or song

45 from old or moderne Bard in hall, or bowre

  Bacchus that first from out the purple grape

crush't the sweet poyson of mis-used wine   50

after the Tuscane mariners transform'd

coasting the Tyrrhene shore, as ye winds listed

50 on Circes Island fell (who knows not Circe

the daughter of ye Sun, whose charmed cup

whoever tasted lost his upright shape

& downward fell into a groveling swine)

This nymph that gaz'd upon his clustring locks

55 wth ivie berries wreath'd, & his blith youth

had by him [,] ere he parted thence, a son

much like his father, but his mother more   60

wch therfore she brought up and Comus nam'd

who ripe & frolick of his full growne age

60 roaving the Celtick, & Iberian feilds

at last betakes him to this ominous wood

      & in thick shelter of black shades imbowr'd

      excells his mother at her mightie art

      offring to every wearie travailer

65   his orient liquor in a crystall glasse

      to quench the drouth of Phœbus, wch as they tast

      (for most doe tast through fond intemperate thirst)   70

      soone as the potion works thire humaine count'nance

      th'expresse resemblance of the gods is chang'd

70   into some brutish forme of Wolfe[,] or Beare

      or Ounce, or Tiger, Hog, or bearded goate

      all other ꝑts remaining as they were

      and they, so ꝑfect is thire miserie

      not once ꝑceave thire foule disfigurement

75   but boast themselves more comely then before

      & all thire freinds, & native home forget

      to roule wth pleasure in a sensuall stie   80

      Therfore when any favour'd of high Iove

      chances to passe through this advent'rous glade

80   swift as the sparkle of a glauncing starre

      I shoote from heaven to give him safe convoy

      as now I doe: but first I must put off

      these my skie robes spun out of Iris wooffe

      and take ye weeds and liknesse of a swayne

85   that to the service of this house belongs

      who wth his soft pipe[,] & smooth dittied song

      well knows to still the wild winds when they roare   90

      & hush the waving woods, nor of lesse faith

      and in this office of his mountaine watch

90   likeliest & neerest to the præsent aide

      of this occasion[.] But I heare the tread

      of hatefull steps[,] I must be veiwlesse now.

                  Exit

Comus enters wth a charming rod in one hand & a glasse of liquor
in the other wth him a rout of monsters like men & women but headed
like wild beasts thire appell glistring, they come in making a
riotous and unruly noise wth torches in thire hands[.]   100

Co: The starre that bids ye shepheard fold
     now the top of heav'n doth hold
95   and the gilded Carre of day
     his glowing axle doth allay
     in the steepe Atlantick streame
     & the slope sun his upward beame
     shootes against the northren Pole
100 pacing toward the other goale
     of his Chamber in the East
     meane while welcome Ioy & feast   110
     midnight shout[,] & revelry
     tipsie dance & Iollitie
105 braid yor locks wth rosie twine
     dropping odours, dropping wine
     Rigor now is gon to bed
     & Advice wth scrupulous head
     strict age, & sowre severitie
110 wth thire grave sawes in slumber lie
     Wee that are of purer fire
     imitate the starrie quire   120
     who in thire nightly watchfull spheares
     lead in swift round the months & yeares
115 the sounds & seas wth all thire finnie drove
     now to the moone in wavering morrice move
     and on the tawny sands & shelves
     trip the pert fairies, & the dapper Elves[.]
     by dimpled brooke[,] & fountaine brim
120 the wood nimphs deck't with daisies trim

thire merry wakes & pastimes keepe

what hath night to doe wth sleepe   130

Night has better sweets to prove

Venus now wakes, & wakens Love[.]

125   Come let us our rights begin

tis only daylight that makes sin

wch these dun shades will ne're report

haile goddesse of nocturnall sport

dark-vaild Cotytto, t'whome the secret flame

130   of midnight torches burne, mysterious Dame

that neere art call'd but when the dragon womb

of Stygian darknesse spetts her thickest gloome   140

and makes one blot of all ye aire

stay thy clowdie Ebon chaire

135   wherin thou rid'st wth Hecat' & befreind

us thy vow'd preists till utmost end

of all thy dues be don[,] & none left out

ere the blabbing Easterne scout

the nice morne on th'Indian steepe

140   from her cabin'd loopehole peepe

and to ye telltale sun discry

our conceal'd sollemnity[.]   150

Come knit hands, & beate ye ground

in a light fantastick round[.]

The measure in a wild rude & wanton antick

145   Co: Breake off, breake off, I feele the different pace

of some chast footing neere about this ground

run to yor shrouds wthin these brakes & trees they all scatter

our number may affright. Some virgin sure

(for so I can distinguish by myne art)

150   benighted in these woods; now to my charmes

& to my wilie trains, I shall ere long   160
be well stock't wth as faire a heard as graz'd
about my mother Circe[.] thus I hurle
my dazling spells in to the spungie aire
155 of power to cheate the eye wth bleare illusion
and give it false præsentments[,] lest the place
and my quaint habits breed astonishment
and put the damsell to suspicious flight
wch must not be, for thats against my course
160 I under faire prætence of freindly ends
and well-plact words of glozing courtesie   170
baited wth reasons not unplausible
wind me into the easie hearted man
& hugge him into snares. when once her eye
165 hath met the vertue of this magick dust
I shall appeare some harmlesse villager
whome thrift keeps up about his Countrie geare
but heere she comes[,] I fairly step aside
& hearken, if I may, her buisnesse heere.

the Ladie enters

170 this way the noise was, if my eare be true   180
my best guide now, me thought it was the sound
of riot, & ill manag'd merriment
such as the jocond flute or gamesome pipe
stirrs up among the loose unletter'd hinds
175 when for thire teeming flocks, & granges full
in wanton dance they praise the bounteous Pan
& thanke the gods amisse, I should be loath
to meet the rudenesse[,] & swill'd insolence
of such late wassailers; yet O where else
180 shall I informe my unacquainted feete   190

in the blind mazes of this tangled wood
my brothers when they saw me wearied out
wth this long way [,] resolving heere to lodge
under the spredding favour of these pines
185   stept as they se'd, to the next thicket side
to bring me berries, or such cooling fruit
187   as the kind hospitable woods provide
191   but where they are [,] and why they came not back
is now the labour of my thoughts, tis likeliest
they had ingag'd thire wandring steps too farre   200
and envious darknesse ere they could returne
195   had stolne them from me [.]
226   I cannot hallow to my brothers, but
such noise as I can make to be heard fardest
Ile venter, for my new enliv'nd spirits
prompt me, & they phapps are not farre hence [.]

         Song [.]
230   Sweet Echo, sweetest nymph that liv'st unseene
       within thy ayrie shell
         by slow Mæanders margent greene   210
and in the violet-imbroider'd vale
       where the love-lorne nightingale
235   nightly to thee her sad song mourneth well

Canst thou not tell me of a gentle paire
       that likest thy Narcissus are?
         O if thou have
       hid them in some flowrie Cave
240   tell me but where
Sweet Queene of parlie, daughter of the spheare
So maist thou be translated to the skies   220
And hold a counterpoint to all heav'ns harmonies

Comus looks in and speaks

Co: can any mortall mixture of earths mould
245   breath such divine enchaunting ravishment
    sure something holy lodges in that brest
    and wth these raptures moves the vocall aire
    to testifie his hidden residence
    how sweetly did they flote upon the wings
250   of silence, through the empty vaulted night   230
    at every fall smoothing the raven downe
    of darknesse till she smil'd, I have oft heard
    my mother Circe wth the Sirens three
    amidst the flowrie-kirtl'd Naiades
255   culling thire potent hearbs, & balefull druggs
    who as they sung[,] would take the prison'd soule
    & lap it in Elisium, Scylla wept
    and chid her barking waves into attention
    and fell Charybdis murmur'd soft applause
260   yet they in pleasing slumber lull'd the sense
    and in sweet madnesse rob'd it of it selfe   240
    but such a sacred, & home felt delight
    such sober certainty of waking blisse
    I never heard till now. Ile speake to her
265   and she shall be my Queene. Haile forreine wonder
    whome certaine these rough shades did never breed
    unlesse the goddesse that in rurall shrine
    dwell'st heere wth Pan or Silvan, by blest song
    forbidding every bleake unkindly fogge
270   to touch the prospering growth of this tall wood
La: Nay gentle shepheard ill is lost that praise   250
    that is addrest to unattending eares
    not any boast of skill, but extreme shift
    how to regaine my sever'd companie

275   compell'd me to awake the courteous Echo

               to give me answer from her mossie Couch

Co: what chance good Ladie hath bereft you thus

La: dim darknesse, & this leavie labyrinth

Co: could that divide you from neere ushering guides

280   La: they left me weary on a grassie terfe

Co: by falshood, or discourtesie[,] or why   260

La: to seeke i'th valley some coole freindly spring

Co: and left yo͏ʳ faire side all unguarded Ladie

La: they were but twaine, & purpos'd quick returne[.]

285   Co: ρhapps fore stalling night prævented them

La: how easie my misfortune is to hit!

Co: imports thire losse[,] beside the præsent need

La: no lesse then if I should my brothers loose.

Co: were they of manly prime, or youthfull bloome

290   La: as smooth as Hebe's thire unrazor'd lipps.

Co: tow such I saw[,] what tyme the labour'd oxe   270

              in his loose traces from the furrow came

              & the swink't hedger at his supper sate

              I saw em under a greene mantling vine

295   that crawls along the side of you small hill

              plucking ripe clusters from yᵉ tender shoots

              thire port was more then humaine as they stood

              I tooke it for a faerie vision

              of some gay creatures of the element

300   that in the colours of yᵉ rainbow live

              & play i'th plighted clouds, I was aw-strooke   280

              & as I past, I worship't, if those you seeke

              it were a journy like the path to heav'n

              to helpe you find them. La: Gentle villager

305   what readiest way would bring me to that place

Co: due west it rises from this shrubbie point[.]

La: to find out that good shepheard I suppose

in such a scant allowance of starre light
would overtaske the best land-pilots art
310 wth out the sure guesse of well-practiz'd feet[.]

Co: I know each lane, & every alley greene   290
dingle, or bushie dell of this wide wood
& every boskie bourne from side to side
my dayly walks & ancient neighbourhood
315 and if yor stray attendance be yet lodg'd
or shroud wth in these limits[,] I shall know
ere morrow wake[,] or the low-roosted larke
from her thatch't palate rowse, if otherwise
I can conduct you Ladie to a low
320 but loyall cottage, where you may be safe
till furder quest[.] La: Shepheard I take thy word 300
& trust thy honest offer'd courtesie
wch oft is sooner found in lowly sheds
with smoakie rafters, then in tapstrie halls
325 & courts of princes[,] where it first was nam'd
& yet is most prætended. in a place
lesse warranted then this[,] or lesse secure
I cannot be, that I should feare to change it
Eye me blest providence, & square my tryall
330 to my proportion'd strength[,] shepheard lead on.

the tow brothers 310

1 bro: unmuffle yee faint starres, & thou faire moone
that wont'st to love the travailers benizon
stoope thy pale visage through an amber cloud
and disinherit Chaos, that raignes heere
335 in double night of darknesse[,] & of shades[.]
or if yor influence be quite damm'd up
wth black usurping mists, some gentle taper

though a rush candle from the wicker hole
of some clay habitation visit us
340   wth thy long levell'd rule of streaming light   320
and thou shalt be our starre of Arcadie
or Tyrian Cynosure. 2 bro: or if our eyes
be barr'd that happinesse, might wee but heare
the folded flocks pen'd in thire watled cotes
345   or sound of pastorall reed wth oaten stopps
or whistle from ye lodge, or village cock
count the night watches to his featherie dames
t'would be some solace yet, some little cheering
in this lone dungeon of innumerous bowes.
350   but O that haplesse virgin our lost sister   330
where may she wander now, whether betake her
from the chill dew[,] amoungst rude burrs & thistles
phapps some cold banke is her boulster now
or 'gainst the rugged barke of some broad Elme
355   leans her unpillow'd head fraught wth sad feares
356   or else in wild amazement, and affright
so fares as did forsaken Proserpine
when the big rowling flakes of pitchie clowds
359   & darknesse wound her in. 1 bro: peace brother peace
366   I doe not thinke my sister so to seeke   340
or so unprincipl'd in vertues booke
and the sweet peace y^t goodnesse bosoms ever
as that the single want of light & noise
370   (not being in danger, as I trust she is not)
could stirre the constant mood of her calme thoughts
& put them into misbecomming plight
vertue could see to doe what vertue would
by her owne radiant light[,] though sun & moone
375   were in the flat sea sunke, and wisdoms selfe
oft seeks to sweet retired solitude   350

where wth her best nurse Contemplation

she plumes her feathers, & lets grow her wings

that in the various bustle of resort

380   were all to ruffl'd, and sometymes impair'd

he that has light w^thin his owne cleere brest

may sit i'th center, and enjoy bright day

but he that hides a darke soule, & foule thoughts

walks in black vapours, though the noontyde brand

385   blaze in the summer solstice. 2 Bro: tis most true

that musing meditation most affects   360

the pensive secrecie of desert cell

farre from the cheerefull haunt of men or heards

and sits as safe as in a senate house

390   for who would rob an Hermit of his weeds

his few books, or his beads, or maple dish

or doe his gray hairs any violence

but beautie like the faire Hesperian tree

laden wth blooming gold[,] had need the guard

395   of dragon watch wth uninchaunted eye

to save her blossoms[,] & defend her fruite   370

from ye rash hand of bold Incontinence.

you may as well spread out the unsun'd heapes

of misers treasure by an outlaws den

400   and tell me it is safe, as bid me hope

danger will winke on opportunitie

and let a single helplesse mayden passe

uninjur'd in this wide surrounding wast.

of night, or lonelinesse it recks me not

405   I feare the dread events that dog them both

lest some ill greeting touch attempt the pson   380

of our unowned sister. 1 Bro: I doe not brother

inferre, as if I thought my sisters state

409   secure, w^thout all doubt or question, no

I could be willing though now i'th darke to trie
a tough encounter wth the shaggiest ruffian
that lurks by hedge or lane of this dead circuit
to have her by my side, though I were sure
she might be free from perill where she is
410   but where an equall poise of hope[,] & feare
does arbitrate th'event[,] my nature is   390
that I encline to hope, rather then feare
and gladly banish squint suspicion[.]
my sister is not so defencelesse left
415   as you imagine brother[,] she has a hidden strength
wch you remember not[.] 2 bro: what hidden strength
unlesse the strength of heav'n, if you meane that
1 bro: I meane that too, but yet a hidden strength
wch if heaven gave it, may be term'd her owne
420   tis chastitie, my brother, chastitie
she that has that is clad in compleate steele   400
and like a quiver'd nymph wth arrowes keene
may trace huge forrests, & unharbour'd heaths
infamous hills, & sandie perilous wilds
425   where through the sacred rays of chastitie
no salvage feirce, bandite, or mountaneere
will dare to soile her virgin puritie
yea even where very desolation dwells
429   by grots, & caverns shag'd with horrid shades
& yawning denns[,] where glaring monsters house
430   she may passe on wth unblensh't majestie   410
be it not don in pride or in præsumption
nay more no evill thing that walks by night
in fog, or fire, by lake, or moorish fen
blew meager hag, or stubborne unlayd ghost
435   that breaks his magick chaines at curfew tyme
no goblin, or swart faerie of the mine

has hurtfull power ore true virginity[.]
doe yee beleeve me yet, or shall I call
antiquity from the old schooles of Greece

440 to testifie the armes of Chastitie   **420**
hence had the huntresse Dian her dred bow
faire silver-shafted Queene for ever chast
wherwith she tam'd the brinded lionesse
& spotted mountaine pard, but set at nought

445 the frivolous bolt of Cupid, gods & men
fear'd her sterne frowne, & she was Queen o'th' woods
what was that snakie headed Gorgon sheild
that wise Minerva wore, unconquer'd virgin
wherwith she freez'd her foes to congeal'd stone?

450 but rigid looks of chast austeritie   **430**
& noble grace that dash't brute violence
wth suddaine adoration[,] and blank aw
so deare to heav'n is sainctly chastitie
that when a soule is found sincerely so

455 a thousand liveried angells lackey her
driving farre off each thing of sin[,] & guilt
and in cleere dreame & sollemne vision
tell her of things that no grosse eare can heare
till oft converse wth heav'nly habitants

460 begins to cast a beame on th' outward shape   **440**
the unpolluted temple of the mind
and turnes it by degrees to the souls essence
till all be made immortall. but when lust
by unchast looks, loose gestures, & foule talke

465 & most by leud lascivious act of sin
lets in defilement to ye inward parts
the soule grows clotted by contagion
imbodies, and imbrut's till she quite loose
the divine propertie of her first beeing[.]

470	such are those thick & gloomie shadows dampe	450
	oft seene in Charnell vaults, & sepulchers	
	hovering, & sitting by a new made grave	
	as loath to leave the bodie that it lov'd	
	& link't it selfe by carnall sensualtie	
475	to a degenerate, & degraded state.	
	2 Bro: how charming is divine philosophie	
	not harsh, & crabbed as dull fooles suppose	
	but musicall as is Apollo's lute	
	and a ppetuall feast of nectar'd sweets	
480	where no crude surfeit raigns. 1 bro: list[,] list, I heare	460
	some farre-of hallow breake the silent aire	
	2 Bro: me thought so too, what should it be. 1 bro: for certaine	
	either some one like us night founder'd heere	
	or else some neighbour woodman, or at worst	
485	some roaving robber calling to his fellows[.]	
	2 Bro: heav'n keepe my sister. agen, agen & neere[.]	
	best draw, & stand upon our guard. 1 bro: Ile hallow	
	if he be freindly he comes well, if not	
	defence is a good cause[,] & heav'n be for us	

	he hallows & is answer'd[,] the guardian dæmon comes in	470
	habited like a shepheard[.]	

490	That hallow I should know, what are you speake	
	come not too neere, you fall on iron stakes else	
	Dæ: What voice is that? my yong Lord? speake agen[.]	
	2 Bro: O brother tis my fathers shepheard sure	
	1 bro: Thyrsis? whose artfull streines have oft delay'd	
495	the huddling brooke to heare his madrigall	
	and sweetned every muskrose of the dale	
	how cam'st thou heere good shepheard, hath any ram	
	slip't from the fold[,] or young kid lost his dam	480

or straggling weather the pen't flock forsook
500 how couldst thou find this darke sequester'd nooke[?]
Dæ: O my lov'd maisters heire, & his next joy
I came not heere on such a triviall toy
as a stray'd Ewe, or to ꝑsue the stealth
of pilfering wolfe, not all the fleecie wealth
505 that doth enrich these downs is worth a thought
to this my errand, & the care it brought[.]
but O my virgin Ladie where is she
how chance she is not in yoᵣ companie   490
1 bro: To tell thee sadly shepheard, wᵗʰout blame
510 or our neglect wee lost her as wee came[.]
Dæ: Ay me unhappie then my feares are true[.]
1 bro: what feares, good Thyrsis preethee breifly shew
Dæ: Ile tell you, tis not vaine[,] or fabulous
(though so esteem'd by shallow ignorance)
515 what the sage poets, taught by th' heav'nly Muse
storied of old in high immortall verse
of dire chimæra's and inchaunted Isles
& rifted rocks whose entrance leads to hell   500
for such there be, but unbeleife is blind[.]
520 wᵗʰin the navill of this hideous wood
immur'd in cipresse shades a sorcerer dwells
of Bacchus & of Circe borne, great Comus
deepe skill'd in all his mothers witcheries
and heere to every thirstie wanderer
525 by sly enticement gives his banefull cup
wᵗʰ many murmurs mixt, whose pleasing poison
the visage quite transforms of him yᵗ drinks
and the inglorious likenesse of a beast   510
fixes insteed, unmoulding reasons mintage
530 character'd in the face[.] This have I learn't
tending my flocks hard by i'th hillie crofts

that brow this bottome glade [,] whence night by night

he & his monstrous rout are heard to howle

like stabl'd wolvs, or tigers at thire prey

535   doing abhorred rites to Hecate

in thire obscured haunts of inmost bowers [.]

yet have they many baits, & guilefull spells

t' inveigle [,] & invite th' unwarie sense   520

of them yᵗ passe unweeting by the way.

540   this evening late by then the chewing flocks

had tane thire supper on the savourie herbe

of knot grasse dew-besprent, and were in fold

I sate me downe to watch upon a banke

with ivie canopied, & interwove

545   wᵗʰ flaunting hony suckle, & began

wrapt in a pleasing fit of melancholy

to meditate my rurall minstrelsie

till fancie had her fill, but ere a close   530

the wonted roare was up amidst the woods

550   and filld the aire wᵗʰ barbarous dissonance

at wᶜʰ I ceas't, & listend them a while

till an unusuall stop of suddaine silence

gave respit to the drousie frighted steeds

that draw the litter of close-curtain'd sleepe

555   At last a sweet [,] & sollemne breathing sound

rose like the soft steame of distill'd p̃fumes

and stole upon the aire, that even silence

was tooke e're she was ware, & wish't she might   540

deny her nature & be never more

560   still to be so displac't. I was all eare

and took in streins that might create a soule

under the ribbs of Death. but O ere long

too well I might p̃ceave it was yᵉ voice

of my most honour'd Ladie yoʳ deare sister

565 amaz'd I stood, harrow'd wth greife & feare
and O poore haplesse nightingale thought I
how sweet thou sing'st, how neere the deadly snare
then downe the lawnes I ran wth headlong hast   550
through paths & turnings often trod by day
570 till guided by myne eare I found the place
where that damn'd wisard hid in sly disguise
(for so by certaine signes I knew) had met
alreadie ere my best speed could prævent
the aidlesse innocent Ladie his wisht prey
575 who gently askt if he had seene such tow
supposing him some neighbour villager
longer I durst not stay, but soone I gues't
yee were the tow she meant, wth that I sprung   560
into swift flight till I had found you heere
580 but furder know I not. 2 Bro: O night and shades
how are yee joyn'd wth hell in triple knot
against th' unarmed weaknesse of one virgin
alone, & helplesse, is this the confidence
you gave me brother? 1 bro: yes, & keepe it still
585 leane on it safely [,] not a piod
shall be unsaid for me, against the threats
of malice, or of sorcerie, or that power
wch erring men call chance this I hold firme   570
vertue may be assail'd but never hurt
590 surpris'd by unjust force, but not enthrall'd
yea even that wch mischeife meant most harme
shall in the happie triall prove most glorie [.]
but evill on it selfe shall back recoyle
& mixe no more wth goodnesse, when at last
595 gather'd like scum [,] & setl'd to it selfe
it shall be in æternall restlesse change
selfe fed, & selfe consum'd [,] if this faile

the pillar'd firmament is rottennesse   580
and earths base built on stubble. but come lets on
600   against th' opposing will & arme of heav'n
may never this just swoord be lifted up
but for y^t damn'd magician, let him be girt
wth all the greisly legions that troope
under the sootie flag of Acheron
605   harpyes & Hydra's[,] or all the monstrous buggs
twixt Africa[,] & Inde, Ile find him out
and force him to restore his purchase back
or drag him by the curles[,] & cleave his scalpe   590
downe to the hipps. Dæ: alas good ventrous youth
610   I love thy courage yet[,] & bold emprise
but heere thy swoord can doe thee little stead
farre other arms[,] & other weapons must
be those that quell the might of hellish charms
he wth his bare wand can unthred thy joynts
615   & crumble all thy sinewes. 1 Bro: why preethee shepheard
how durst thou then thy selfe approach so neere
as to make this relation. Dæ: care, & utmost shifts
how to secure the ladie from surprisall   600
brought to my mynd a certaine shepheard lad
620   of small regard to see to[,] yet well skill'd
in every vertuous plant, & healing herbe
that spreds her verdant leafe to th'morning ray
he lov'd me well, & oft would beg me sing
wch when I did[,] he on the tender grasse
625   would sit[,] and hearken even to extasie
& in requitall ope his letherne scrip
& shew me simples of a thousand names
telling thire strange[,] & vigorous faculties   610
amoungst the rest a small unsightly root
630   but of divine effect[,] he cull'd me out

631   the leafe was darkish [,] & had prickles on it
638   he call'd it Hæmony [,] & gave it me
        & bad me keepe it as of soveraine use
640   gainst all enchauntments, mildew blast, or dampe
        or gastly furies apparition
        I purs't it up, but little reckoning made
        till now that this extremity compell'd
        but now I find it true, for by this meanes   620
645   I knew the fowle enchanter though disguis'd
        enter'd the very limetwigs of his spells
        and yet came off, if you have this about you
        (as I will give you when wee goe) you may
        boldly assault yᵉ necromancers hall
650   where if he be [,] wᵗʰ dauntlesse hardyhood
        & brandish't blade rush on him, breake his glasse
        and shed the lushious liquor on the ground
        but sease his wand, though he & his curst crew
        feirce signe of battaile make [,] & menace high   630
655   or like the sons of Vulcan vomit smoake
        yet will they soone retire [,] if he but shrinke [.]
1 Bro: Thyrsis lead on apace I follow thee
        and some good angell beare a sheild before us [.]

        the scene changes to a stately pallace set out wᵗʰ all manner of
        deliciousness, tables spred wᵗʰ all dainties [.] Comus appes wᵗʰ his
        rabble, & the Ladie set in an inchanted chaire [,] to whome he offers
        his glasse wᶜʰ she puts by, and goes about to rise [.]

Co: nay Ladie sit, if I but wave this wand
660   yoʳ nerves are all chain'd up in alablaster   640
        and you a statue, or as Daphne was
        root bound, that fled Apollo. La: foole doe not boast
        thou canst not touch the freedome of my mind

wth all thy charmes [,] although this corporall rind

665   thou hast immanacl'd, while heav'n sees good [.]

Co: why are you vext Ladie, why doe you frowne

heere dwell no frowns [,] nor anger, from these gates

sorrow flies farre. see heere be all the pleasures

that fancie can beget on youthfull thoughts

670   when the fresh blood grows lively [,] & returnes   650

brisk as the Aprill budds in primrose season [.]

and first behold this cordiall julep heere

that flames [,] & dances in his crystall bounds

wth spirits of baulme, & fragrant syrops mixt [.]

675   Not that Nepenthes wch the wife of Thone

in Ægypt gave to Iove-borne Helena

is of such power to stirre up joy as this

678   to life so freindly, or so coole to thirst [.]

poore ladie thou hast need of some refreshing

688   that hast bin tir'd all day wthout repast   660

& timely rest hast wanted [.] heere faire virgin

690   this will restore all soone. La: t'will not false traitor

t'will not restore the truth & honestie

that thou hast banisht from thy tongue wth lies

was this the cottage [,] & the safe abode

thou toldst me of? what grim aspects are these

695   these ougly headed monsters? Mercie guard me!

696   hence wth thy brewd enchauntments foule deceaver

701   were it a draft for Iuno when she banquets

I would not taste thy treasonous offer, none   670

but such as are good men can give good things

and that wch is not good [,] is not delicious

705   to a well govern'd & wise appetite [.]

Co: O foolishnesse of men! that lend thire eares

to those budge doctors of the stoick furre

and fetch thire precepts from the Cynick tub

praising the leane, & sallow abstinence[.]
710 wherfore did nature powre her bounties forth
wth such a full, & unwithdrawing hand
covering the earth wth odours, fruits, & flocks   680
thronging the seas wth spawne innumerable
but all to please & sate the curious tast
715 and set to worke millions of spinning worms
that in thire greene shops weave the smooth-haird silke
to deck her sons, and that no corner might
be vacant of her plentie[,] in her owne loynes
she hutch't th'all worshipt ore[,] & precious gems
720 to store her children wth. if all the world
should in a pet of temperance feed on pulse
drinke the cleere streame, & nothing weare but freize   690
th'all giver would be unthank't[,] would be unprais'd
not halfe his riches knowne, & yet despis'd
725 and wee should serve him as a grudging maister
as a penurious niggard of his wealth
& live like natures bastards[,] not her sons
who would be quite surcharg'd wth her owne waight
and strangl'd wth her wast fertilitie
730 th'earth cumber'd[,] & the wing'd aire dark't wth plumes
the heards would over multitude thire Lords
the sea orefraught would swell, and th'unsought diamonds   700
would so emblaze the forehead of ye deepe
and so bestudde wth starres y^t they below
735 would grow enur'd to light[,] & come at last
736 to gaze upon the sun wth shameless browes.
756 La: I had not thought to have unlockt my lips
in this unhallowd aire, but that this Iugler
would thinke to charme my judgement[,] as my eyes
obtruding false rules pranck't in reasons garbe.
760 I hate when vice can boult her arguments

and vertue has no tongue to check her pride.   710

Impostor doe not charge most innocent nature

as if she would her children should be riotous

with her abundance, she good cateresse

765   means her provision only to the good

that live according to her sober laws

and holy dictate of spare temperance.

If every just man that now pines wth want

had but a moderate & beseeming share

770   of that wch lewdly-pamper'd Luxurie

now heap's upon some few wth vast excesse   720

natures full blessings would be well dispens't

in unsupfluous even proportion

and she no whit encomberd wth her store

775   and then the giver would be better thank't

his praise due paid, for swinish gluttonie

ne're looks to heav'n amidst his gorgeous feast

but wth besotted base ingratitude

779 806   cramms[,] & blasphems his feeder. Co: come[,] no more

this is meere morall babble, & direct

against the canon laws of our foundation   730

I must not suffer this, yet tis but the lees

810   and setlings of a melancholy blood[.]

But this will cure all streite, one sip of this

will bath the drooping spirits in delight

beyond the blisse of dreames. be wise[,] & tast.

The brothers rush in with swoords drawne[,] wrest his glasse of

liquor out of his hand[,] and breake it against the ground his rout

make signe of resistance[,] but are all driven in[.] the Dæmon is

to come in wth the brothers[.]

Dæ: what have you let the false enchaunter scape?   740

815 O yee mistooke, yee should have snatcht his wand
and bound him fast; w^thout his rod revers't
& backward mutters of dissevering power
wee cannot free the Ladie that sits heere
in stonie fetters fixt[,] & motionlesse.
820 yet stay, be not disturb'd, now I bethinke me
some other meanes I have that may be us'd
wch once of Melibæus old I learnt
the soothest shepheard that ere pip't on plaines
There is a gentle nymph not farre from hence   750
825 that wth moist curbe swaies the smooth severne streame[,]
Sabrina is her name[,] a virgin pure
whilome she was the daughter of Locrine
that had the scepter from his father Brute[.]
she guiltlesse damsell flying the mad ꝑsuite
830 of her enraged stepdame Guendolen
commended her faire innocence to the floud
that stayd her flight wth his crosse flowing course
the water nymphs that in the bottome playd
held up thire pearled wrists & tooke her in   760
835 bearing her straite to aged Nereus hall
who piteous of her woes, reard her lanke head
and gave her to his daughters to imbath
in nectar'd lavers strewd wth Asphodil
and through the porch & inlet of each sence
840 dropt in ambrosiall oyles till she reviv'd
and underwent a quick immortall change
made goddesse of the river, still she retaines
her maiden gentlenesse, and oft at eve
visits the heards along the twilight meadows   770
845 helping all urchin blasts, & ill luck signes
846 that the shrewd medling Elfe delights to make
848 for wch the shepheards at thire festivalls

caroll her goodnesse loud in rustick layes
850 and throw sweet garland wreaths into her streame
of pancies[,] pinks[,] & gaudie daffadils[.]
and[,] as the old swaine said, she can unlock
the clasping charme[,] & thaw the nu̅ming spell
if she be right invok't in warbled song
855 for maidenhood she loves[,] & will be swift 780
to aide a virgin such as was her selfe
(in hard besetting need) this will I trie
and adde the power of some adjuring verse[.]

Song[.]

Sabrina faire
860 listen where thou art sitting
under the glassie[,] coole[,] translucent wave
in twisted braids of lillies knitting
the loose traine of thy amber-dropping haire
listen for deare honours sake 790
865 Goddesse of the silver lake
listen & save[.]

The verse to sing or not[.]

Listen and appeare to us
in name of great Oceanus[,]
by th'earth shaking neptunes mace
870 and Tethys grave majestick pace
by hoarie Nereus wrincled looke
and the Carpathian wizards hooke
by scalie Tritons winding shell 800
and old sooth-saying Glaucus spell
875 by Leucothea's lovely hands

         & her son that rules the strands

         by Thetis tinsel-slipper'd feet

         and the songs of Sirens sweet

         by dead Parthenope's deare tomb

880   and faire Ligeas golden combe

         wherw^th she sits on diamond rocks

         sleeking her soft alluring locks

         By all the nymphs that nightly dance   810

         upon thy streams wth wilie glance

885   rise[,] rise & heave thy rosie head

         from thy corall-paven bed

         and bridle in thy headlong wave

         till thou our summons answerd have[.]

               Listen & save[.]

       Sabrina rises attended by the water nimphes

          and sings[.]

890   By the rushie-fringed banke

            where grows the willow, & the osier danck   820

              my sliding chariot stayes

         thick set wth Agat, and the azurne sheene

         of turkis blew, & emrauld greene

895   that in the channell strayes

         whilst from off the waters fleet

         thus I set my printlesse feet

         ore the couslips velvet head

           that bends not as I tread

900   gentle swaine at thy request

           I am heere   830

     Dæ: Goddesse deere

         Wee implore thy powerfull hand

         to undoe the charmed band

905   of true virgin heere distrest

through the force, & through the wile
of unblest inchanter vile.

Sab: Shepheard tis my office best
to helpe ensnared chastitie

910 brightest ladie looke on me
thus I sprinckle on thy brest   840
drops that from my fountaine pure
I have kept of precious cure
thrice upon thy fingers tip

915 thrice upon thy rubied lip
next this marble venom'd seate
smear'd wth gumms of glutenous heate
I touch wth chast palmes moist & cold
now the spell hath lost his hold

920 and I must hast ere morning howre
to waite in Amphitrites bowre   850

Sabrina descends and
the ladie rises out
of her seat [.]

Dæ: Virgin daughter of Locrine
sprung of old Anchises line
may thy brimmed waves for this

925 thire full tribute never misse
from a thousand pettie rills
that tumble downe the snowie hills
Summer drouth, or singed aire   860
never scorch thy tresses faire

930 nor wet Octobers torrent flood
thy molten crystall fill wth mud
may thy billowes rowle a shoare
the beryll & ye golden ore

may thy loftie head be crownd
935 wth many a towre, & terrace round
and heere & there thy bankes upon
wth groves of mirrhe, & cinnamon.

      song ends[.]   870

Come Ladie while heav'n lends us grace
let us fly this cursed place
940 lest the sorcerer us intice
wth some other new device[.]
not a wast[,] or needlesse sound
till wee come to holyer ground
I shall be yor faithfull guide
945 through this gloomie covert wide
and not many furlongs thence
is yor fathers residence   880
where this night are met in state
many a freind to gratulate
950 his wish't præsence, and beside
all the swayns that neere abide
wth Iiggs[,] & rurall dance resort
wee shall catch them at thire sport
and our suddaine comming there
955 will double all thire mirth[,] & cheere
come let us hast the starres are high
but night sitts monarch yet in the mid skie 890

the scene changes then is præsented Ludlow towne & the
Præsidents Castle[,] then come in Countrie dances[,] & the like &c.
towards the end of those sports the Dæmon wth ye 2 bro. & the
Ladie come in[.] the spirit sings[.]

Back shepheards[,] back enough yor play
till next sunshine holyday
960 heere be wth out duck or nod
other trippings to be trod
of lighter toes, & such court guise
as Mercury did first devise 900
wth the mincing Dryades
965 on the lawns, & on the leas

2 song præsents them to thire father & mother[.]

Noble Lord & Ladie bright
I have brought yee new delight
Heere behold so goodly growne
three faire branches of yor owne
970 Heav'n hath timely tri'd thire youth
thire faith, thire patience, & thire truth
and sent them heere through hard assayes 910
wth a crowne of deathlesse praise
to triumph in victorious dance
975 ore sensuall folly, & intemperance

they dance. the dances all ended
the Dæmon sings or sayes[.]

To the Ocean now I fly
and those happie climes that lie
where day never shuts his eye
up in the broad feilds of the skie[.]
980 There I suck the liquid aire 920
all amidst the gardens faire
of Hesperus & his daughters three
983 that sing about the golden tree[.]

988 there æternall summer dwells

and west winds wth musky wing

990 about the cedar'ne alleys fling

nard, & casia's balmie smells

Iris there wth humid bow

waters the odorous banks y^t blow

flowers of more mingled hew   930

995 then her purfl'd scarfe can shew

yellow, watchet, greene[,] & blew

996 and drenches oft wth manna dew

998 beds of Hyacinth & roses

999 where many a cherub soft reposes[.]

1012 Now my taske is smoothly don

I can fly[,] or I can run

quickly to the earths greene end

1015 where the bow'd welkin slow doth bend

and from thence can soare as soone   940

to the corners of ye Moone

Mortalls that would follow me

love vertue[,] she alone is free

1020 she can teach you how to clime

higher then the sphærie chime

or if vertue feeble were

heaven it selfe would stoope to her[.]

Finis   948